A Broken Thing

A BROKEN

THING

Poets on the Line

Edited by Emily Rosko
and Anton Vander Zee

UNIVERSITY OF IOWA PRESS,
IOWA CITY

University of Iowa Press, Iowa City 52242
Copyright © 2011 by the University of Iowa Press
www.uiowapress.org
Printed in the United States of America

Design by Ashley Muehlbauer

The University of Iowa Press is a member of Green
Press Initiative and is committed to preserving natural
resources.

Printed on acid-free paper

Library of Congress Cataloging-in-Publication Data
    A broken thing: poets on the line / edited by Emily Rosko
and Anton Vander Zee.
        p.   cm.
    Includes bibliographical references and index.
    ISBN-13: 978-1-60938-054-0 (pbk.)
    ISBN-10: 1-60938-054-1 (pbk.)
    1. Poetics.   2. Poetry—History and criticism.
I. Rosko, Emily, 1979–   II. Vander Zee, Anton.
PN1055.B766 2011
808.1—dc22   2011007472

Thus a poem is tough by no quality it borrows from a logical recital of events nor from the events themselves but solely from that attenuated power which draws perhaps many broken things into a dance giving them thus a full being.

—WILLIAM CARLOS WILLIAMS, *Kora in Hell*

Table of Contents

Acknowledgments and Permissions

Highest thanks go to the contributors to this collection. They have taken considerable time and care with their essays—both those who revised their essays that appeared in the 2008 symposium on the line from *Center: A Journal of the Literary Arts*, and also the great many who joined this project in its present form. Thanks to Jeffrey Pethybridge for the incisive feedback and ideas he offered as the introductory essay came together, and to Roland Greene, Albert Gelpi, Nicholas Jenkins, and Robert Kaufman for their keen attention to earlier incarnations of many of the ideas that found a home in the first part of the introduction. Deep appreciation goes to Alice Fulton, Lynne McMahon, and Sherod Santos. We would like to thank Joseph Parsons, Holly Carver, Lisa Raffensperger, and their colleagues at the University of Iowa Press. Our external reader, Lisa Steinman, offered a generous reading of the manuscript and made many helpful suggestions along the way. Thanks as well to the English Department at the College of Charleston for generous financial and professional support.

A Broken Thing

Introduction

NEW MINDS, NEW LINES

Anton Vander Zee

In a short letter to Kenneth Burke from November 1945, William Carlos Williams thanks his friend for his hospitality on a recent visit and proceeds to reflect on one particularly meaningful exchange: "I liked your manner of explanation when you lowered your voice and spoke of the elementals that interest us both, the humane particulars of realization and communication" (East 88). Such thoughts made it into his half-remembered dreams, for he continues: "I woke in the night with a half-sentence on my metaphorical lips: 'the limitations of form.' It seemed to mean something of importance." Burke, in his response dated a few days later, suggests that the substance of Williams's formal concern reminds him of their discussions from the 1920s, which, he writes, "were always about 'form,' though God only knows what we meant by it" (90).

The limitations of form must have been particularly pressing for Williams near the end of 1945, just three months after Hiroshima and one month into the Nuremberg trials. Narratives of twentieth-century American poetry often describe a highly aestheticized and experimental 1920s giving way to a more socially engaged posture in the 30s and 40s as artists responded to economic depression and world war. An oversimplification to be sure, but a useful one when we consider how this apparent divide between the art of the 20s and 30s establishes the contours of the durable struggle that we see reflected in the Williams-Burke exchange, and that the most significant works of art since then engage: how to move from word to world, from poetics to politics, and from the limitations of form to life itself. Then, as now, a strong commitment to form persisted despite, against, and alongside multiple crises that remind us constantly—even in the middle of the night in half-remembered dreams—of form's limitations in light of what Wallace Stevens called "things as they are" (165).

In the arena of poetry and poetics over the last century, no idea has been more generative, variable, and contentious than the idea of form. And no technical aspect of form has more emphatically sponsored and substantiated this marked formal expansiveness than the line in poetry. But what, exactly, is the line? Should it be defined in strictly prosodic terms? Is there value in identifying certain line-genres as Chris Beyers does in *A History of Free Verse* (2001), or as Allen Grossman attempts more economically in his *Summa Lyrica* (1980)? Or should we instead attend to what Stephen Cushman names the numerous fictions of form—those ways in which American poets since Whitman have tended to "overvalue the formal aspects of their art, investing those aspects with tremendous significance," resulting in a poetry that "distinguishes itself not only by the unique ways in which it foregrounds signifiers but also by the unique ways in which it promotes the significance of its own formation" (4–5)?

Perhaps all of the above, for these questions suggest a certain lack of conceptual literacy and critical consensus regarding the line that *A Broken Thing* does not seek to correct. Instead, this general disagreement marks out a uniquely charged area of poetic as well as critical concern that reflects what the poetry of the last century is, in some elemental way, *about*. The line, in its many ulterior projections, might be an engine for certain ideals of progress—political, ethical, or otherwise. For some, it touches upon the most fundamental epistemological and ontological questions. One finds it caught up in theories of language, and in the very beginnings and endings of things. Remarkably, the line has become an aesthetic, sociopolitical, and, at times, metaphysical variable even as it remains deeply invested in the formal minutiae of rhythm and metrics, rhyme and sound. More than ever, the line *is* poetry, the radical against which even alternate and emerging poetic forms that foreground the visual or the auditory, the page or the screen, can be distinguished and understood. Extending Burke's statement to the present context, the line does indeed seem to mean something of importance, but God only knows what—and how—we mean by it.

So yes, the line is overtaxed; it presumes to do too much, and it knows it. What might seem an overextension, however, suggests a core strength of the line that the essays in *A Broken Thing* collectively embody: its ability to be both critical and self-critical, holding its own elaborate fictions of form at a skeptical, questioning distance. This blend of bold confidence and a self-critical undertow saturates the last century of American poetry. Indeed, the most important American poetry of the twentieth century could be said to display either of the following traits, and often both simultaneously: a penchant for developing ambitious claims about what formal strategies such as the poetic line can accomplish, and a deeply rooted formal concern about such claims. This concern signals a certain anxiety in the face of such ambitious claims for poetry. But it also suggests a certain persistent care, attention, and commitment.

The seeds of such meta-lyrical reflection can be traced back to poetic self-consciousness itself, which, one could argue, is as old as written poetry. But, for our purposes, a more distinct formal concern, particularly in relation to the line, emerges markedly in romantic poetry, where the pieties and prescriptions of received forms were increasingly challenged and stretched to reflect new social experiences and emerging philosophical paradigms. Consider William Blake's brash pronouncement in his prefatory note for *Jerusalem* (1804). Looking back to John Milton's famous statement on the bondage of rhyme at the start of *Paradise Lost*, Blake writes that his original choice of Miltonic blank verse for his prophetic book "was not only awkward, but as much a bondage as rhyme itself" (300). Pushing beyond blank verse, Blake suggests a looser line in terms that would seem perfectly at home in discussions of contemporary free verse: "I therefore have produced a variety in every line, both of cadences and number of syllables. Every word and every letter is studied and put into its fit place." Manipulating the raised copper on his plate to produce a distinctly bolder script, and including profuse capitals for emphasis on the illuminated page, Blake concludes by forging an integral relationship between formal innovation and national identity, if not political revolution: "Poetry Fetter'd, Fetters the Human Race. Nations are Destroy'd, or Flourish, in proportion as The Poetry Painting and Music, are Destroy'd or Flourish."

In William Wordsworth's *Prelude*, the poet's reflection on the fickleness of muse and mind alike offers a much quieter lesson about the failures of the blank-verse line. After considering the accepted subjects for epic utterance—those stories of quest and combat, both fantastic and historical—Wordsworth attempts to justify the fraught ambition behind his autobiographical epic of the poetic mind. Yearning to connect word and world, to "invent / A tale from my own heart" that might still end in some "philosophic song / Of Truth that cherishes our daily life," Wordsworth's hopes are dashed on the shores of self, on what George Oppen would later call the shipwreck of the singular:

But from this awful burthen I full soon
Take refuge and beguile myself with trust
That mellower years will bring a riper mind

And clearer insight. Thus my days are past
In contradiction; with no skill to part
Vague longing, haply bred by want of power,
From paramount impulse not to be withstood,
A timorous capacity, from prudence,
From circumspection, infinite delay.
Humility and modest awe, themselves
Betray me, serving often for a cloak
To a more subtle selfishness; that now
Locks every function up in blank reserve,
Now dupes me, trusting to an anxious eye
That with intrusive restlessness beats off
Simplicity and self-presented truth. (42–43)

One imagines T. S. Eliot's Prufrock here: the infinite delay, the anxious eye/I, the intrusive restlessness. But Wordsworth is not left pinned and wriggling on a public wall, but is rather locked up within the limitations of form. In Wordsworth's "blank reserve," we hear the near-anagram "blank verse," which constrains his poetic desires, leaving him to beat off, via rote counting out of poetic feet, the clarifying force of simplicity and self-evident truth. The formal anxiety here, in its specificity and unease, arrives almost inaudibly next to Blake's confident dismissal of the blank-verse line, but it nevertheless provides a pointed critique of Milton's optimistic description (in the prefatory remark on "The Verse" at the start of *Paradise Lost*) of the blank-verse line, its "sense variously drawn out" across heavily enjambed lines, released from the binds of rhyme (355). Unshackled, however, Wordsworth confronts a different kind of limit: a "subtle selfishness" and a "timorous capacity" that constitute not only a shadowed description of his chosen line—that blank reserve—but also an allegory for his restless state of mind seeking connections with the wider world.

In the context of American poetry, we note an important glimpse of a more socially critical formal concern in Phillis Wheatley's proto-romantic paean to the mind's poetic potential in "On Imagination," likely penned during the 1770s. Extolling the virtues of this welcome captivity, she writes:

Now here, now there, the roving Fancy flies,
Till some lov'd object strikes her wand'ring eyes,
Whose silken fetters all the senses bind,
And soft captivity involves the mind. (65)

Wheatley's troping on the heroic couplet is certainly not innocent. Here, fancy roves freely, and no one owns the personified imagination's beloved objects; silken fetters captivate only mind and sense, not soul and person. The neat couplets explode Alexander Pope's facile notions of a versifying mimesis: her lines are not an icon of action or thought, but instead offer a complex formal reckoning of what it meant for a former slave in a slaveholding society to write in the language and form of the enslaver. This makes her song of praise—her "unequal lay," as she names it in the poem's last line, again exploiting poetic convention to offer a pointed critique—indelibly elegiac even when most exuberant. Wheatley's subtle interrogation of the heroic couplet and its associations previews the kind of devastatingly self-conscious and insinuating formal intelligence wielded nearly three centuries later by poets such as Gwendolyn Brooks. It is a kind of weeping—to adapt a line from Brooks—with form.

Then we come to Whitman, where so much of this business begins. Midway through "Song of Myself," Whitman decisively shrugs off formal constraints to make way for his long line and its multitudinous contradictions: "To be in any form, what is that? [. . .] Mine is no callous shell" (215). And yet not so decisively: for isn't there some quiet nostalgia in the trotting iambic perfection of the first clause—"To be in any form"—and also some deep conflict in the statement if we press on in its clear echoes of Hamlet's indecision? And if form, in terms of a measured metrics, appears only sporadically (though always in a charged, if disguised, way) in Whitman's work, it returns explosively as a political and metaphysical variable in his long-lined synthetic chants of "Form, Union, Plan" (246). Throughout his work, Whitman models the expansiveness of formal ideas that would influence so many future poets, even as he offers a glimpse—particularly in the contracted and increasingly metrical forms that his late work takes—of the inventive endurance of traditional verse forms.

When Whitman asks what it is to be—to write, to exist—in any form, he inadvertently poses a question that would consume both poets and critics of poetry for the next century and beyond. Even as form pulled away from its traditional metrical and generic connotations, and even as poets began to think more rigorously about their work in relation to extra-aesthetic or extra-technical concerns, ideas of form began to take precedence. Though criticism of twentieth-century poetry by default addresses certain facets of this phenomenon, the critical narratives that emerge too often inhabit a partisan sense of formal efficacy that merely retraces the steps of stock narratives involving either the value or vacuousness of so-called innovative and traditional poetics relative to their supposed ideals, political or otherwise. Rather than join the fray, the present introduction aims to explore the integrity and complexity of this development itself—in particular relation to the line in poetry—and to direct attention to a rich and varied formal concern that remains just as pressing in the twenty-first century.

No single poet could ever exhaust the varied sources of the line or approximate the unique expression it achieves in each poet, in each poem. From Chinese ideograms to Mayan hieroglyphs, from abstract sculpture to cubist collage, from serial music to jazz, from the open field to fractal amplifications, from physiology of the body to the stress of inner thought, and from organic visions of nature to the functions of machine and code, the line in poetry has multiple, intersecting origins and inspirations. If one thing defines how poets approach the line, it is this very acquisitiveness and curiosity. Though one could turn to any number of modernist poets to examine their idiosyncratic fictions of form, William Carlos Williams's obsession with *measure* makes him a seminal figure for thinking about the line. His presence hovers both explicitly and implicitly over the essays in this collection as a model theorizer, idealizer, and self-conscious scrutinizer of the line.

In *Book II* (1946) of Williams's *Paterson*, the poet emerges into the eponymous city's streets in an effort to connect with the life and language of its inhabitants. An internal voice, however, keeps the poet locked in his own mind, stifling his desired engagement with the world:

Outside

        outside myself

                there is a world,

he rumbled, subject to my incursions. (43)

The first three lines here—a preview of the famous triadic line in which Williams would invest such hope—formally enact through their spacing a sense of expansive connection and release. But the fourth line, snapped back close to the left margin, forces a retreat as the poet moves from the world outside to the world inside: the mind's anxieties, its divided consciousness, its doubt, finally, that the triadic line can induce a true transformation. Those three steps threaten to become *merely* formal. Yet this crisis of form—this finely orchestrated breakdown of Williams's formal ambition—while it might seem to indicate a failure, invites the reader to imagine the difficulties of emerging humanly and authentically into a world marked by class divisions and scarred by war.

Or take this more explicit reflection on what is at stake in thinking about the line later in *Book II*:

Without invention nothing is well spaced,
unless the mind change, unless
the stars are new measured, according
to their relative positions, the
line will not change, the necessity
will not matriculate: unless there is
a new mind there cannot be a new
line, the old will go on
repeating itself with recurring
deadliness: without invention
nothing lies under the witch-hazel
bush, the alder does not grow from among
the hummocks margining the all
but spent channel of the old swale,
the small foot-prints
of the mice under the overhanging
tufts of the bunch-grass will not
appear: without invention the line
will never again take on its ancient
divisions when the word, a supple word,
lived in it, crumbled now to chalk. (50)

This brief passage contains not only a theory of the line, but a theory of poetry. The business of stars being new measured according to relative positions suggests the profound implications that Williams sensed in Albert Einstein's theory of relativity—not only poetic, but moral and intellectual as well. Williams submits that we need (if we catch the echoing stellar pun) a new a-line-ment, a new measure. The argument, then, seems clear: if we can make it new, if we can invent, we can progress. The line in poetry must reflect—and reflect upon—those changes if it is to maintain any connection to things as they are. It is an indelible statement on the various potentialities of the line, and one that seems as relevant as ever.

But they remain, inevitably, potentialities—everywhere qualified by the conditional and hedged in *via negativa*: "without," "nothing," "unless," "cannot." Against the rigorously projective and forward-looking aspects of this passage,

Williams offers a kind of reverse dialectic: from making it new (invention, a new mind), to making it romantic/pastoral (nature's witch-hazel, the burgeoning alder), to making it, in a word, "ancient." Why does Williams care what lies under the witch-hazel, a plant whose supposedly magical and healing properties are well documented in folk lore? What does it mean to suggest that invention might "take on" the "ancient divisions" and return to some primal state of the "supple word," where idea and thing, perhaps, were one? Don't these reversions to the past and to superstition lead only to that marked "deadliness"—one can't help but see and hear *dead lines*—of the old repeating itself over and over? The old and the ancient, the myth and the magic, it seems, carry on uneasily with the new, are even revived in and through the new. Williams's forward-looking idealism is thus highly tempered and qualified, a sense enacted in miniature by certain lines read in isolation as a singular integer of meaning: "a new mind there cannot be a new." And yet there *must* be.

This anxious concern runs through Williams's prose as well, a medium he liked to think of as his laboratory for poetics. In his 1939 essay "Against the Weather: A Study of the Artist," Williams offers a series of questions as to what the artist is, and what he or she should do, before suddenly breaking off and inserting the following: "I've been writing a sentence, with all the art I can muster. Here it is: A work of art is important only as evidence, in its structure, of a new world which it has been created to affirm" (*Selected Essays* 196). A few years later, he would write, "What we are trying to do is not only to disengage the elements of a measure but to seek . . . a new measure or a new way of measuring that will be commensurate with the social, economic world in which we are living" (283). The poem, it seems, must be both world-creating and world-reflecting, all the while (looking back to the passage from *Paterson* above) calling back to its ancient roots. These are the kind of hyperbolic—one might say romantic—contradictions for which Williams is well known. This is what gives his poetry such a rich cognitive congestion, though one should also note a more problematic dissonance that emerges in the condescending awkwardness with which he handles gender, class, and race relations throughout his work. This gap between ideals and reality leads, more often than not, to a charged incommensurability, magnifying the distance between the poet and his ideals on the one hand, and the person he is and the world in which he lives on the other. His work, his lines, show the strain of a formal commitment constantly grating against its limitations. In this broad sense, he is our contemporary.

Williams, in the words we borrow for the epigraph to *A Broken Thing*, writes that "a poem is tough by no quality it borrows from a logical recital of events nor from the events themselves but solely from that attenuated power which draws perhaps many broken things into a dance giving them thus a full being" (*Imaginations* 16–17). A stunning description of the problems and possibilities inherent in the making of a poem, Williams's statement also suggests a model for the myriad micro-essays assembled here—these variously informal, dynamic, suggestive, partial, broken things that we have brought into a kind of critical and poetic dance. One cannot offer a cold history of the line, treating its many pasts and multiplying presents as so many instances of poetic thought or signposts of a historical moment. Rather, we must be open to the ways that lines continue to hold us and claim us in some curious way that cannot, and should not, be exorcized or explained away. A poem lies somewhere between a determined now and an open future. This capacity to stretch beyond the extant makes poems such a difficult and necessary pleasure—this blank reserve, this attenuated power, this complex allegory of a present shaded by the past, and shading into something else still. Lines do not mean solely in their brevity or their length, in their becoming or their brokenness; lines live in and through the descriptions we give them. Now, I want to honor these descriptions by offering an overview of the debates that have emerged around poetic lines. Indeed, the history of American poetry in the twentieth century could be told by the compounding, and often confounding, discussions of its lines. *A Broken Thing* extends this history, charting a rich diffusion of theory and practice into the twenty-first century with the most diverse, wide-ranging, and engaging set of essays on the line in poetry to date.

With free verse as we currently understand it over a century old, the thought of compounding discussions about new lines has elicited some sensible skepticism. Ed Dorn, in an interview from the late 70s, discusses the "constant and chronic exacerbation about the legitimacy of the line," the justification for which he found overdone in an era that had witnessed the "passing of strict meter" (92). As for the perennial question of the line, he declares that "the only thing we can hope for is that it will just die of old age as a question."

Well, it may have matured, but it certainly hasn't died. The decade following this interview witnessed two of Denise Levertov's seminal essays on the line from 1979 ("On the Function of the Line" and "Technique and Tune-up"), as well as three separate publications taking up the topic: *A Field Guide to Contemporary Poetry and Poetics* (1980, revised 1997) included a symposium on the line, as did the literary journal *Epoch* during the same year, and a special free-verse issue of the *Ohio Review* from 1982 contained much pointed back-and-forth about the line. A more theoretically informed and critical set of responses to these main-stream reflections on the line appeared in *The Line in Postmodern Poetry* (1988). Sponsored both by the academic and aesthetic sea change accompanying the rise of what Mark McGurl has recently dubbed *The Program Era* (2009), and by the genuine integrity and complexity of the topic itself, these varied reflections on line trace the contours of the most fundamental debates in the arena of poetry and poetics from the 50s to the 80s. Before concluding with a rough sketch of the nearly seventy contributions to the present collection, it is important to gauge how this new set of essays, arriving nearly a quarter century after the most recent concerted set of reflections on the line, extends and revises the concerns of these prior reflections.

Field's "The Poetic Line: A Symposium" begins with Sandra McPherson's response to a piece Hayden Carruth published in the *Hudson Review*, and the essays that follow loosely track the rather limited contours of that debate with responses from seven additional poets. The catalyst for these essays was Carruth's craggy dismissal of two poems by Charles Simic and John Haines, which he found riddled by a "complacent suggestiveness, passiveness, [and] inertness" that no manner of lineation could save (qtd. in McPherson 75). Responding in kind, McPherson, Haines, Simic, and Louis Simpson offer valiant defenses of the free-verse line. They write of the poet's innate sense for the line, its impulsive unfolding, containment, and releasing of energy, its proximity to the psychic life of the poet. This manner of thinking about the line imposes some severe limitations on what it means for the line to be, as McPherson writes, "a unit to work in" (75). Less a made thing, a purposefully broken thing, the line is more an index of idiosyncratic feeling or a mimesis of our physiology.

The *Field* symposium has its more contrary participants as well, such as James Wright, who voices his displeasure with any poetry in which form registers merely personal whim: "every God-damned fool in America quivers with the puce longing to win life by printing at us that he is sensitive. He and Viva know that rhyme and rhythm are out. Twitch is in" (82). We need, according to Wright, a poetry with intelligence, a poetry that contains its own criticism. Instead, he writes, "the endless bad poems of our time distribute themselves automatically between masturbation and the exquisite phoniness of middle-class revolution" (82). Donald Hall, more coolly conservative and with less vitriol, doubles down on some of Wright's reservations, suggesting that "the Line . . . is an *intellectual force*" (88).

In a clarifying statement that encompasses both sides of this debate between body and mind, impulse and intellect, Donald Wesling has argued that "all poetry restructures direct experience by means of devices of *equivalence*," but that more than metrical prosodies, "free verse claims and thematizes a proximity to lived experience. [Poetry] does this by trying to replicate, project, or represent perceptual, cognitive, emotional, and imaginative processes" ("Free Verse" 426). Such a formal mimesis—whether emotional or intellectual—may be an unavoidable ingredient in the line at times. But it does not account for devices of equivalence that attempt to capture non- or anti-subjective processes, nor does this notion of equivalences offer a way of dealing with what Robert Duncan identified as a poetry of linguistic impulse, a category he offered as a necessary, even corrective, addition to Levertov's limiting, if influential, ideas about an organic form rooted in body, mind, and nature. In short, the formal mimesis Wesling describes fails adequately to register the dynamism and range of poetry flourishing on the margins of the mainstream verse—a mainstream that the *Field* group seems circularly to both represent and discuss.

To its credit, *Epoch's* 1980 "A Symposium on the Theory and Practice of the Line in Contemporary Poetry" moves beyond certain constraints of the *Field* debate. With a more critical edge, and with nearly thirty essays that are more broadly representative at least in terms of aesthetics if not identity, this symposium offers a crucial model for *A Broken Thing*. The symposium includes statements by a range of poets and scholars including Margaret Atwood, Seamus Heaney, Donald Davie, Sandra Gilbert, Robert Morgan, and Howard Nemerov, among many others. The editors gave each contributor a series of prompts that ranged from more craft-centered inquiries to questions of how the poet's use of the line might accommodate any other emotional, intellectual, or social concerns. Rory Holscher and Robert Schultz's valuable introduction offers a way of thinking about the line that remains very relevant for *A Broken Thing*, as when they direct attention to the minutiae of form: "In such seemingly esoteric considerations as how the line is turned," they write, "we discuss how the world turns" (166). If Denise Levertov's and Charles Olson's sense of the line persists quietly in the *Field* symposium, their example is even more evident as intellectual and practical models in *Epoch's* symposium. Various echoes of Olson's projective sense of energy and open-field poetics reverberate throughout. Levertov's core ideas regarding how the line tracks the stress of inner thought, and her notion of line as a script for performance, inform a number of the essays as well. "Energy" emerges as a dominant trope in the *Epoch* symposium, as the line becomes a kind of pacing device that contains and creates energy, momentum, and expectation. The line, here, actively shapes the content to the form, melding manner and matter.

Despite these kindred concerns, however, much of the *Epoch* symposium remains focused on policing the boundaries between free and formal verse, and especially between prose and poetry. This more conservative aspect of the symposium prompted a typically sharp reply from Marjorie Perloff. In her essay "The Linear Fallacy," published partly in response to the symposium, she sought to remind poets that lines should not be considered sufficient to poetry: they must be necessary. Too many poets, she argues, forget the question that should be most basic to poetry, whether formal or free: "when is lineation the right and inevitable form of verbal discourse? What necessary deformation of language, what foregrounding of semantic units does this particular exemplar of 'art by line' achieve?" (864). Riffing on Frost's famous tennis metaphor, she pointedly warns that the line has become the net of free-verse forms, just another tradition to serve blindly.

As Perloff notes, however, a few voices in the Epoch symposium do provide a more critical and self-critical tone. Don Byrd's passionate piece imbues technique with a palpable social urgency that moves beyond the merely poetic: "We need massive flowing and breaking intensities, not tension; we need universal participation in the pleasure of sight, sound and intellection, not elegance; we need the analytic disruptive exercise of the mind, not wit; we need the awkward spectacle of the untried move, not grace" (Holscher 180). But he calls even this earnest plea into question, inquiring after its value beyond academic debates about the line: "what are we going to say to a race that may be lucky to last another three generations? And are we going to say it in lines?" (180). Such a disarming question forces us to face our poetic and critical idealizations of the line and poetry alike. Christopher Bursk, in his brief essay, seems resigned, even quietly resentful, in the face of a poetry that fails to live up to its ideals. Craft, for him, amounts to an artful evasion; poetry, an aesthetic escape. Discussions of craft help us avoid, not address, the most crucial questions: "It is much easier for me to tell you how to break your lines," he writes, "than for me to say to you that your poem about your father's death is shallow and evasive" (Holscher 176). Touching on deeper social concerns, he writes how it saddens him that the Epoch symposium "so strongly reflects our society's concern with technique and not our society's lack of genuine concern for its fate and the fate of the oppressed within it. It is sad," he continues, "that this symposium is not on justice in the poem" (176). Ezra Pound wrote that technique is the test of one's sincerity. It seems that we too-readily miss the statement's aphoristic wisdom when we place the emphasis on the intricacies of technique or ideals of sincerity and authenticity. It is the middle term—test—that underscores the utter difficulty of any neat accommodation between poetry and life. As Bursk reminds us, it is a damn hard test.

And it is a test that the contributors to *The Line in Postmodern Poetry* (1988) take very seriously. Consisting of a handful of critical essays by James Scully, Marjorie Perloff, and Stephen Henderson among others—and supplemented by "L=A=N=G=U=A=G=E Lines," an embedded, independent anthology of shorter, more experimental reflections by poets aligned with that school—*The Line in Postmodern Poetry* offers a trenchant reply to the general drift of the *Epoch* and *Field* symposia. With the goal of replacing the Olsonian and Levertovian moment of kinetic, physio-cerebral mimesis with a sense of postmodern poetry as "the very embodiment of a socially imposed and encoded praxis" (xv), editors Robert Frank and Henry Sayre pitch the aggressively disruptive noise of postmodernism against free verse's suspect music. Free verse had ceased to become a sincere, expressive force, and instead had become a bag of transparent tricks for the rendering of authenticity: "The free verse line, like expressionist brushwork," they write, "has come to signify an authentic self-expression, but is used everywhere, at least potentially, in bad faith" (xvii). Thus, the primary focus of *The Line in Postmodern Poetry* is a poetry haunted not by the ghost of meter—a common theme in discussions of free verse—but by the specter of insincerity.

James Scully's long essay, which was later included in his superb *Line Break: Poetry as Social Practice* (1988, 2005), gives voice to certain concerns shared by all the contributors when he notes that "writers . . . attempt to solve those problems they have set for themselves, but set in concert with their historical circumstances, social values, class outlook, jobs, and the innumerable opaque or transparent 'aesthetic' and 'extra-aesthetic' encouragements and discouragements visited on them." Echoing Perloff's argument above, he asserts that "for writers as writers the strict intramural question will be whether their technical capabilities have risen to the occasions of those problems: problems that are multifaceted, complex" (Frank 98).

Just as the critical reflections in *The Line in Postmodern Poetry* tend to view writing in relation to a much more diffuse set of concerns, they also tend to be more diverse and representative, filling notable gaps in earlier symposia. Stephen Henderson's essay "Worrying the Line: Notes on Black American Poetry," for example, documents how black American poetry in the 60s and 70s worked to carve out a distinct voice rooted in music and oral traditions while simultaneously struggling "with stylistic and thematic concerns inherited from the larger body of American and Western poetry" (60). These poets strove to discover ways to render the "highly charged inventive quality of black American vernacular on the printed page," and "how to indicate its dynamic range, its mixture of elegance and wit, its tonal contrasts with Standard English, its plasticity" (60)—and how to do all this through the shaping and modulation of the line. At a key point, his essay describes a feature of black oral and musical style known as *worrying the line*. He explains:

> While it subsumes the verbal analogue of jazz sound or sonority, it is closer to the analogue of jazz phrasing. [. . .] Worrying the line is essentially a kind of analytical play on words, on parts of words, on qualities of words. It is as firmly entrenched in current vernacular as it is in folk speech. Originally, it referred to the personal practice of altering the pitch of notes in a given passage, or to other kinds of ornamentation often associated with melismatic singing in the black tradition. In the verbal parallel, a word or phrase is broken up and the fragments sometimes distorted to allow for affective or didactic comment. (69)

Examining the work of Carolyn Rodgers, Amiri Baraka, Nikki Giovanni, and Bob Kaufman in relation to Langston Hughes and Sterling Brown—among many others—Henderson introduces an experience and art of the line that was entirely absent in the previous symposia. Similarly, Garrett Hongo's reflection on the evolution of his own line, pitched between Chinese poetry, Asian American history, and the adopted musics of jazz and blues, further opens the field.

The embedded or appended anthology that concludes *The Line in Postmodern Poetry* includes some of the collection's most original meditations on the line. Bruce Andrews, in an essay he reprises and expands in *A Broken Thing*, offers a vision of line as transgression and transversal. The line, he writes, is an "explanation in action that keeps crossing the line into a politics outside (its articulation into contested hegemonies, fields of force) and bringing it back inside to challenge the constitution (and possibilities) of meaning as well as form" (178). His ideas of lineation oppose more traditional notions that signal neat boundaries and neater subjectivities. But crucially, he abandons neither the idea of lineation itself, nor its importance within experimental poetics. Lyn Hejinian's essay similarly resists inflexible experimental ideals that discard lineation wholesale, as when she writes that she "think[s] about the line more than about any formal element in my writing" (191). She writes powerfully of the line as "the standard (however variable) of meaning in the poem, the primary unit of observation, and the measure of felt thought" (191). The line here is not an ideological sign, but the beginning of possibility: "Lines, which may be rigid or relaxed, increasing or decreasing, long or short, ascending (questioning) or descending (decisive), predisposed (necessary) or evolving (speculative), representative of sequence or of cluster, redistribute meaning continuously within the work" (192).

Even Charles Bernstein's sardonic poem-essay in iambic pentameter speaks beyond the confines of a narrowly ideological poetry. His poem "Of Time and the Line" reflects an academic culture of high-theory and ideology critique, but it also speaks not so much against it as productively beyond it: "When / making a line, better be double sure / what you're lining in & what you're lining / out & which side of the line you're on" (215). This would seem, initially, a casually mocking ditty on Robert Frost's finger-shaking advice in "Mending Wall," perhaps showing how free verse now stands in place of the sturdy metrical tradition once represented by Frost. Such a reading, however, dishonors both Frost and Bernstein. Indeed, Frost's warning about walling in and walling out, and to whom you're likely to give offense, announces a political and ethical injunction speaking beyond the local disputes of metrical versus free verse. It seems that Bernstein, here, mocks neither Frost nor the new free-verse establishment. He mocks, rather, the broader posturing of lines of defense that too often define (and confine) the poetry world. He plays the suggestive fool here, not just a partisan joker.

The intervening decades between this burst of critical activity in the 80s and the present moment have witnessed a few notable developments in thinking about the line in poetry. In Bernstein's edited collection *Close Listening: Poetry and the Performed Word* (1998), Perloff takes the occasion to return once more to the line. Her contribution to that volume, "After Free Verse: The New Nonlinear Poetries," urges a move beyond a narrow conception of linearity that, for her, marks the watered-down free verse in poetry anthologies such as *Naked Poetry* (1969). Identifying a clear formal evolution beyond the limited play of the line, she writes: "Just as early free-verse poets called metrical form into question . . . what is now being called into question is the line itself (98)." She looks to the critical and creative works in the "L=A=N=G=U=A=G=E Lines" anthology discussed above to buttress her claim. After offering a sound bite from Bruce Andrews that captures all of his wrangling with traditional notions of the line, but none of his genuine recasting of linear concerns, she asks: "who would have thought that fewer than forty years after Olson celebrated the 'LINE' as the embodiment of the breath, the signifier of the heart, the line would be perceived as a boundary, a confining border, a form of packaging?" (99). She goes on to cite Bernstein's aforementioned iambic pentameter poem, "Of Time and the Line," as a kind of final deconstruction of linearity where parody obviates criticism. To be sure, healthy rhetoric against the line by various experimental camps persists in "L=A=N=G=U=A=G=E Lines" alongside a genuine concern for the line. But Perloff misses Bernstein's subtle commentary on the shrill tone of this debate, a debate that seems somehow stale already in 1988. Furthermore, she fails to mention Lyn Hejinian's piece, which certainly does anything but call the line into question. In this sense, Perloff seems to animate a debate between dueling camps that the authors she addresses had already begun to think beyond and beneath in crucial ways. And in any case, Olson himself did think of the line fundamentally as a kind of boundary and confining border (albeit in a more productive sense) as when he wrote that "Limits / are what any of us / are inside of" (21). Looking back to Wheatley's "silken fetters," Wordsworth's "blank reserve," Williams's "attenuated power," and Brooks's "weep[ing] without form," an awareness of constraint and limitation remain central to almost any enduring experiment with the line. Shifting attention to the page is certainly necessary, just as it is important to emphasize how inapt a narrow definition of the line becomes in the face of various sound, concrete, and new-media poetries. But to discard the line entirely, to insinuate a broader movement beyond it, misses its undiminished importance.

While Perloff remains invested in various ideologies of lyric, James Longenbach's recent pocket-book *The Art of the Poetic Line* (2008) tries to dodge questions of ideology altogether. In what might as well be a response to Perloff, he writes that "some poets have argued that the rejection of line carries a kind of political charge, just as poets once felt that the rejection of rhyming verse for blank verse or blank verse for free verse carried a political charge. This may be true in a particular time at a particular place. But it cannot be true categorically" (95). Fair enough, but it is the examination of lines in particular times and places—gauging how they are both constrained by a tradition and a historical moment, and yet strain to stretch and think and sing beyond that moment—that underscores poetry's enduring power. Instead of engaging this messiness, Longenbach proceeds from more general observations about technique to discussions of poems that exemplify those techniques. Though he develops an enormously useful vocabulary for describing three different kinds of line endings—annotating, parsing, and end-stopped—he too often reduces the line to a holding pen for syntax, the alterations and breakages of which seem to provide a kind of pure formal pleasure. Given its almost exclusive emphasis on sound and the pleasure and potential of broken syntax, Longenbach's piece remains rather deaf to the world. He writes, in a tidy bit of common sense that is hard to refute, that the "line has a meaningful identity only when we begin to hear its relationship to other elements in the poem" (5). Yes, but we also need to hear its relationship to an array of implicit and explicit elements in the world around the poem. We need to attend to the sound of the social that poetry, even in its most subtle formal maneuvers, alternately reflects and refuses.

Alice Fulton, in her work on fractal poetics, deftly captures the infinite formal density of the line, though she never forgets form's integral connection to things as they are: "Any line," she writes, "when examined closely (or magnified) will reveal itself to be as richly detailed as was the larger poem from which it was taken; the poem will contain an infinite regression of details, a nesting of pattern within pattern" (58). And yet poems, she emphasizes, are complex "linguistic models of the world's workings," an observation as important for thinking about poetry and science as it is for poetry and the social.

More recently, in *Blue Studios* (2006), Rachel Blau DuPlessis distills the most incisive work mentioned above in her probing discussion of the line in poetry as a charged segmentivity. Though her interests here are anchored in Frankfurt School aesthetics, she offers a useful clarification of how fundamental the line is to all poetry: "Something fairly straightforward, but highly distinctive, separates and distinguishes poetry from nearby modes like fiction and drama that also unroll in time and use sequencing tactics of various kinds," she writes. While *narrativity* encompasses what is central to the novel, and *performativity* approximates the concerns of various dramatic forms, *segmentivity*, which she defines as "the ability to articulate and make meaning by selecting, deploying and combining segments," fundamentally characterizes poetry. DuPlessis continues:

> Both of these now-familiar neologisms indicate the practice of sequencing event, gesture, and image. Poetry also sequences; it is the creating of meaningful sequences by the negotiation of gap. . . . Poetry can then be defined as the kind of writing that is articulated in sequenced, gapped lines and whose meanings are created by occurring in bounded units, units operating in relation to pause or silence. . . . The acts of making lines and making their particular chains of rupture, seriality, and sequencing are fundamental to the nature of poetry as a genre. Fundamental to what can be said of poetry as poetry. (199)

Many contributors to *A Broken Thing* share DuPlessis's commitment to ideas of form in both theory and practice, in both word and world, implicitly endorsing her sense that lines are where "materiality and mystery join dialectically," embodying a "lively tension between eloquent stasis and driven becoming" (205, 203).

A defining feature of *A Broken Thing* in relation to the preceding collections and essays mentioned is its lack of defensiveness. Though echoes of old debates persist in a few of the essays, these essays are, for the most part, unconcerned with policing boundaries between experiment and tradition, between prose and poetry, between good poetry and bad poetry. "Free verse" itself—that vague varietal of twentieth-century poetry that has vexed American poets ever since the modernists simultaneously maligned its connotations while exploiting the liberties it offered—has become a much more neutral descriptor here. That said, we should note the reaction that many poets who have committed themselves, often radically and with great innovation, to more traditional or metrical forms might have to the collection's title: *A Broken Thing*. Doesn't the title seem to value the line solely for its potential to break? Such a notion, one could argue, sponsors a very narrow conception of the line. That we foreground the work of William Carlos Williams, an early master of the free-verse broken line, and even go so far as to yank the title directly from his experimental *Kora in Hell*, certainly makes this all seem like a sly partisan move that belies the supposedly ecumenical vision of its editors. It is a valid point: one can enjamb the metrical line, can stretch the line, and one can elide, substitute, and behead metrical units. And there is certainly a line-break *between* lines. But one rarely *breaks* a metrical line—that's part of a different game called free verse.

To answer this critique, one could argue that, for better or worse, the language of the "line-break" has taken on a much broader sense nearly synonymous with enjambment, which occurs in free and formal verse alike. Or, one could argue that the rhetoric of brokenness—from the recovered shards of Greek lyric poetry to the romantic cult of the fragment and beyond—echoes something crucial within the history of poetry. But a more direct defense of the language of brokenness reveals a dominant fiction about form that has guided us throughout this project, and that many of the essays included here speak to as well. After what Walter Benjamin would call the catastrophe of history, poetry as broken reflects a world as broken, even as its constructive powers collect and collate and—if only rarely and with great difficulty—transcend. We like to think that this more philosophical sense of brokenness is not utterly at odds with a poetics that seeks to reclaim the body of poetry, and for which gestures of wholeness guard against the inclination to rupture. Thus, we hope that poets and critics inclined to balk at our title will take it not as a unilateral declaration of free-verse hegemony, but as an invitation to repair, to counter this force of brokenness. As though in answer to this hope, many of the contributors who reflect on the metrical line here do just that, as they prize integrity above brokenness, form above fragment. If nothing else, a common ground persists as the line exceeds its trappings as a partisan counter, becoming a poetic variable for all manner of extra-aesthetic concerns. Such concerns are less predictable and more wide-ranging than ever, and it is on this stage—where fictions of form converge and collide—that this conversation about contemporary poetry and poetics takes its place.

Noting a similar sense of a post-partisan poetics, Donald Wesling, a careful thinker on the line of both traditional prosodies and non-metrical forms, writes that "there seems to be something like a critical consensus that we appear to have arrived at a historical point of demarcation, a point at which polemics end and a renewed understanding and appreciation of poems and their diverse prosodies begin" (*Scissors* 325). Mirroring this shift of critical opinion, we are tempted to borrow the language of hybridity that Cole Swensen eloquently deploys in her introduction to the recent anthology *American Hybrid* (2009). In *A Broken Thing*, too, there is what she calls a "thriving center of alterity," a healthy disregard for aesthetic divisions. Such hybridity, Swensen implies, is not a concession, not a collapsing toward the middle, nor is it a neatly dialectical movement to the next new thing. Similarly, the essays in *A Broken Thing* lack the cohesion of any concerted movement in any particular direction, and this is one of the collection's primary strengths. The essays here—the result of nearly 200 personalized solicitations—offer a diffuse hybridity, a dynamic hodgepodge that we hope captures the breadth of poetic practice rather than isolates or idealizes any narrow tendency. Our unique moment of hybridity—sponsored by the professionalization of writing and the growth of small, independent presses, and also, more profoundly, by the trenchant conceptualizations of hybrid identities and poetics that have emerged over the past three decades—shows a slackening of partisan posturing *about*, but no less commitment *to*, poetic form.

In its tendency toward a rigor of range, *A Broken Thing* shares much with Donald Hall's classic anthology *Claims for Poetry* (1982). Though Hall's anthology does not share the concentrated focus of *A Broken Thing*, it deserves special mention for its prescient defense of the kind of hybridity and ecumenism discussed above. Emerging on the heels of the *Field* and *Epoch* symposia, *Claims for Poetry* harbors none of the early conservatism that had tended to mark his career ever since he unfurled his landmark anthology *New Poets of England and America* (1957), which fell decidedly on the reactionary side of the unfolding anthology wars of the 60s and 70s. Instead, *Claims for Poetry* forswears allegiance to any single tendency, offering an arbitrary alphabetical list of over thirty essays by poets as different as

A. R. Ammons, Wendell Berry, Robert Duncan, Sandra Gilbert, John Hollander, X. J. Kennedy, Audre Lorde, Jackson Mac Low, Ron Silliman, Mark Strand, and Alice Walker. Donald Hall's eloquent defense of his anthology speaks to our purpose just as well. He writes of the dynamic "accidents of juxtaposition" that the arbitrary ordering affords. With such a motley crew, one cannot possibly neatly navigate what he calls the "collage of contentions"; one can only catalog their divergent claims for poetry: "conflicting, overlapping, contentious; avant-garde, reactionary; immemorial, neoteric; light, heavy, angry, funny, political, aesthetic, academic, psychological, innovative, practical, high-minded, abstract, frivolous, pedagogic" (xi). With no overlap in authors, and with nearly twice as many essays, we hope that A Broken Thing will become as indispensible as Claims for Poetry, both for new generations of poets and for scholars eager to track developments in twenty-first-century poetry and poetics.

MAPPING THE LINE

Emily Rosko

We have such lines here—to name a few: lines of sight and lines of thought; the line as musical and textual scoring, as voicing and orality; the line as geneal-ogy and elegy; materialities of the line, both in the world and in cyberspace. As Lisa Steinman generously noted in an early response to the essays assembled here, "to consider the tropes used to describe lines of poetry—and to notice that they are tropes—is precisely the kind of insight this diverse collection al-lows." Needless to say, it is difficult adequately to survey the essays included here, which represent a diversity of practice and a historical arc that take us, quite literally, from Hammurabi's Code to hypertext and Twitter. The attempt that follows remains a knowingly partial gloss, what Robert Creeley might call a quick graph. We encourage each reader to make her or his own map.

Near the start of the collection, Marianne Boruch articulates a common theme throughout these essays. "The line against the larger wealth of the sentence," she writes, "is a rebel thing which undercuts order. With it comes all that can't be fully controlled: the irrational, the near-deranged, the deeply personal and individual utterance." Sarah Kennedy supplies us with a more visceral image that we might keep in mind when considering the line's critical, even violent, energy. Her figure for lineation was conceived in a grocery store parking lot in the face of a howling, growling dog unleashed in the bed of a 4×4: "The poetic line: a big dog in a truck." Conceding that "lines of poetry are musical in their rhythmic cadences, yes, and they make meaning(s), yes, and they are often beautiful, yes," she continues to argue that "what makes a line of words a poetic line rather than just part of a sentence broken halfway across the page is that tensive moment at the last word, when the entire animal rushes to the boundary in full gorgeous fury." For many others, however, it is not this more pointed danger, but how the line holds us close in its cadence, how the line shades into music. "Whether we attend to the fact or not," Tim Seibles begins, "poetry has deep roots in song. Beyond their meanings, words are sounds, *notes* if you will." Whether we view the line as a marker of subversive, even dangerous, power or as the pure pulse of poetic song, as a matter of technical mastery or as an invitation to philosophical and social reflection, these essays as a whole remain interested in the grounding question of how and why poets do or do not break lines. The varied and inventive answers to this grounding question contained herein offer so many crucial windows into how poetry means, and why it continues to matter.

Sturdy conversations underscoring the centrality of the poetic line find new life here. Timothy Liu combines a lively anecdote with his take on a classic pedagogical lesson involving the transposition of poems into prose and vice versa. Robert Wrigley makes no fuss about it and declares that the poetic line, whether free or metered, is the only tool: "All the other attributes poetry is said to possess," he proffers, "are bullshit." Other poets—including Bruce Bond, Scott Cairns, and Thomas Lux—reinvigorate these fundamental genre distinctions with powerful statements about how the line remains fundamental to poetry, how it holds a provocative agency that involves the reader in the poem's unfolding: its momentary plays against concision, to borrow Cairns's apt phrase with its Frostian echoes. Indeed, many of the essays here touch on that central tension between sense and syntax, but they often give this traditional binary a new twist, a new language. Cole Swensen, for example, thinks of "the crux of poetry as twofold—as excess and as incommensurability: the shape of sense and the shape of language simply aren't the same, and poetry is the form that, above all others, refuses to make light of that difference. And so it must, instead, address it. Poetry has historically addressed it through the line-break."

Confessing that she has become wary "of thinking about the poetic line solely . . . as single-voiced encounters playing with expectation and the ephemeral" where emphasis falls always at the line's end, Catherine Imbriglio describes how she has come to think of "the entire line, not just beginning and end words, as setting up tensions between the temporal and the spatial, with *each* line having a hard-core relation with *every other line and every space* in the poem, not just the ones before and after it." Concurring that we often tend to overvalue line-breaks over the line itself, V. Penelope Pelizzon turns our attention to the beginnings of lines, and, through a reading of Frank Bidart, she examines how the rhythm of a line can be established or productively disrupted by what she terms "soft" or "strong" entrances. Molly Peacock puts pressure on the middle of lines as a place to delicately fold in rhyme. Annie Finch, who has previously pursued T. S. Eliot's notion that one might discover the metrical code, the ghost of meter, in free verse, foregoes the dug-in defensiveness of New Formalist polemics as she argues for the presence of something like a line-break after each poetic foot. Tellingly, even though she sardonically reflects on how the line has too often become the lone tool for free-verse poets, she defines her sense of metrics not against, but in positive relation to, that dominant facet of the free-verse line. Kevin Prufer looks not only to the ghost of meter in free verse, but to the uses of freedom within fixed forms. Expanding the kinds of things that fall within the purview of the line, Terese Svoboda describes how the line lurks even in prose as well.

Departing from the concerns of technique, other contributors more philosophically defend the value of the poetic line as the singular unit of meaning in poetry. For Heather McHugh, the line models a finely honed and necessary attention, even shelter, in terms that echo Frost's famous definition of poetry as a momentary stay against confusion. "The poetic line," she writes, "is an advertency constructed to contend with a world of inadvertencies—inadvertencies that, otherwise, could swamp us." Graham Foust sees the poetic line as an integer of consciousness, where it figures as both the enactment of a "thinking subject" and, at the line-break's pause, the poet's consciousness thrown back on the "thought-about object." Placing equal weight on the importance of every line in a poem—of each line's purposeful integrity—Alberto Ríos reminds us: "A line is a moment that has value right then, and which deserves some of our time." Noting a very similar meditative potential in the line, Kazim Ali offers the following figure: The poem is "not mere rhetoric or reportage or description, but pure mystery, an aspirant to the divine. A book of poems is an abbey of aspirants, each reciting a line to herself in meditation." Suggesting how mysterious and private poems can appear, even to their writers, and questioning any poetics that would seek to tell us what a poem ought or ought not do, John Gallaher concludes that the poem itself must teach us how to read it: "The poem becomes a one-time use definition of line-break, line, stanza, and so forth."

The philosophical graces the physical in Susan Stewart's fluid essay in which she embraces the breath, the voice, the hand, and the body's dance, all of which underlie a line's making. Drawing attention to the gendered language of poetic discourse and its limited binary logic, she jests: "All my endings would be feminine unless they were masculine." Catherine Barnett weaves in a subtle feminist critique to the work of lineation when she admits that "there is an energy in breaking that is perhaps too often sworn or wooed or won out of women. I spend an awful lot of time trying to fix things, trying to make things. I am glad to be able to break." This visceral physicality that accompanies the making and breaking of lines is key for Carl Phillips as well: "There's the strange, undeniable pleasure both in controlling and in being controlled," he writes.

Arielle Greenberg blends the physicality of the line with its potential for an expansive rhetoric as she considers what she calls the "*hyperextension* of the line," which involves "pushing the line past the point of sentence unit into something that feels at once fragmented and stretched." Cynthia Hogue, moving more explicitly from formal to social reflection, explores how the calculated spatial suspension that enables many of Williams's punning lines becomes devastating in Leslie Scalapino's revisions of them in the context of the recent wars in Iraq and Afghanistan. "The line," Hogue reminds us, "is telling, not only in what it says but what it doesn't say." Paisley Rekdal further argues how lineation supports meanings that are not explicitly voiced, enabling broader explorations of identity and cultural critique, something she finds exemplified in the increasingly fragmented lines of Myung Mi Kim's "Food, Shelter, Clothing."

In the same way that Rekdal turns to Kim, or Hogue to Scalapino, many of the contributors here root their reflections in a fine attention to the work of other poets. This crucial dialogue comes to life in Dana Levin's comparative look at Allen Ginsberg's hurtling, uncontainable line and the contrastive appreciation it inspires for the radical enjambments of a poet like Michael Dickman. "I could meditate for quite some time on 'I'm not dead but I am,'" she tells us, reflecting on a line from Dickman. Joanie Mackowski distinguishes the "productively destabilizing free-verse lines" in Forrest Gander's work against the more gimmicky line-break one encounters all too often. Shara McCallum turns to poems by Gwendolyn Brooks and Yusef Komunyakaa to show "how the line in free verse, chafing against or in concert with the sentence, creates a rhythm that corresponds to the inflections of an actual, human voice." Touching on poets as different as Longfellow and May Swenson, William Carlos Williams and Carl Sandburg, Ravi Shankar unpacks notions of pace, tradition, risk, and sport that chart the possibilities of lineation. Wayne Miller revisits Emily Dickinson's use of the line, offering striking close readings that show how her dash often does the work of a line-break. Looking to the work of Lily Brown and G. C. Waldrep to demonstrate the fundamentally re-orienting quality of our best poetry—a quality that becomes a kind of ethical charge—Joshua Marie Wilkinson argues that in such poems we "discover new techniques of the poetic line" that have the ability to "undo what we have unwittingly come to expect from poetry, from language, from one another."

Many poets here reevaluate poetic traditions or trace deep histories of the line, theoretical, formal, or otherwise. Jenny Mueller and Karla Kelsey offer the kind of incisive reappraisals of modernist and language-poetry practices that too often escape critical attention. As the sole contributor to endorse the syllabic line, Robyn Schiff argues that the formal constraint presented by syllable-counting demands "the most physical encounter with words both orally and textually." Joshua Clover's more theoretical piece pursues Theodor Adorno's influential claim that "the unresolved antagonisms of reality appear in art in the guise of immanent problems of artistic form" (8). Turning to the emergence of the free-verse line and the burgeoning problematic of form that resulted in the early twentieth century, Clover suggests one answer to the question of "why this particular mutation of the line appears as an immanent problem of poetic form around the turn of the century." Taking us back to the speculative origins of the line, Johanna Drucker turns to ancient Babylonian inscription, highlighting the way the graphic line was used at times in cuneiform writing to divide signs into semantic units. This stunning piece of poetic archeology beautifully supplements her essay from *The Line in Postmodern Poetry* on "The Visual Line."

While many contributors here look to the practice of their peers, others reflect upon the sense of the line that motivates their own work. There are lively accounts of personal encounters with the line and its difficult potentialities by Brent Cunningham, John O. Espinoza, Kimiko Hahn, Raza Ali Hasan, Martha Rhodes, and Dana Roeser. Meanwhile, poets such as J. P. Dancing Bear, Patrick Phillips, and Mary Ann Samyn track the idiosyncratic ways that the line becomes a measure and a means for composition in their own work. For their part, Ben Lerner and Donald Platt offer candid insights into what motivates and sustains a broken line in their work. Harnessing speech acts, such as the stutter, false start, and interruption, and also using a technique that he calls "braiding lines," Lerner writes that his goal with each line is to "focus attention on the activity of thinking over the finished thought." As a practitioner of a highly particular use of the line across a career, Platt explains that his line use (of alternating long and short lines arranged in tercets) offers a generative constraint with which to shape poetic thought. Platt is an interesting exception among poets insofar as the line—his line, across a body of work—is not a variable but a constant, a kind of signature.

Other contributions, more difficult to typify, range from the cutting-edge to the colloquial, from the experimental to the everyday. Evie Shockley, with John Cage's mesostic form in mind, proposes exchanging strict linearity for more "circuitous routes" as she details this operation in one of her own poems. At the forefront of new-media poetics, Stephanie Strickland argues that in digital poetry the line does not break but embodies "an entire interactional system," thriving dynamically and simultaneously across multiple digital dimensions. Playing with the ways the line is woven into everyday language and cliché, H. L. Hix raids the colloquial for insights into the poetic. Noah Eli Gordon offers four cryptically Blakean allegories, each concluding with riddle- or koan-like keys that often obscure as much as they clarify, as when he concludes the first allegory with the chiastic observation that "the line fears its love of tradition and loves its fear of innovation." Charles Bernstein supplies the most micro of contributions here, with a poem consisting of three sections of three, four, and five lines, all knocking the language of cliché off center just enough to force insight: "you / break it / you / thought it," the middle poem scolds. Good advice indeed, for, as he concludes: "a / line is / a / terrible thing / to waste."

The line lives in these essays most often as a spur to thought, a barometer of historical change, and an index of current creativity. "I wonder, above all else," Kathy Fagan writes in her essay here, "what a poet's up to with a line. I adore how charged the choices are. How vital to the body of the poem and its meaning, and how ferociously poets, experienced or not, cling to lineation." The obverse, of course, is true as well, and a number of essays here demonstrate that a poet's questioning or even rejection of lineation remains just as vital to the body and meaning of the poem. This broken thing does not require our critical care, some suggest; it requires fundamental realignment, if not utter obliteration. Bruce Andrews revisits and refines his 1988 piece that appeared in *The Line in Postmodern Poetry*, filling out his previous essay via generous inter- and intra-sentence glosses that highlight the reception, rather than production, of lines. Against normative lines—lines of control, property, policing, decorum—he pitches the line as a "countering, an unorthodoxy on [& of] lines of space & time." Yet he maintains a sobering sense of how poetic lines and the theorizing that surrounds them so often fail to gauge and reconfigure the social: "but don't we want to get off the surface," he writes, interrupting his own heady theoretical riff more than two decades later. Gabriel Gudding tosses aside even this strained and tested idealism that one glimpses in Andrews, stocking his representative poetry workshop full of straw people and offering a list of poetic offenses. His essay is a rollicking catalogue of lyric hyperbole where the line exists as a "fascist reliquary," a "vomito-aesthetic concrescence of a larger, mystifying ideology." Such vitriol makes one wonder whether his gracious pastoral coda voices his earnest hope or his own cynically deferred dream. A striking rhetorical counterpoint to Gudding's piece, Emmy Pérez's essay weighs the relevance of the poetic line against social realities that exist much closer to home: "How to teach about the poetic line, about desire and syntax, about a poem's formal considerations as equally significant to the exploration of content, as a search for social justice and possibility," she asks, "when students and I are standing in Hidalgo, Texas, touching the new concrete border wall?" Voicing a strained hope that the poetic and the political might be integrally related, her essay demands much of us as line-makers and line-readers, but even more as human beings straddling a fraught border.

Confronting a very different sort of material reality, a few notable entries here interrogate how the page imposes limits to the poetic line. Hadara Bar-Nadav raises the question of whether a prose poem has line-breaks—breaks that are determined by page size and formatting, such that a prose poem in one venue offers radically different meanings than it might in another where more generous margins alter the arbitrarily encoded endings. Rachel Zucker forces a different understanding of what we mean by the economy of the line when she discusses how she decided to pay a press so that her poems could appear in a wide-trim book size that could accommodate her long lines. Christina Davis echoes this concern for the page and how a poet's lines operate within set dimensions when she asks of Dickinson's work: "Who are we to say that her lines are not as long as Whitman's in proportion to their original, originating space?" In her essay, Mei-mei Berssenbrugge discusses this idea of space and how she felt the accommodating wideness of a line pulled across a horizontal page: "To register many small colorations or distinctions, I needed a long, pliant thread. I was also transforming some philosophical ideas into the lyric, and I needed room." In appreciation of Berssenbrugge's line, Christine Hume begins her tribute to this crucial figure with a rhetorical question: "Remember rotating a journal sideways for the first time to read the Mei-mei Berssenbrugge line?" Such a question kindles a kind of wonder that the poetic line can alter not only how we use the page, but how we conceive of it and hold it.

In what remains a distinguishing aspect of this collection, a number of poets have exchanged theoretical or lyrical prose reflections for enactments of the line itself in works driven by image, collage, association, accumulation, and, of course, line-breaks. Responding to a reading by poet Raúl Zurita, Norma Cole reflects on lines not broken but shattered, where "everything opens up"—a phrase that suggests both certain possibilities of form and also a violent entry into a shattered world-historical reality. For Sarah Gridley and Sarah Vap, explorations of the line blend autobiography and literary pastiche, as when Vap hears in the line a directive to "*Go back*" as she traces a personal (and a universal) genealogy through parents and children, landscape and nature. Fanny Howe's unique poetic creation embodies an argument for plain poetry as a tool for writing instruction in the classroom: "If the children could see / the points where breath / and length come together / they might decipher / the necessity of syntax," she argues. "They might feel the stirrings / of love for harmony / and complexity / that exists in grammar."

Given the enormous wealth and range of poetic thought in this collection, it is important to note what appear as recurring intensities. First, a preponderance of pastoral imagery courses through these essays. Urban landscapes—so fundamental to poetic modernism from Charles Baudelaire to Langston Hughes, and crucial as well to the lines of postwar poets such as Frank O'Hara and George Oppen—are almost entirely absent. These contributions do much more than equate poetry to nature, of course, and it is stunning to note the richness of the eco-minded figures that flower here, as when Laura Mullen describes the line as "a scored portion of shared sky." For Camille Dungy, the variable motion of ocean waves correlates with the poetic line, and for Donald Revell, the poetic line embodies a "motile" movement, which he senses palpably in nature. Although urban architecture constitutes part of Eleni Sikelianos's explorations, she moves beyond the city in favor of nature's line models such as "the jointed segments in arthropods."

A second distinct node of concern has to do with the somber tone that recurs throughout. Where Olsonian discussions of the line's energy course through *Epoch*'s symposium, an unmistakable elegiac quality resides in many essays here. Though never an absolute focus, it lingers in the background just as it lingers in life, as when Jenny Mueller imagines the free-verse line in age: "What does one make of this wild child so many years on, now that it is bald not in birth but in dotage? Writing with this line today, we rarely associate it with the shock of the new—if by 'new' we also mean youthful. In fact, the modern line feels quite old, bearing as it does the freight of modernism's appalled hopes." It seems that after periods of prosodic bickering, there is a return to a more authentic and grounded reflection on matters of form. Furthermore, though one cannot definitively announce a shifting ground, one wonders to what extent these concentrations on elegy and death suggest some anxieties about the role of poetry in culture itself, just as the emphases on organic imagery occur alongside an increasingly imperiled Earth. Or perhaps this elegiac temper highlights a certain aging of the very terms we use to discuss poetic concepts. As Ed Dorn reminds us, this talk of the line is an aged and aging discourse.

For all the discovery and energy engendered in the line, then, it might finally seem a vehicle of loss. The line is something—to borrow a line from Robert Creeley's "The Innocence"—always "partial, partially kept," a presence verging on an absence (118). But the line also summons the desire to begin again, somewhere. And so we begin, *A Broken Thing*.

WORKS CITED

Adorno, Theodor W. *Aesthetic Theory*. Trans. Robert Hullot-Kentor. Minneapolis: University of Minnesota Press, 1997.

Beyers, Chris. *A History of Free Verse*. Fayetteville: University of Arkansas Press, 2001.

Blake, William. *William Blake: The Complete Illuminated Books*. New York: Thames & Hudson, 2000.

Creeley, Robert. *The Collected Poems of Robert Creeley, 1945–1975*. Berkeley: University of California Press, 1982.

Cushman, Stephen. *Fictions of Form in American Poetry*. Princeton, NJ: Princeton University Press, 1993.

Dodd, Wayne, ed. "Free Verse Issue." Special issue, *Ohio Review* 28 (1982).

Dorn, Ed. "Strumming Language." *Talking Poetics from Naropa Institute*. Ed. Anne Waldman and Marilyn Webb. Boulder: Taylor and Francis, 1978. 83–97.

DuPlessis, Rachel Blau. *Blue Studios: Poetry and Its Cultural Work*. Tuscaloosa: University of Alabama Press, 2006.

East, James, ed. *The Humane Particulars: The Collected Letters of William Carlos Williams and Kenneth Burke*. Charleston: University of South Carolina Press, 2003.

Frank, Robert, and Henry Sayre, eds. *The Line in Postmodern Poetry*. Urbana: University of Illinois Press, 1988.

Friebert, Stuart, David Walker, and David Young, eds. *A Field Guide to Contemporary Poetry and Poetics*. 1980. Revised, Oberlin, OH: Oberlin College Press, 1997.

Fulton, Alice. *Feeling as a Foreign Language: The Good Strangeness of Poetry*. Saint Paul, MN: Graywolf Press, 1999.

Grossman, Allen. *The Sighted Singer: Two Works on Poetry for Readers and Writers*. Baltimore: Johns Hopkins University Press, 1992.

Hall, Donald, ed. *Claims for Poetry*. Ann Arbor: University of Michigan Press, 1982.

———. "The Line." In Friebert, *A Field Guide*, 88–90.

Holscher, Rory, and Robert Schultz, eds. "A Symposium on the Theory and Practice of the Line in Contemporary Poetry." *Epoch* 29 (Winter 1980): 161–224.

Levertov, Denise. *New and Selected Essays*. New York: New Directions, 1992.

Longenbach, James. *The Art of the Poetic Line*. St. Paul, MN: Graywolf Press, 2008.

McGurl, Mark. *The Program Era: Postwar Fiction and the Rise of Creative Writing*. Cambridge: Harvard University Press, 2009.

McPherson, Sandra. "The Working Line." In Friebert, *A Field Guide*, 75–80.

Milton, John. *The Major Works*. Ed. Stephen Orgel and Jonathan Goldberg. Oxford: Oxford University Press, 1991.

Olson, Charles. *The Maximus Poems*. Berkeley: University of California Press, 1985.

Perloff, Marjorie. "After Free Verse: The New Nonlinear Poetries." *Close Listening: Poetry and the Performed Word*. Ed. Charles Bernstein. Oxford: Oxford University Press, 1998. 86–110.

———. "The Linear Fallacy." *Georgia Review* 35.4 (Winter 1981): 855–868.

Rosko, Emily, and Anton Vander Zee, eds. "Symposium on the Line: Theory and Practice in Contemporary Poetry." *Center: A Journal of the Literary Arts* (2008): 47–145.

Scully, James. *Line Break: Poetry as Social Practice*. Willimantic, CT: Curbstone Press, 1988.

Stevens, Wallace. *The Collected Poems of Wallace Stevens*. New York: Knopf, 1971.

Swensen, Cole. Introduction to *American Hybrid*. Ed. Cole Swensen and David St. John. New York: W. W. Norton, 2009.

Wesling, Donald. "Free Verse." *The New Princeton Encyclopedia of Poetry and Poetics*. Ed. T. V. F. Brogan and Alex Preminger. Princeton, NJ: Princeton University Press, 1993. 426–427.

———. *The Scissors of Meter: Grammetrics and Reading*. Ann Arbor: University of Michigan Press, 1996.

Wheatley, Phillis. *The Collected Works of Phillis Wheatley*. Ed. John Shields. Oxford: Oxford University Press, 1989.

Whitman, Walt. *Complete Poetry and Collected Prose*. New York: Library of America, 1982.

Williams, William Carlos. *Imaginations*. New York: New Directions, 1970.

———. *Paterson*. Ed. Christopher MacGowan. New York: New Directions, 1995.

———. *Selected Essays*. New York: Random House, 1954.

Wordsworth, William. *The Prelude: 1799, 1805, 1850*. Ed. Jonathan Wordsworth, M. H. Abrams, and Stephen Gill. New York: W. W. Norton, 1979.

Wright, James. "A Response to 'The Working Line.'" In Friebert, *A Field Guide*, 81–83.

On the Line

Kazim Ali

When we talk about the line we should talk about the line separate from came before it or after it, otherwise it is merely a sentence in prose with a break for visual effect.

As in Michael Palmer's "Notes for Echo Lake 4": "whose is the voice that empties."

Or Jorie Graham's "Underneath (13)": "explain to me remains to be seen."

Or does the line require separate life, separate from the poem, text without context.

The line itself, ornate and gorgeous, creates a texture defined by the space between one line and the next.

Something exists in the here and now with no dependence on before or after.

Few "prose poems" seem to work with the single sentence as a carrier of poetic weight and instead work primarily with the paragraph as a basic unit, which seems to me to be just another way to frame a moment as complete but not explore the fleetingness, uncapturability, and pure tragic drama of a single moment that passes and has to pass.

Hence a "prose poem" really is just prose, the beginning of an essay that writer has chosen not to finish, or the beginning of a fiction that an American ear has not had enough guts to see as such.

Why should one bother, when working with the single line as a compositional unit in poetry, with a traditional Western structure of SUBJECT-VERB-OBJECT.

Don't we all already know that the human being is master of the universe and will act upon the planet / the poem / the colonized subject any way he pleases?

It is time for art to start reimagining and reorienting the conceptual understanding of the universe.

A moment needs to be seen anew.

In other words a poem doesn't have to be a transmission from mouth to ear or page to mind but can be a place in which things actually *happen*.

The poetic line ought not be buckled to conventional syntax, it ought to demonstrate the actual powers of poetry to move the mind beyond the mundane, as in Jorie Graham's truncated Wyatt quote that opens *The Errancy*—"Since in a net I seek to hold the wind."

—or Broumas and Begley's ecstatic inventions in *Sappho's Gymnasium*—"Lord let me all I can wild cherry."

It ought to be able to do more, be more, transcend the pedantic definition of language as a carrier of discursive meaning and by its motion enable the mind to follow and have an understanding that is past intellectual and enters conceptual.

In my work I don't seek to move from beginning to end of a certain poem. Such predetermined motion is meant for paragraphs and stanzas.

To proceed line by line means not to feel yourself forward in the dark but to throw yourself with abandon into the arms of darkness.

Led by language, led by intuitive leaps of thought, a poem does not presume.

Not mere rhetoric or reportage or description, but pure mystery, an aspirant to the divine.

A book of poems is an abbey of aspirants, each reciting a line to herself in meditation. The lines could be heard as a chorus, in any order, simultaneously, or backwards to forwards.

Now everyone is joining in the effort of creating one-line poems, via Twitter posts.

Paul Virilio: "There is no here anymore, only now."

What he meant was a collapse of geography and distinction of place.

Or rather than collapse a conflation of all places into one place: the screen.

But what are the possibilities of a new form?

Olga Broumas: "transitive body this fresco I mouth."

Agha Shahid Ali: "of what shall I not sing and sing?"

Anne Shaw is Twittering (prettier sound than "Tweeting," don't you agree?— meaning is determined, after all, by sound) a project of individual one-line poems:

"help to winter me a small belief"

"i (in)visible"

"you bereft believer say you will return"

As in the court culture described in The Tale of Genji, poetry and letter writing each become a public art, deliciously shared and responded to.

But also allows a bravery.

One can cast a thought into the silence.

And then another.

By discrete moments, little swabs, a life can appear.

What Stein could have Twittered. The thought leaves me breathless. But would she have. And if she would have could she have. And if she could have she could have but you still could not say she would have.

A line is one single line and Stein needed a lot of them, dropped one after the other.

And what is the appeal then of a single line uttered in a poetic landscape governed now by the book, the thought of a book as an entity, a unit, and in an information landscape, saturated as Virilio says, with immediacy.

And it seems, increasingly, for any book—the form of the novel, the form of a memoir, blog, Web page—modes of information distribution are created and controlled by institutions in support of state and superstate (financial) power.

Even though you must think that when information flows, any communication of the individual spirit is always counter to the centralizing urge.

I said things in my book *Bright Felon* the only way I could. Slowly. One line. And then another.

If Virilio is correct and there is only a now, then wouldn't a chorus of coruscating voices from every last place in the world help us to believe once more in place, in actual human lives, bodies that really matter?

In Arabic, "word," "breath," and "spirit" are all the same: "ruh."

Yoko Ono dreamed a film in which every single person in the world smiled.

What if every human body that existed was given a chance to breathe one utterance of how she felt, what he was doing, what she dreamed of.

Once more from Anne Shaw: "begin again in whether"

The poet is a tricky channeler then to be able to discern music, to order the lines on a page, or to seek other more transgressive models for poetry, as it occurs.

It is not that meaning is less important than music in poetry, but that when we say "meaning" we don't know what we mean.

WORKS CITED

Ali, Agha Shahid. *The Country Without a Post Office: Poems 1991–1995*. New Delhi: Pauls Press, 1997.

Broumas, Olga, and Begley, T. *Sappho's Gymnasium*. Port Townsend, WA: Copper Canyon Press, 2000.

Graham, Jorie. *Swarm*. Hopewell, NJ: Ecco Press, 2001.

Palmer, Michael. *Codes Appearing: Poems 1979–1988*. New York: New Directions, 1988.

Shaw, Anne. Twitter. <http://twitter.com/anneshaw>.

Reading Lines Linear How to Mean

Bruce Andrews

Reading struggles to make meaning, meaning anew & embodied, or to make matter "matter." But, ideally: without letting too much "in the way of" presuppositions getting in the way of a reading experience & judgment, without their being kept too much "in line."[1]

1. First: the line can be an obstacle, a straightening barrier to experience's full efflorescence. *Lines linear outline*, a faux transparency of truth in packaging: *clear boundaries' effect*, its damper on our freedom of apprehension (prior to judgment), so we *notice the package from its perimeter*, or mistake the insides for the lining, as lines propose or valorize a *consistency*, an *evenness*, those *seemingly internal contours which end up packaging the insides so that they can react or point or be subordinated, as a homogenized unit, to what's outside*. A vertical axis (of reference: either representational or personally expressive) pulls our attention outward, but all the more easily (& seemingly without the violence of any command) if the internal packaging does its conservative work. The lining as containment, as a framing — an innocent jumble of material gets framed for crimes it hasn't yet committed, or expressions & references it's not even invested in. Magnetic pull of a limiting, pre-set (& seemingly non-public, privatizable) outside which forces or reduces our reading experience — helped along by the lining (& its supplement) of the insides. *Lines as signatures of meaning by inscription* — as if we're being asked to immobilize ourselves as we "second the motion" or, more likely, second a lack of motion; to become the hapless con who dutifully countersigns the author's signatures or the referential set-up's indexing, to end up reinforcing the coercive verticality of the text. We get inscribed. We get positioned, carefully, right above the line (as if we are in danger of falling off, going "wayward" — instead of being "wards" of "the way") — "*relationships by force*," by indexical overpowering, with circumstances turning us into clues (or clue

hunters) before we even get a chance to act for ourselves. Before the fact, but prepped for apprehension, as if *after the fact, marking off an internal hierarchy of value identified with parts or tags, disciplining the already constituted body.* Plus — doing this "ahead of time": if not disenfranchising our potential readings, then at least gridding or anticipating or preempting them, not doing justice to time [& its stand-ins, matter & materiality], but "just in time." *Too late.* Don't these function as colonizings? — operated by leash of closures of (prior or predictable) time or of outward (— someone else's, but not a collective public) space. Also: as if the two are mutually allegorizing. Readers [judges] set up (or locked in, locked up) to be in circumstances "behind the time" &/or in "outer space." *How far inside are we?* However far it is, it feels as if it's enforced, that we're usually getting "delivered." And marked (off & out) by outer lines. *Boundary as dividing* — marked by all the divvying up, the way danger zones are prepositioned — *"you step over that line & you're asking for trouble"* — *privatizing property,* broadcasting a mirage of sovereignty, of ownership, but *without* granting actual *(internal) authority.* Because internal authority is never secure, never solid enough. It depends upon a relationship to the outside, to external contexts, which it usually has trouble admitting to. *Territorial markers and confinements, ghost towns, congested metropolis on a grid. Readability underscores the openness.*

2. What is the experience? The readability? The judgment? *Words divide* — micro-level: the vectors of possibles (meaning & weight & movement) ricochet outward. A centrifuge of words & syllables & letters. Yet typically, at least in their normative [catalog] version, *lines unite.* This tilts toward containment, *a compact, to slim down & centripetalize & package up a single reading, helping offer that overall intonational curve so useful for language-learning & memory.* Once you unify the perspectives [/the vectors], it enables [/empowers] a shutting down of time & materialized openness, a closure on the horizontal axis. *A constructed continuity you find your way through,* to track & trail *a "power line," piping to convey a fluid.* [Yet we could recast the verb "convey" to underscore our subjection to constraint & fixing & imprinting, as it keeps time in line *in moves,* as if the reassuring *horizontal rows* are making regularity (or power lines) for us & of us.] As *if to create a loop or equivalences* — as in: our experience gets looped [the shadow of the eternal return]; our experience gets equivalented [the shadow of capital]. (Narrative, the cliché notion of how temporal closure operates.) To turn (at least potential) fluidity into *a static & isolating* [spatial compression — facilitated by freezing "time" up] & *securing closure of purpose.* But not our purpose — we who are dwarfed. Readers, getting a fix, fixed at the intersection of space & time — as axes, as lines. *It makes for size.*

3. So, for a reading, what could set itself up as a different kind of apprehension & ground for judgment — as a countering, an unorthodoxy on [& of] lines of space & time? What would facilitate new starts: *Better, constant crease & flux, a radical discontinuity as lack, jeopardizes before & after, stop & start, a dynamic in fragments, suggesting an unmappable space, no coordinates, troubling us to locate ourselves in formal terms. Polyrhythms' spatial counterpart, lack of (regular, traditional) closure as generative, tensions restored. It foregrounds an artificial, constructed process, a de-natured measure of kinetic shifts, registers of differentiation. This pluralism of incident, refusing all packages — not "cut to fit" — a luxurious anarchy, a fuller flowering or specificity of internal rhythms & semantic redistributions.*

4. Let's consider a centrifugal experience for readers — an enabling of (a potentially critical) judgment. To point or be thrown outward, crosshatching & relativizing. *Lines everywhere* [versus "any one where," or: Take Me to Totalityville] to be readable *as patches or territorial/spatial orchestrations, skeleton of volume, made* fragile or abstracted down to *structure exposed* [imaginatively empowered] *inside-out. Re*[-ad-]*vantaged* — reading operations experienced in motion. [No longer just a presupposed (either passive or static, let alone eternalized) reception.] *Refusing the normatively linear & its discipline (and delineation) in favor of a constructed conversation* — injecting heterogeneity inside (to transform things: into *celebratory form,* into a *participatory regime). To erase* those previously imposed *boundaries,* to *break up compactness* & containment, *in favor of a difference* & a less generic, *more individualized interior.* In a context: the inside is also outwardly framed or hinged or directed, not nearly so based on claims or promises of an autonomy, or an autarky, *an internal legitimacy.* This is a judgment call.

5. Yet, what about social circumstance, or social matter? If we don't go "all out" in our emphasis on reading experience, aren't we left with writing which is *still too self-enclosed* or seemingly self-legitimating? *A formally "contemporary" writing may propose the bogus immediacy of gesture as a codeless transparent revelation of the body, as if its markings were natural, neutral, to be taken for granted.* Because it's still claiming the autonomy of the text's body, the author's body — (or the silliness of imagining that these two, as if joined at the hip in some fancy celebration of freedom, can capture or map the social body). *Attention to a freer play of line, as formal course of writerly conduct ornamentally preening in its autonomy, may distract us from what's outside, from the regulatory limits & constraint of meaning as a horizon. Discontinuous breaks & patches can discombobulate the surface,* but don't we want to get off the surface?: *they can also be brought into the project of articulating an external context by embodying its complexities, with meaning's outer structure (language/society) as model and limit* — & *as ground for unlearning, contest & prescription.* By readers.

Self-governing is not free-floating — [that brand of formalism needs to be decommissioned] — instead: *its value hinges on that contextual understanding of structures & systems of significance & their horizons.* But that understanding is not guaranteed or even typical. It needs to be actively facilitated via readerly pressure & play. *An explanation in action that keeps crossing the line into a politics outside (its articulation into contested hegemonies, fields of force) & bringing it back inside to challenge the constitution (and possibilities) of meaning as well as form. "That's not a line, that's an idea."* That's not a writer's trophy; it's a reader's garden or maze.

1. Italicized material is the entire essay "Lines Linear How to Mean," from the symposium "L=A=N=G=U=A=G=E Lines" which Charles Bernstein and I edited about twenty years ago for the collection *The Line in Postmodern Poetry,* edited by Robert Frank and Henry Sayre (University of Illinois Press, 1988). The original short piece, like most of my early literary theorizing/conceptualizing, focused on production and its radical possibilities; the new version highlights issues centered around reading and reception.

Who Is Flying This Plane? The Prose Poem and the Life of the Line

Hadara Bar-Nadav

The prose poem is undeniably a contested form, one that led Karen Volkman, in her essay "Mutable Boundaries: On Prose Poetry," to refer to prose poetry's status as "shady and suspect to the mainstream poetry world." One need only look to the curious omission of prose poetry from such books on form as Mark Strand and Eavan Boland's *The Making of a Poem: A Norton Anthology of Poetic Forms* (2000) for confirmation of Volkman's statement. On the other hand, prose poetry has been too narrowly conceived and consequently misrepresented by some of its proponents. In *The Prose Poem: An International Anthology* (1976), Michael Benedikt defines the prose poem as "poetry, self-consciously written in prose, and characterized by the intense use of virtually all the devices of poetry. The sole exception is the line break" (47). Mary Ann Caws, in an entry for *The New Princeton Encyclopedia of Poetry and Poetics*, similarly decrees the prose poem a "controversially hybrid" genre "without the line breaks of free verse" (977). Rather than consider the prose poem a poetic form or genre without line-breaks, I would argue that the prose poem indeed contains line-breaks that are given over to chance operations and the margins established by a particular writer, journal, or publisher, or those set by or on a computer, typewriter, or printing press.

This revaluation of the prose poem as containing line-breaks that are imposed by the margin may surprise some. But when a prose poem breaks at the right margin, do we not stop for a brief moment, holding that last word on our tongues or in our ears, a slight lingering before we return to the left margin and take up the next line? In a prose poem, the line-break *is* the right margin. Certainly, a poem changes when lines are broken differently, and the shape of a poem shifts with the margins of a given publication, effectively reshaping and revising the poem.

Some might consider the prose poem a never-ending line, one that, if the page or computer screen allowed, would go on forever. However, I want to distinguish the prose poem from the long line—the insistence of breath in Walt Whitman and Allen Ginsberg or the embodied intellectual projects of Cole Swensen's *Ours* (2008) or Anne Carson's *Autobiography of Red* (1998). Some book publishers and literary journals accommodate the long line by producing oversized books or changing their print orientation from horizontal to vertical. Such a gesture generally would not be made to accommodate prose poetry. Unlike poets writing in the long line who write through the right margin, prose poets use the margin; they write both *through and against* the margin, even as it is arbitrarily assigned.

As one who writes prose poetry, I have come to enjoy that risk-taking right margin, the one that contains magical line-breaking properties and makes the poem come back to me anew. And I also enjoy the caginess of the prose poem, that inherent tension in the mission of its line to continue on forever (despite the margin) and to be turned (because of the margin).

One of the finest examples of the prose poem's capacity to simultaneously work through and against its margins is Claudia Rankine's *Don't Let Me Be Lonely: An American Lyric* (2004). Dominated by the prose-poem form, Rankine's book-length work was uniquely formatted by Graywolf in an off-sized book, approximately 5.5 inches wide and 10 inches long, with one-inch margins on the right and left. The book looks more like a pamphlet than a typical book of poetry, leaving just 3.25 inches for the text. Rankine's prose poem is compressed by these narrowly defined margins that make language press in on itself. Her squeezed lines suggest how narrow the vision of America (and poetry) may be, even as the poem simultaneously presses outward with its large vision of America, poetry, racism, illness, and loss.

For years I secretly thought about the life of the line in prose poetry, but a recent experience inspired my writing this essay. Being MLA trained, I default to one-inch margins, and the given confines of these margins actually helped me compose the prose poem "I Would Have Starved a Gnat." The very margins that had helped me compose the poem were blown open when the poem appeared in *Crazyhorse*. Below are the two versions (in each version the poem was justified on both sides). Even as I paste the original version I submitted, I repeat to myself the end-words as a guide to maintain the line-breaks: "Your"—"kiss"—"See"—"of"—"body"—"moist"—"half":

This lean of bone and tilt. All odd angles to the sun. Flut. Flet. Flatten me with your mad flit. Your fast tying hands. All odd angles and eminent collapse. Now on our knees. Now bowing. Please, kiss my littlest one. A video found in a bunker underground. I once was a night. Once nightly news. See the vultures and gnats flock to our shivering. *Food's necessity on me—like a Claw—*. A gathering of wingly things so all you see is weather. Turning iridescent. Turning black. The kingdom of the body blown to ash. Buttons of us left in the sun. The crown and the teeth. The aftermath. No moist benevolent thing between us. Take me. Take half.

And here's the same poem as it appeared in *Crazyhorse*:

This lean of bone and tilt. All odd angles to the sun. Flut. Flet. Flatten me with your mad flit. Your fast tying hands. All odd angles and eminent collapse. Now on our knees. Now bowing. Please, kiss my littlest one. A video found in a bunker underground. I once was a night. Once nightly news. See the vultures and gnats flock to our shivering. *Food's necessity on me—like a Claw—*. A gathering of wingly things so all you see is weather. Turning iridescent. Turning black. The kingdom of the body blown to ash. Buttons of us left in the sun. The crown and the teeth. The aftermath. No moist benevolent thing between us. Take me. Take half. (59)

The end words in the *Crazyhorse* version suggest less of a narrative, but are resonant in other ways: "flit"—"bowing"—"Once"—"a"—"Turning"—"and"—"half." Looking at these end words, the poem seems even more exploded or destroyed. This later version has a more intense tonal emptiness, and the line-break after the word "turning" suggests a kind of ironic self-consciousness about the prose poem form (that turns with or without an intentional turning), which I had in fact not originally intended.

When I was composing the poem, pushing against and through the one-inch margins helped me to write its ending. The weight of the previous lines seemed to bear down on the poem's closure. The final attenuated line hung halfway between each margin in a kind of no-man's-land that led me to articulate it: "Take me. Take half." Those four final words seemed suspended in mid-air like an explosion, which simultaneously pronounced the absence of the rest of the line. The version from *Crazyhorse*, however, extends that final line almost all the way to the right margin and offers a visual weightiness and completeness that by contrast creates tension in this poem about loss. Both versions are satisfying in different ways and both have different resonances thanks to their variously imposed line-breaks.

I could easily conclude that the habit of working within one-inch margins has influenced my poetry (just as William Carlos Williams's writing on prescription pads is said to have influenced his poetry). The margin helps me anticipate when a line will end, even if I am not always conscious of it. Although Benedikt points to prose poetry as being "self-consciously written," Russel Edson, one of the prose poem's most ardent advocates, playfully challenges this mode of intentionality (Benedikt 47). Edson comments on the surrealist and absurdist tendencies of prose poetry in his essay "Portrait of the Writer as a Fat Man," and explains, "The pilot is asleep. . . . This aeroplane seems to fly because its pilot dreams" (98).

The prose poem has a body, a shape; it is a carriage made of words whose lines will be formed, reformed, and transformed. And the poem will be born anew.

WORKS CITED

Bar-Nadav, Hadara. "I Would Have Starved a Gnat." *Crazyhorse* 74 (2008). 59.

Benedikt, Michael, ed. *The Prose Poem: An International Anthology*. New York: Dell, 1976.

Carson, Anne. *Autobiography of Red: A Novel in Verse*. New York: Random House, 1998.

Caws, Mary Ann. "Prose Poem." *The New Princeton Encyclopedia of Poetry and Poetics*. Ed. T. V. F. Brogan and Alex Preminger. Princeton, NJ: Princeton University Press, 1993. 977–979.

Edson, Russell. "Portrait of the Writer as a Fat Man." *Claims for Poetry*. Ed. Donald Hall. Ann Arbor: University of Michigan Press, 1982. 95–103.

Rankine, Claudia. *Don't Let Me Be Lonely: An American Lyric*. St. Paul, MN: Graywolf Press, 2004.

Swensen, Cole. *Ours*. Berkeley: University of California Press, 2008.

Volkman, Karen. "Mutable Boundaries: On Prose Poetry." *Poets.org*. The Academy of American Poets. 5 May 2009. <http://www.poets.org/viewmedia.php/prmMID/5910>.

Three Takes on the Line

Catherine Barnett

GLASS HALF BROKEN

On my bookshelf I keep two broken glasses. Where they are broken they catch the light. That they are broken calls up the "what was," a past wholeness. Perhaps because I came to poetry after writing and editing prose I am especially drawn to the break, the ways poetry is a "ruin" of prose, the way what is missing—even in the momentary missing that is the end of a line—is simultaneously present and absent. At the Louvre, the *Winged Victory* has no head, no arms—we go looking for them, then make them in our seeing. The viewer fills in her missing parts and is simultaneously moved by their absence.

I love to fix; I didn't know how much I loved to break until a teacher encouraged me to try writing a poem. I didn't know exactly what line was, only that I could break it. And then fix it, affix it, by or to what follows. Or not. My experience tells me some things cannot be fixed.

Charles Wright talks about the "making" of a line, preferring "making" to "breaking." I think it's a matter of temperament whether you want to break or make. There is an energy in breaking that is perhaps too often sworn or wooed or won out of women. I spend an awful lot of time trying to fix things, trying to make things. I am glad to be able to break.

PRESERVE YOUR OPTIONS

Maybe it's not so much that I like breaking the line as that I like the chance to keep beginning. I have never been good at endings, neither at making conclusions nor at following through. The promise of a break, the allure of breaking a line, lets me feel I never need to settle, or be certain, too fixed. My father taught us—I am not always happy to have learned this lesson—to "preserve your options."

Poetry gives me endless options, and where and how to end the line is, for me, one of the most energizing possibilities, uncertainties, because it holds within it the possibility of beginning again at the next line, and that little vertical fall is fuel, libido, a little vertigo—and because it holds within it the possibility that the line won't end, not / this / time. Preserving your options is only a poor man's strategy for forestalling death. A line-break is the same. Mortality confronts you at every line. Is this it? Is this it? Is / this / it?

Not long ago I overheard a conversation at my local diner between a woman and her boyfriend. He asked the woman please to be certain that the dash on his tombstone be very long. He wanted to show that a lot had been achieved between the beginning and the end: this could be how one conceives of line. Can I, through strategies of compression, shove so much into a line that my dash, though short, be long?

The fact that a line *ends* calls to mind the less negotiable ending we have always to contend with.

THE AFTER-SILENCE

Line makes language into *material*; it's like Jean Valentine's "red cloth . . . on the ground." Line also makes its opposite—white space, the silence out of which the line arises, the silence into which it falls—more palpable. Coming to poetry from prose, I am still most excited by the "after-silence" that marks the end of every line, by the energy I get from discovering when and where this after-silence resides.

How long does it last? Listen to Williams fighting "against time," trying to speak to his wife, whom he'd betrayed:

And so
         with fear in my heart
                  I drag it out

and keep on talking
         for I dare not stop.
                  Listen while I talk on

against time.
         It will not be
                  for long. (311)

These lines enact a continual confrontation with the after-silence that accompanies each urge to "keep on talking."

Some after-silences are louder than others, some more choked and death-inflected; some are acts of great intimacy, others acts of aggression. How a poet manages his or her lines, with their necessary silences, guides our listening.

As a poet and as a reader, I both crave and dread this after-silence, anticipating it even as I guard against it. "There's Ransom in a Voice—," writes Emily Dickinson. "But Silence is Infinity" (548).

WORKS CITED

Dickinson, Emily. *The Complete Poems of Emily Dickinson*. Ed. Thomas H. Johnson. New York: Little, Brown and Company, 1961.

Valentine, Jean. "Red Cloth." *The Nation* 22 April 2009 <http://www.thenation.com/doc/20090511/valentine2>.

Williams, William Carlos. *The Collected Poems of William Carlos Williams*. Vol. 2. New York: New Directions, 1967.

3/4/5

Charles Bernstein

Don't break
it—
spend it.

~

you
break it
you
thought it.

~

a
line is
a
terrible thing
to waste.

Two Lines

Mei-mei Berssenbrugge

A line of poetry on a page exists in space, but I think of it as a kind of timing, a measured flow of poetic energy, a dynamic. My sense of a line is given, as my way of walking or my voice is given and bodily. I walk a path from here to the edge of the woods, I read or speak a line, taking time. My line that required the page to go into landscape orientation was written in the wide landscape of New Mexico (subtle colorations of open, parallel ridges receding into distances, sun moving across during a day). As a person looking at the horizon, my sight line is perpendicular to the horizontal line of mountains. This compares to a person looking at a line of writing on a page, and the line length, the horizontal, is generated by your body's sense of extension, or periphery. To register many small colorations or distinctions, I needed a long pliant thread. I was also transforming some philosophical ideas into the lyric, and I needed room. I maintained the line's tension with internal rhymes and internal caesurae.

During a collaboration with artist Kiki Smith, while cutting up a poem to lay out on the page, I came upon a new lineation. Today, I use a line that varies in length, because each sentence is a line. Line length is determined by the length of the sentence, and I allow the line to break at the page margin and wrap around until the sentence comes to an end. Then I double space before the next "line." There is a dynamic tension between the extending sentence and the mini-breaks at the page margins, which adds geology to my landscape, and can also be architectural. Most recently, this lineation has given me enough structure to allow the poem to become very soft and still be contained.

The Summons of the Line

Bruce Bond

Take any novel. Now break it into the closest approximation of iambic pentameter that you can manage. Why is it bound to fail now? The answer brings us closer to what it is that makes a poem a poem, to the distinctive power of poetry implicit in the artful approach to the parts that make up the poem—most conspicuously, of course, the line. A novel broken into lines may be a poem, but not a good one, for many reasons. Principal among them is the squandering of time. The line encourages us, as do all poems of shimmer and evocation, to slow down. It is thus a summons, a call to our attention, a wager, a waver, a risk of the author's credibility, suggesting as it does that the language is under enough pressure to deserve more time, to yield more upon careful and repeated reading.

If not serving the traditional function of the mnemonic via traditional form, the line nevertheless facilitates and inspires memory. Perhaps more important to a poem than our absolute recall of it is our desire to recall it, to inhabit each line as one more room in the House of Memory. To know it by heart. And part of the heartbreak that is a poem's beauty; part of what weds a language to its form, thus making it a poem; part of what wins over the reader's faith in the search, the scrutiny, the *there* there, is deployment of richly resonant patterns of emphasis. Meaningful pairings, a harvest of enjambments, word play, tonal complication, reversals of expectation—all are made possible by both the continuity that is the line itself and the discontinuity that is the line-break. As a continuity, each line has a beginning, middle, and end—a sense of measured attention to whatever elements of language we choose to measure: weight, tone, music, image, syntax, the body of the poem and where that body takes us. As a discontinuity, the line-break is a form of the space that unites, like the air that touches the objects in a room.

Of course, the play between continuity and discontinuity governs all the arts, even novels, and, most obviously perhaps, forms of music. All art is the art of surprise. Any jazz player will tell you: too much change is boring. It takes the raising of an expectation to break an expectation. Imagine Mozart, the light breaking of an expectation that keeps the music fresh while strengthening the unity of expression, the sense of one thing growing from another, the logic that dreams. However illusory, it is a high art that wears its art lightly, a high art that takes our breath away with some resolution that only in afterthought feels like the absolute necessity, inevitable even—in the case of poetry, the best possible words in the best possible order. It is the larger pursuit of meaning in general that seeks freedom from both too much structure and too little, freedom from stricture, freedom from the arbitrary. Anything less would be stingy with pleasure and all it has to teach us. To teach by pleasing, that is what art is capable of, to engage us freely in a kind of dialogue of poem and the reader's co-creation.

As I mentioned, the line is particularly attractive since it gives our freedom a space to inhabit. Thus, the break as breath, if not literal then the figurative space, the little death that replenishes speech, the absence out of which presence is born. We, of course, could reverse the metaphor with the notion of speech as exhalation and thus as a spending of the breath. That too. With the line comes the foregrounding of the author's breath, the correlative to the musical phrase that longs to make an impression upon the silence that follows, to echo across the silence in a kind of counterpoint of the spoken and unspoken, the unspeakable no less. If this makes me post-postmodern or just plain modern, to foreground speech and thus a speaker, so be it. Why squander the immediacy of the music in our mouths? To dissociate language from a speaker or writer may be intriguing, but rarely very moving. It is a kind of nervous system torn from the body, spread out against a graph. A poem lives in a body. Ideas made sensuous, that's what Stevens called a poem. And as such, it is what makes the world into something we can love. Why not involve that body deeply down to the rich resources of the thinking heart? Why not a tune to cheer us? At least these are opportunities that the line offers. A good poem makes the most of its evolving possibilities in a way that surprises itself into a revelation of some kind. And so the line as the pulse, the throb of opportunity. Blake's grain of sand. Not to be wasted. Not to be ignored.

Secret Life

Marianne Boruch

Line. Of course—the major element in the great divide between poetry and prose, one of those first-glance definitions: a set of lines might well *equal* a poem, no matter what those lines contain. But this notion misleads. After all, it has been said endlessly that prose "chopped up into lines" isn't necessarily a poem. And poems do occur without lines. And sometimes even outside of poetry itself, if we are to believe Wallace Stevens on the subject.

Still. Still, the presence of line is a key reason poems *mime*, on the page, what's true, meaning what complicates, and therefore what resembles things as they really are. For starters, line is an architectural device that suggests what is profoundly interior, bringing up pause, hesitation, the heard and visual sense—*oh, I get it*—of something coming into being, right now. That interiority works directly against the bright, light, rational feel of the sentence—the very *public* sentence threaded down the page to make those lines.

It's ironic. The famously secret life of the poem is both revealed and protected by that good-doggy social contract of the complete sentence (oh, hard-working subject, verb, object!), even the ghost of one, via the fragment. Because the line against the larger wealth of the sentence is a rebel thing which undercuts order. With it comes all that can't be fully controlled: the irrational, the near-deranged, the deeply personal and individual utterance. Thus poetry. And the line—kept *almost* in line by the commonplace sentence—enacts its own small, large drama in direct cahoots with the strange, the unending.

A Momentary Play against Concision

Scott Cairns

A sufficiently textured line (that is, a troubled and troubling line) is the poet's best defense against the narrow tyranny of syntax.

Such a richly laden line (better yet, a poem whose every line performs in this way) also serves to guard against the poem's being replaced by its paraphrase or paraphrases, and frustrates the widespread disposition that a poem is to be approached as a difficult allegory, an encrypted message, a code to be cracked. This is a disposition often accompanied by another: believing that the poem, thus decrypted, thus cracked, can thereafter be dismissed.

This is why poems must be framed so as to say more than one thing—to say many things, and to keep on saying—if only as a matter of survival.

Assuming that in much verse (as in most prose) a poem's primary sense (occasioned by its more transparently referential activity) is provided by *the sense of syntax*, the verse poem's continuing riches—its sequential, provisional meanings—can be occasioned by *the sense of the line*, as each line, in turn, avails a momentary opacity that can suggestively extend, or complicate, or otherwise enrich the syntactical overlay of meaning constructed in the course of a given visit to the poem on the page.

Duly appreciated, this dynamic obtains for the poet, as well as for the reader, an understanding that the poem offers a place where meaning might be made, and made again. Committed to such a process, one learns to apprehend one's own sentences opening, one's own initial sense of things being challenged and altered. Moreover, in a sufficiently well-made poem, this dynamic serves the poet even beyond the period of composition, as visits to previously completed poems are rewarded with subsequent discovery.

It is self-evident that the "line of poetry" that simply moves the syntax along—as in a commonplace "line-phrasing" prosody—does no work, allows no play, and is therefore hardly a poetic line at all.

Finally, a series of well-worked lines (lines crafted so as to continue to *do* work) is the poet's greatest assurance of his saying more than what he intends. It is her protection against her poems becoming simple expressions of previously received matter, and his guarantee that he will not simply repeat what he thinks he already knows. More than anything else, then, the actual, real-time labor of attending to the line—mid-composition—is the labor that makes poetry a worthwhile vocation for the poet. Duly engaged, our working the lines avails for us in the midst of composition a glimpse of more than we meant to say; it is in working the lines this way that a poet realizes how poetry is chiefly a way of knowing, and not a way of saying what is already known.

Notes on the *Point de Capital*

Joshua Clover

The Argument: *Lacan's remarkable observation that "the sentence completes its signification only with its last term"(231), and thus that realization flows backward from the period—the* point de capiton, *or "quilting point"—is most significant for poetry, exactly because poetry proffers the false period of the line-break, with its incomplete completion of the phrase.*

STROPHE

a. The mutations of the English verse line in the twentieth century are many and various but can be coordinated by a crude fact: the abandonment of the line as a quantitative instrument measuring similar and repeating units of sound. That mode of lineation persists as a residual, but loses its capacity to define poetry and increasingly appears as antiquarian. Similarly, lines continue to measure; it is the quantitative regularity of repetition that is demobbed. No single counterexample serves to contradict this general tendency.

b. If this change is small, it tilts the balance of poetics decisively. What was already immanent in poetry—the line's incompleteness in the midst of the sentence—asserts itself absolutely.

c. The confrontation which has always characterized poetry, between sentence and line, period and carriage return, *point* and *counter-point*, now takes on the signal quality of underscoring language's slippage. The contingency of a line's meaning, the continuous activity of reinterpretation, the simultaneous motion by which each step forward throws the mind backward as well—all of this is the experience of linguistic slippage.

d. It is this situation that is indexed by metonymy's claim against metaphor in twentieth-century poetics—a development that is itself, thusly, a cause-consequence of the mutation in the line.

e. Metonymic slippage (*glissement*) ascends in twentieth-century poetry from ghost to king. The poem becomes a kind of alembic for this experience, testing, clarifying, intensifying. Meaning asserts itself as process rather than object; poetry shifts its allegiance from Parmenides to Heraclitus. The line was once a thing about which one could speak; now, *panta rhei*.

f. It is only at the period, Lacan's *point de capiton*, that the slippage is briefly halted, the retroactive double-motion rests, and meaning is quilted into place. Even this is temporary: the poem's renewed insistence on meaning as process reminds us not to take the completed sentence as truly fixed, nor the poem. To say that poems have always been ambiguous, meanings multiple, is to miss the particularities of twentieth-century poetics almost entirely.

ANTISTROPHE

a. One sees immediately that this development in the history of the line must make its successful claim at much the same time as the *Course in General Linguistics*, delivered as lectures between 1906–1911. The ascendant logic of the line is the logic of the signifier, extended from sign to syntax.

b. Structural linguistics provides poetry an uncanny complementarity to the decline of rhyme and meter: a kind of baton-pass in the history of the materiality of the signifier. As if the desire for the sensual characteristics of language must be sated somewhere.

c. But one sees as well that this Saussurean-Lacanian operation of retroactive realization that characterizes poetry—this relation between the period and the meaning—is not a purely linguistic fact (for Lacan thusly a psychoanalytic fact). It is the signal structure shared by language and capital.

d. Meaning and value (in the terms of political economy) circulate in much the same way: in flux, indeterminate in the midst of a moving structural relation, until coming to rest imperfectly at the period and the moment of sale, respectively.

$$M_s - M_f - M_b - M_i - C \cdots P \cdots C' - M'_i - M'_b - M'_f - M'_s$$

M=Money	i=industrial
C=Capital	b=bank
P=Production Process	f=other financial institutions
	s=speculative markets

e. Price is value's quilting point.

f. And so poetry provides the scene in which to think the operation of the *point de capiton* as a matter of political economy: the *point de capital*.

CATASTROPHE

a. Adorno: "The unresolved antagonisms of reality reappear in art in the guise of immanent problems of artistic form. This, and not the deliberate injection of objective moments or social content, defines art's relation to society."

b. We must then ask the question of why this particular mutation of the line appears as an immanent problem of poetic form around the turn of the century.

c. This appears as a question of modernism only insofar as it poses the question of why modernism wished to confront this problem, this thought about language and value.

d. There is a corollary question about postmodernism: can one think the further, late-modern changes in the line as attempts to grasp changes in late capitalism, as the value form attempts a new freedom of its own?

e. Answers to these questions are not necessary to recognize that the great object of thought for poetry in the twentieth century, via this mutation of the line, is *structure in motion*.

f. It is not a thought that can come to rest, any more than value comes to anything more than a temporary rest at the *point de capital*—as *structure in motion* is also a trade name for history, the real which resists symbolization absolutely

. . .

WORKS CITED

Adorno, Theodor W. *Aesthetic Theory*. Trans. Robert Hullot-Kentor. Minneapolis: University of Minnesota Press, 1997.

Lacan, Jacques. *Ecrits: A Selection*. Trans. Alan Sheridan. New York: Routledge, 2001.

Forever Amber

Norma Cole

I heard a real poet[1] reading his work yesterday. Shattering. When I looked at it in the book, I saw that there were no line-breaks. Not broken, shattered.
The sea captain tried to escape last night, but he was quickly captured by the pirates
1) off the coast of Somalia
2) in the Gulf of Aden
Perfume overcomes the trigger, the trauma, the shattering.
dream→Trauma
der Traum
As the man said, a little stimulation causes the line to break.
Wraps around
A tiny song:
Man with umbrella in backpack
So it won't rain
Nothing is reliable—look, my wrist doesn't move, the lines break, are broken, no safety here/near (when my cane, its curve resting on the table edge, falls down—crash—no one starts, stares. I pick it up
or will
)
Shooting schedule: shots of shots: e.g. 1-second shots of shooting (guns) from familiar or unfamiliar western, adventure, period, dramatic, comedy etc. movies
In blood we trust
uncertain ground→coherence of vibration
travelers' reports→disruption
other logics

Everything opens up. Pretending to read in order not to talk, moving from thought to thought to thought. The line? What about it?
Your thoughts were elsewhere.
Why stop with one?
Have three.
(melt away)
I think I'll stop here
but then go on
read "beer and sun"
for "bees and sun"
jingle of a bell on a bike
thumbtack, its shadow on the wall
the shattering—hear it
?

1. Raúl Zurita.

Remarks / on the Foundation / of the Line: A Personal History

Brent Cunningham

"For if I cut, I can of course choose where I want to cut."
—WITTGENSTEIN

Around the end of 1999, I stopped breaking lines of poetry. More precisely, I lost my conviction that there was any basis for why or, especially, *where* lines broke.

Naturally this crisis did not happen overnight. It took place as a slow flowering of doubts and confusions. I saw that various accounts of the line were *already* in my head, apparently having arrived there some time ago, propping up a habit I had never much interrogated. The more I examined these accounts the less I trusted them.

("Thinking," then, as a kind of rethinking, always *in media res*, with previous thoughts and assumptions as its object. But how do the initial thoughts and assumptions get in there if not through some process of consideration? Do they enter *directly*?)

The first assumption I rejected (on the basis of its pure tautology) was that lines of poetry broke because that was what lines of poetry did. Tradition might have certain limited uses, but for me tradition-for-tradition's-sake was the very thing to be fought against in art. More appealing was the argument set out by Charles Olson and Robert Creeley that the line was related in some way to the unit of breath (this argument appealed to them, I think, because they were each in different ways concerned to find a way out of Cartesian mind/body duality, so that the line-as-breath proposed an agreeable physiological "presence" for poetry's seemingly cerebral activities). But the trouble with the breath-line was that it led inexorably to the notion that writing had to mimic oral structures, since the breath is so fused to speaking and to voice. I wasn't interested in a poetry that decided to see itself as the lesser score to a more actual oral performance. When I heard, from certain people, that poetry was at root an oral art form and must always be, I felt this was a ridiculous restriction. It's not that I wanted to say that mind and body were separate, or that I wanted to deny that heartbeats and breathing likely formed the basis of the human sense of rhythm, but I didn't want to enter writing with line=breath as a given. Why not use poetry as a locale to explore *what else* might contribute to rhythmic pulsation, or to explore aspects of bodily existence unrelated to rhythm? To use a rough analogy, I had once understood the act of pointing as a purely visual phenomenon. Then, as I started teaching my daughter to look at what I was pointing to, I found myself tapping on various things to draw her attention with the sound, and I realized there was an important aural element hidden inside of "pointing." To restrict poetry to the oral seemed like restricting pointing to sight. Why not keep the field open for other possibilities?

I considered other theories of the line, from the variable foot of William Carlos Williams to Oulipian formal constraints. But no account had the force of appeal to me. Why break *now*? What initiates it? What justifies it? Every answer felt arbitrary and contrived.

(Then again: isn't everything in poetry arbitrary and contrived? Why should breaking a line feel more arbitrary than not breaking it? I want to say: because breaking is an action, a decision, while not breaking is not. If you're typing what you consider a poem and fail to depress the "return" key, i.e., if you do nothing, gradually your poem will become prose. At the very least it will become prose poetry. So prose is "natural," while poetry has to be put in, formed, and thus *justified*. Just as we don't blame lions for eating zebras, we don't blame prose writers for not breaking their lines. Only poets are held accountable. Only their lines must have *reasons*.)

So I found myself writing prose poetry. Again, not by choice, but because of confusion about how and when to act; in short, from inertia. In ethics, such inertia can take the form of a positive command: if you don't know, it is proper not to act. ("First, do no harm.") But more often inertia is an unhappy state the subject is trying, agonizingly, to escape. (Think of Hamlet.)

(Something to notice: "inertia" is an idea derived from the physical sciences, generally from Newton's first law of motion. When we use it to describe a person, a Hamlet, so confused they make no active or willful decision, the term is quietly conflating two distinct things. A person's mental indecision is imagined to be similar "in some way" to an apple on the ground physically holding still. But this is not true. An apple on the ground is not motionless because it is confused.)

(Or: *isn't* the apple confused? Is it wrong to say the apple is "confused" between the force of gravity and the ground's density? One underlying question here is whether the conflation of two distinct worlds in a single term is actually a deception—even though Wittgenstein, for example, thinks it is. Isn't conflation what all metaphorical language does? We could call it a deception of language and say that we are being misled, or we could call it an illumination of language and say we are seeing things newly.)

(Still it often *feels* deceptive if we don't notice such conflations, but only later realize they were happening.)

In brief, then: embroiled in the problem of the line was the problem of deciding. This problem of deciding is itself really a problem of valuing (i.e., of valuing anything in particular over anything else, valuing a break *here* rather than *here*). But this "inertia" I was in, so irritating and uncomfortable to the mind, almost akin to madness, could be seen as precisely the "opening" to other possibilities I claim to value. Isn't it *good* to be confused about where the line should break? Isn't it *bad* to go around, like a certain former president, deciding just to show you are a decider? In poetry circles, I often hear people say they reject all formal or aesthetic principles, programs, theories, philosophies, etc. They tend to hold this position in the name of freedom or spontaneity, against systems and the regulated. Meanwhile, and simultaneously, I am skeptical that people can actually make meaningful acts without solid principles, in a truly free space, if by free we mean undetermined. Isn't every action, even the action of inaction, willed and organized by the mind? Is it, for instance, possible to will a line to break without any reason or "basis" to that break? Mustn't the intent, the will itself, be triggered by something? Physical need, a series of thoughts, always *something*, always some value, even if the value does happen to be freedom. Madness, for instance, also operates using principles. People who work with the insane will tell you they don't lack a kind of logic of their own. In a way it's that they're *too* logical. (Everything as logical, therefore everything as *inaccurate*.)

Such thoughts did nothing, naturally, to overcome my inertia. In a sense, these loops and questions were the inertia itself. (Inertia as endless mirror: you want to act, therefore you mistrust your reasons for acting, because those reasons may be "forced" just for the sake of acting.) (Again, like a certain former president.)

In this way, inertia is at root a *complicating* force, necessarily reflexive. You can't decide, but you also can't decide if you actually value deciding. You doubt, but you are also unsure if doubting is good or bad. You notice yourself thinking, but also you wonder if such noticing is the problem or the solution.

Poetry, in one conception, is a kind of platform. The things you put on it are like objects you are supposed to notice a little more than other objects. As you stare at them, it is almost certain they will grow more complicated, because, of course, you cannot help staring at your staring at them. But this is strange: why would you want to put objects on a platform and observe them? What would be the point?

(Or say there isn't a point. I am only describing, as Wittgenstein would say, what already happens, i.e., what poems already presume is happening. For us, this is past choosing: if poems didn't compel your noticing them, why would you be here?)

(Still, could you, as an experiment, manufacture a different relationship to poems than this kind of observation platform? Well, that depends: can you ask your observation to stop observing what draws it in? Isn't your observation you? Who is available to ask your observation to redirect its activity?)

Whenever the mind falls into inertia, it must look for a way out. Discomfort is discomfort. So it goes back over the steps that first got it there. (Think of Hamlet.) (Thought as a kind of rethinking.) My first assumption was that breaking lines was an action, a decision. But why is it? Or: what makes it more of a decision than, say, typing a word? Isn't the return key a key just like the letter keys? (A little wider, I see.) (And with "Enter" printed on it, in my case.) Is it because no one "types" the return key? We "strike" the return key, or we "hit" the return key, and this "breaks" the line. Contained in our idea of a line-break (even in the very notion of "breaking" the line) there is, perhaps, a hidden belief that letters and words are pre-formed and present in the mind, overabundant, ready to spill forth naturally and without motivating force. By contrast, a hard return, a break, any pause or ending, must be *brought in* from somewhere more violently distant.

Of course this *can't* be right. Distant from what? Brought in from where? Where does interruption come from? Since thought is continuous, isn't every pause or ending a deception? Or, to put it differently, aren't breaks something like symbols or possibly microcosms of a lived moment of *surrender*, standing for the moment that human observation gets so tired of making things complicated, of cycling reflexively through doubts, that it gives up (without *really* stopping or breaking or even deciding) and simply moves on?

And that, approximately, begins the history of how I started breaking lines again.

Suppose children are taught that the earth is an infinite flat surface; or that God created an infinite number of stars; or that a star keeps on moving uniformly in a straight line, without ever stopping. Queer: when one takes something of this sort as a matter of course, as it were in one's stride, it loses its whole paradoxical aspect. It is as if I were to be told: Don't worry, this series, or movement, goes on without ever stopping. We are as it were excused the labour of thinking of an end. (Wittgenstein 141e)

WORK CITED

Wittgenstein, Ludwig. *Remarks on the Foundations of Mathematics.* Trans. G. E. M. Anscombe. Ed. G. H. von Wright, R. Rhees, and G. E. M. Anscombe. Cambridge, MA: MIT Press, 1967. Epigraph from 149e.

A Line Apart

J. P. Dancing Bear

Over the several years that I have been hosting a radio show dedicated to poetry, I've had numerous poets sit down before the microphone and read their poems. In interviewing the hundreds of poets that I have been honored to have as guests, one of the things that has struck me most is the process by which some of the poets attempt to make audible the line-breaks. When I ask them about it, they almost always give an answer that lets me know, and everyone else listening, that every word, every breath is accounted for and is not accidental. This answer cuts across all schools and aesthetics.

But I've also encountered other poets with a different philosophy regarding poetry. Some poets do not believe the line-break should be audible. They also disagree with importance placed on individual lines. For some, the line is a means to an end—nothing else. Much the same way that a word is to a line, they see a line is to a poem. I have had the fortunate opportunity of workshopping my poems with C. J. Sage over the last ten years and one thing (among many) that she has taught me to look at is the importance and relevance of the individual line. Her attention to detail and sound will oftentimes lead to lengthy discussion of a single line and its "weight" to the overall poem.

It is a focus not easily lost when it comes to reading poems by other writers, published or unpublished. I find myself marking a line for further rumination as I am reading a poem. Then I go back and consider the line on its own. I read it several times. When a line is perfect, it has the completeness of a highway on-ramp—it has its own structure, its own intelligence, and it transports the reader to something larger.

While jotting down lines as I was reading so many poems, I began to wonder what the heck I would do with all of these lines. I felt a little like a guy who had collected snapshots of his favorite on-ramps. Then I thought about it in a different way: what if the on-ramp was a launch ramp; what if the individual line could send you somewhere else should you apply imagination and a little aim? So I spent the better part of a year writing a collection of poems that start with a single line from someone else's poem. I set some additional rules for myself: the poet had to be living (although, sadly, one has died since I started), and it could not be a beginning or ending line to a poem. This caused me to focus on the middle lines, those lines that some see as a means to the end of the poem and little else. My attempt was to praise and exalt the line. The project became a celebration of the line itself.

And with that examination of individual lines, I have learned that a line has a life of its own. That instead of a line being an I-beam or a femur, it could be part of synergy—something that, taken away from its original surroundings, could grow new ones—the salamander's tail growing a new body.

For me, the best lines have a complete thought in them. It may not be the complete thought of the sentence they are found in, but a completeness nonetheless. For example, "The air is limned with secrets, and we are painted tenderly / and awkward" (151) is a sentence from Ralph Angel's poem, "Like Animals." I begin my poem with Angel's line:

The air is limned with secrets, and we are painted tenderly
upon the cave walls, where our Monet dedicates
his fragile brushes to the least rough surface he can feel
with his pale palm and failing eyes.

I borrowed another line from Jason Bredle's poem, "The Idiot's Guide to Faking Your Own Death and Moving to Mexico." Here is its original context:

According to Hercules, if we make an angel
out of ourselves, that is what we are; if we make
a devil out of ourselves, that too is what we are.

Bredle strategically places the line-break so that the reader can think about "if we make an angel" first, before following up with "out of ourselves." I began my poem, with Bredle's line, as follows:

According to Hercules, if we make an angel
then we will spend our nights picking feathers
from our teeth. (45–46)

My experience with focusing on lines has furthered my awareness of how crucial a line is to a poem. Even though I've gone through the process of showing that a line has the potential to be something to more than one poem, it still relies on a solid structure, it still has that uniqueness that makes it a great line. Now I read poems in several different ways. Now I mark those launch ramps. Now I don't feel like a weirdo for relishing a single line in a poem.

WORKS CITED

Angel, Ralph. "Like Animals." *Exceptions and Melancholies: Poems 1986–2006*. Louisville, KY: Sarabande Books, 2006.

Bredle, Jason. "The Idiot's Guide to Faking Your Own Death and Moving to Mexico." *Verse Daily* 2006 <http://www.versedaily.org/2006/fakingdeath.shtml> .

Dancing Bear, J. P. "Poem Starting with a Line by Jason Bredle." *The National Poetry Review* 4.2 (2007). 45–46.

Furthermore: Some Lines about the Poetic Line

Christina Davis

The poetic line is a primary act of conviction—surrounded by aisles of pause and space. A line steps out of circularity to assert. And what it asserts is: *further.*

⁓

The difference between Dickinson's and Whitman's lines:
the difference between a bird in hand and birds on a wire.

⁓

Free verse has been achieved by Poetry.
But what freedoms have *each of us* achieved
on the level of the line? And what laws
have we each created to protect those freedoms?

⁓

In thinking about my predilection for a minimalist, enjambed line—

A landscape of disappointed bridges
cannot but breed
                        rivers.

⁓

If all lines are broken, what is a line?

⁓

"A line, a white line, a long white line,
A wall, a barrier, towards which we drove" (Eliot 67).

These lines have returned to me throughout my writing life. Earthen, spare, and bone-like in their construction, yet borne forward from such staccato knowns into the Unknown. Removed as they were from a draft of T. S. Eliot's *The Waste Land*, they remain (for me, at least) the ghost-lines of that poem and of poetry itself. We drive words, meanings, attachments toward the verge of what we know not, toward the blank and mortal margin. A poetic line is an inherently drastic stance: the "extreme of the known in the presence of the extreme / of the unknown," as Wallace Stevens once put it (432).

~

As the sunset of one line begins
the sunrise of another.

~

To convince: Latin, for "to overcome, conquer."

When I say *conviction*, I don't mean that you believe in the meaning of the words per se. Though that's not a bad idea. But rather, that you believe in the line you have made as an entity, as a moment of matter. And that it has achieved its own status as a semantic, aesthetic, acoustic, visual thing-in-itself. It has overcome the resistance against its existence. Or, in the words of Marianne Moore:

> If you will tell me why the fen
> appears impassable, I then
> will tell you why I think that I
> can get across it if I try. (178)

~

I've heard it said that those who write with a short Dickinsonian line create an insular, spiritual poem. Whereas those who write with a long Whitmanic line create a broad and social poem. (Yet, in handwritten manuscript—on 85 × 78mm envelope scraps or jaggedly-scissored wrapping paper measuring 90 × 90mm—Dickinson's poems reach across their respective canvases and are often crowded within them like Alice in Tenniel's rendition of the tunnel. Who are we to say that her lines are not as long as Whitman's in proportion to their original, originating space?)

~

In the workshops I attended over the course of a decade, more emphasis was placed on the line-break than the line. An immediate modulation of the minutiae was prized over "the force that through the green fuse drives the flower" (Thomas 10). Through this apprenticeship in breakage, I became a swinger of branches instead of birches; in so doing I lost sight somewhat of totalities and the patience towards the evolution of an entire and forward-borne idea.

While I'm still an advocate of poetic patience, over time I've come to appreciate the essential role that focused experimentation with line-breaks can play as a kind of litmus to test the intentional dimensions of the whole: the line-break samples and re-samples the acoustical contours of the line, varies the line's visual and architectural blueprint, reconfigures the poem's vertical and horizontal dimensions, interrupts or reestablishes the underlying meter/stress/breaths of the line, and, of course, confirms or alters the line's semantic life.[1] Even if we revert to the original line, each time we break a line during revision, we get a better understanding of the manifold potential of the poem.

～

If you break, does it make what came before that
    a line?
If you answer, does it make what came before that
      a question?

～

I'm curious to know what's happened to the stanza and stanza break (//) in all of this emphasis on the line and line-break? Are stanza breaks still the red light to the yellow light of the latter? Is the stanza still the paragraph of the poem? I can't help but think that the line is in the ascendant as the primary cohering force in many a contemporary poem.

～

I am most interested in lines that can live apart from a poem.

In my own poems, I try to guess in advance which line a reader will extract, so that I can create the conditions for its survival. This is one of the great capacities of poetry, the aphoristic afterlife: to come apart and survive apart from the flock of itself. While the poem may be one of mourning, the line itself is capable of reveling in and enduring the End of Among.

~

This year my mother asked me to choose the line that would be engraved

on my father's headstone: a single line for the life.

It is something to work in stone,
to consider each word in terms of eternity.

It's then that all ironies depart, all superfluities. Even a comma seems gaudy when it comes down to the rock. There, beneath the name, like a permanent appositive to the name. There, above the grass, words that must live unostentatiously among the moss and ant-mounds.

The line needed to have the autumn and calm of last words,
but be prepared to be said again. Far from us

and in another mouth. The first words of some next,
unknowable time. In other words,

Poetry. And *what would the first words be?* (Woolf 210).

~

"We go by detachments to the strange Home" (Dickinson 78).

"Till the gossamer thread you fling catch somewhere, O my soul" (Whitman 564–565).

1. I am particularly interested in George Oppen's statement regarding the alliance between the line-break and the construction of the "vertical dimension" of the poem. The more broken the line, he suggests, the less prose-like and conversational—in other words, the more apt to be "speaking to the divinity" and not the reader alone (Oppen 85).

WORKS CITED

Dickinson, Emily. *New Poems of Emily Dickinson*. Ed. William H. Shurr. Chapel Hill: University of North Carolina Press, 1993.

Eliot, T. S. *The Waste Land: A Facsimile and Transcript of the Original Drafts*. Ed. Valerie Eliot. New York: Harcourt Brace, 1971.

Moore, Marianne. *Complete Poems*. New York: Penguin, 1981.

Oppen, George. Letter to Rachel Blau DuPlessis. 13 April 1976. *The Poker* 9 (2009).

Stevens, Wallace. *Collected Poetry and Prose*. New York: Library of America, 1997.

Thomas, Dylan. *Collected Poems of Dylan Thomas 1934–1952*. New York: New Directions, 1971.

Whitman, Walt. *Complete Poetry and Collected Prose*. New York: Library of America, 1982.

Woolf, Virginia. *Between the Acts*. New York: Harcourt Brace, 1969.

The Graphic Line

Johanna Drucker

The graphic line displays a modern aspect when the metrical units of poetic form are matched by their lineation on the page (Schmidt). Graphical conventions of lineation are not modern devices, and when thought of as a basic material support for poetic expression, they track to the origin of writing. The notion of a phrase as a lexical unit extends into Babylonian times. The culture of the ancient Near East, in which writing emerged from earlier sign systems used for accounting, developed the first known use of lines to divide a surface and to group signs into semantic units.

Denise Schmandt-Besserat, renowned archaeologist and scholar of cuneiform, has shown that cuneiform scribes developed graphical conventions for the rational, systematic representation of language. Her work emphasizes the importance of the ground line as a feature that organizes and rationalizes the graphical space in which the relative position, size, scale, direction, orientation, and clustering/proximity of signs gain value. This organization in turn provided conventions adopted for pictorial presentations of narrative. This cultural event took place in the third millennium B.C.E., and like the graphical conventions in Egypt in and around the same time, serves as an example for the ways written texts are organized after.

Other graphic lines are also conspicuous in cuneiform tablets, used to frame and group units of signs in a gridded surface. The lineation of Hammurabi's code on the eighteenth-century B.C.E. stele is a masterwork of graphic design for its regularity, efficiency, and textural beauty. The law code is not poetry, but it uses the enframing techniques of other cuneiform as well as the implied ground line for each lexical unit. The oldest examples of written poetry are cuneiform texts from the middle of the third millennium B.C.E., such as the celebrated hymn by Enheduanna to the goddess Inanna.[1] Lineation and phrasing exist, but not in the forms we use today.

The complex relation between the two modes of transmission—written inscription and verbal phraseology, with its dependence on and engagement with breath, pause, song, hymn, prosody, and poetic forms—has many variations and detours in the history that follows. But the notion of a ground line is foundational to all verbal sign systems that function to register language in a stable communicative system. We know, but often forget, that writing is not a direct transcription of verbal writing, but its own parallel, semi-autonomous system. These insights allow us to track the articulation of graphical conventions in a codependent relation with verbal ones. Because we encounter poetry in conventions that prevail in print culture, we tend to overlook how the forms on which our sense of the poetic line depends have come into being in graphic terms. Look again, and imagine the ground line dissolved, the line-breaks dubiously rendered, and the graphical function becomes strikingly clear.

1. See Roberta Binkley's "Biography of Enheduanna, Priestess of Inanna," and John H. Walton's *Ancient Israelite Literature in Its Cultural Context*.

WORKS CITED

Binkley, Roberta. "Biography of Enheduanna, Priestess of Inanna." <http://www.cddc.vt.edu/feminism/enheduanna.html>.

Schmandt-Besserat, Denise. *When Writing Met Art*. Austin: University of Texas Press, 2007.

Schmidt, Michael. *The Story of Poetry I: From Caedmon to Caxton*. London: Weidenfeld, 2001. <http://www.michaelschmidt.org.uk/ppo06.shtml>.

Walton, John H. *Ancient Israelite Literature in its Cultural Context*. Grand Rapids, MI: Zondervan, 1994.

Shore Lines

Camille Dungy

From where I sit, two miles up a mountain on the California coast just south of Big Sur, I have a magnificent view of the ocean, but I can't see the shore. I can observe the undulations and rhythms of the water, its inexorable drive toward a point (in this case, the maps tell me, Ragged Point). I mark subtle and dramatic shifts in its shade and come, by careful attention, to understand what these shifts suggest about temperature, depth, and the nuance of currents. It is an expansive and engaging view, but I miss the shore.

What I am witnessing might find its literary equivalent in the best works of Nabokov or Morrison, the great prose writers' amazing expanses of undulating language, their subtle and dramatic shifts in tone, depth, and motion, their long but inexorable drives toward a point. Much great prose has plenty of poetic qualities to recommend it. One thing it doesn't have is the same thing my view lacks: the predictable moment of physical return, the abrupt interruption, the edge, the beach, the tide break, the line-break, the shore.

When it comes to a shore, the ocean I am watching will do the same thing over and over again. It will break. It will break in relatively the same way several times. Then it will change. It might break that way once or twice more. Or it will change again. Do that a few times, enough times to lull me. Then it will change again. From the shore, if you know what to watch for, you can discover patterns. Surfers track these patterns to predict which wave in a set they will ride. Steve McQueen did this in *Papillon* and managed, by counting waves until he could predict the most favorable one to jump into, to escape from a prison island.

Poems are not, hopefully, prison islands, but I want to talk about how repetition and variation can work for poems (and readers of poems) when they encounter the anticipated physical moment of return, the line-break, the shore.

Many waves rhyme with each other, meaning they resemble other waves in sound and appearance. One of the things that calms people who visit the shore is this sonic regularity, as well as the swelling of momentum as water gathers force before coming to the locus of return, the tide's break point, the shore. The same goes for a poem. The ear enjoys a good rhyme at the end of a line because we enjoy the rhythmic and sonic regularity those rhymes support. And we enjoy a line that swells and builds momentum as it moves toward its line-break, its moment of physical return.

I could watch the sets all day, excited to see how one break will resemble or differ from the last, how the water will build upon and tumble over itself, how it will look and sound as it rolls over and withdraws back into the main body again. This is what I want to achieve in my poems as well, this degree of motion and momentum. I want the moment of the break to bring pleasure as much from its breaking as from the realization that the break is part of a whole, that each advancing line will bring me great pleasure moving back into the larger body, building momentum, then breaking, then repeating these actions again and again and again.

The best poems deliver what I call the inevitable surprise. We know the line will break, and we might even have an idea of where and how the physical boundary might present itself on the page, and that is part of the beauty, but for that beauty to work to its full potential there must also be much that comes as a surprise.

In the case of an end-rhymed poem, the inevitable might be the fact that we know after a cycle of five iambic feet we must come to an -ay sound. There can be great joy in this anticipation. And if the expectation is thwarted by a poet who presents three iambic feet and an anapest before returning, for a measurable period, to the expected pentameter, then so much the better. Keep us on our toes.

If after a run of end-stopped phrases like "had cream today" and "the girls said hooray" we come to an enjambed line that buries the -ay sound so deeply we nearly forget it, then so much the better. We're always looking for ways to break out of prison.

If we do manage, really, to forget the -ay sound, not for instance to ask, Hey, where's the -ay sound, but to carry on through the poem's interrupted pattern without noticing a break in the pattern, until careful study in a later reading perhaps, then that pattern's break becomes, in its own way, inevitable and it remains also, in its own way, a surprise. Steve McQueen watched the surf break against his prison island over and over until, surprise, he noticed the subtle shift in pattern that always, and inevitably, was there.

Since I think waves can rhyme, it may come as no surprise that I think ideas can rhyme too. I like to end lines this way, following conceptual rhymes, carrying the basic elements of an idea from one line to the next in the same way one might carry a certain element of sound throughout a poem. Just as with sonic rhymes and rhythmic repetition, the execution of rhymed ideas goes a long way toward the pleasure you can garner from a line. As with sonic rhymes, continuity of conceptual rhymes is necessary, but so is variation. A good poem can benefit from the more aggressive wave that follows three delicate ones, the wave that soaks you, that draws even the most timid beachcomber into the water just a little more.

If a poem is broken into lines, you tend to know what's coming: each line will need, in some potentially predictable way, to end. If a poem has good line-breaks, there will still be plenty of opportunity for surprise. That's a huge part of the pleasure of poetry. That's why I love the moment of return, the abrupt interruption, the edge, the beach, the tide break, the line-break, the shore.

Scotch Tape Receptacle Scissors and a Poem

John O. Espinoza

When most young poets write their first poems, they turn out lines that are either long and wormy or stubby as toes. Of course, it's not that writing either length is against any rules, but short lines for the beginning poet tend to be more like shards with splinters for line-breaks, and longer lines tend to be chatty and wordy. As a beginning poet I wrote both these lengths. Early on, my sense of line length and line end was modeled on Gary Soto's *Where Sparrows Work Hard*, which typically had lines of two beats. For the most part, these poems dictated my sense of the line: pick a length and stick to it. It took me a while to learn the value of the poetic line that paid attention to subject and content.

During my undergraduate days in workshop, my drafts were returned to me saturated with blue ink. Words, phrases, and whole lines were crossed out. Prepositions would be added, word pairings inverted, and the thin blue line from Professor Christopher Buckley's pen, wedged like a fence between two words, indicated a line-break. In his own poems, Buckley showed mastery over his lines. In workshop, he taught us about using syllabics and meter, although, at the end of the day, we turned in free verse.

At that age, more thickheaded than arrogant, I wasn't interested in syllables, meters, or poetic feet, other than mine that needed a good rub after walking around campus all day. I was attending UC Riverside, located in the Inland Empire east of Los Angeles where first-generation college-goers didn't attend the university to learn how to write a successful poem. I was a brown kid excited enough about poetry to buy a black-and-white marble composition notebook and spend an additional $6 worth of quarters on foil stickers of Aztec warriors, low riders, *cholos*, and *payasos* to decorate the front and back covers. Back at my apartment bedroom, I wrote poems at dusk, at what cinematographers called the "magic hour." Writing by hand, the lines of my poems always reached the inside trench of the notebook. Besides, the wisdom of Buckley's blue slash upon which I was so reliant would transform a sloppy line into a tight one. The suggestions in his line endings were so simple they were almost mysterious, but I soon began to hear the music and measure of my own breath.

Scotch tape. A receptacle. Scissors and a poem. These were the tools we needed for Alberto Ríos's do-it-yourself editing kit. It was my second year at Arizona State University's MFA program, and I was enrolled in Ríos's popular Magical Realism course where his writing exercises would give my poems and their poetic lines a good licking. The assignment was to take a poem that wasn't quite working for us, triple-space it, scissor out each line, and dump it into a receptacle, so that each day I would pull out a strip and read it like a fortune from a fortune cookie before taping it to my wall. Do this once a day until you're done. Finally, type out this "revision" of the poem, make copies, and bring to class.

Taken out of their context my lines were senseless; I was, after all, primarily a narrative poet. I discovered that I continued to make poor choices in enjambments. Rarely did the lines stand alone, and when they did, the language, like a Triscuit, was flat and bland. Often, subject and nouns masqueraded as lines: "The palm tree," "tabernacle," "almonds. Afterward I." Or maybe a cut-off prepositional phrase: "Under the." Because only one line could be drawn a day, it was torturous to stare directly from where I lay in bed at the poorly written lines taped to my bedroom wall. I wanted to cheat, pull out the strips all at once from the Arizona Diamondbacks ball cap in which they rested in a tangle, to expedite the embarrassment. That would have been a disservice more to myself than my teacher. Ríos wanted us to contemplate our lines, let them dissolve in our mouths like a dinner mint. He wanted us to find our patterns that hindered us from writing good lines, to see how much of the poem depends on how strong the lines are. After the last line was drawn, taped up, after the new version was typed up, and after all the dismemberment and suturing, if the poem still stood to make some sense, according to Ríos, then the lines work. At the end of the assignment, when I trashed these flat, paper worms in the wastebasket, the poem, too, was scrapped.

Before that assignment I realized that I didn't see a poem for its lines and now, like an ailment I didn't know I had before, I am much more sensitive to its workings. I do believe that a poem is the sum of its lines. I do believe Kazim Ali when he discusses the integrity of "the line suspended in space and context separate from what came before it or after it, otherwise it is merely a sentence in prose with a break for visual effect" (51). I believe in poet Kevin Young's notion that the line is a unit of sense, a unit of music, or a unit of breath. Whatever it is, the line should make some sort of sense if it were to be flung and stuck to a wall (or in my case, taped). I believe that most poets believe this, too. I will not claim here that I have some profound insight to offer about the poetic line. In my ten plus years of writing poems I've learned everyone has, not their theory, but their "practice" or "process" or "technique" about how a line should work—from not ending a line after an article, to ending a line on a word that resonates with the theme of the poem. I'm glad too because that's why we have such beautiful and varied poems.

After all these years I follow some simple principles that dictate my working of the line. A line is about language employing a diction that is not too flat or too elevated. It is about imagery that will brand itself in the readers' imaginations with a good metaphor or simile. Can the contents of the line exist in the real world? Can you hold them or photograph them? My lines are about being natural and not pretentious. The line should have the energy and economy to move the reader to the next line. Finally, a line should make a listener nod her head when she hears it. Plain and simple.

WORK CITED

Ali, Kazim. "On the Line: A Short Vociferation." *Center: A Journal of the Literary Arts* 7 (2008). 51–52.

In Praise of Line-Breaks

Kathy Fagan

In a poetry class I'm currently teaching for MFA prose writers, I was reminded yesterday that the word "poet" comes from the Greek for maker, and "verse" from the Greek for plow lines. The analogy is obvious: just as those who work the land reshape it, we poets might rightfully think of ourselves as re-creators of the language. From the air, one sees crops cultivated in traditional rows, spheres, or hemispheres, on flooded plains or hills of orchard: all of it, from that distance, orderly and exquisitely shaped. Even from the ground, controlling patterns can be perceived. As citizens of the planet, we reshape the earth to our own purposes; poets manipulate and mold the language.

It is commonplace to say that poetry differs from prose in that it is written in lines, and that its tensions, pleasures, and challenges derive from the fact that poetry alone is written in sentences *and* lines. Poetry adds up to more than this, of course. If it didn't, prose poetry and lyrical prose would have nothing in common with poetry cast in lines. But the possibilities for line-making within the context of a verse poem have always been abundant enough to hold my interest as a writer, and as a reader I wonder, above all else, what a poet's up to with a line. I adore how charged the choices are. How vital to the body of the poem and its meaning, and how ferociously poets, experienced or not, cling to lineation. It's comparable to nothing else I can think of in the art world, though I have tried to make such comparisons. Ballet, for example, was forever altered when the primacy of the step gave way to line. And to visual artists, line and perspective have long been the building blocks of composition. But line in poetry, certainly in unmetered, unrhymed poetry, is a more fluid, less singular strategy, relying solely on context for meaningful deployment.

James Longenbach, in his fine book *The Art of the Poetic Line*, suggests that we swap out the term "line ending" for "line break." I admire his discussion of line endings and the helpful new names he creates for them: the end-stopped line (self-explanatory), the parsing line ending (unit of syntax), and the annotating line ending (enjambed line). But the term "line ending," not unlike the term "free verse," suggests there is a natural and organic resolution to a line, a completion, and while that may indeed occur in some kinds of poems, it seems to me that in others it most certainly does not. Line-break, on the other hand, suggests a violent wrenching, a kind of deliberate reshaping, far closer to the agrarian metaphor we started with.

I like to remember that what we do as poets, as the makers of lines and reshapers of language, is artificial. Language is mediated cerebrally. Music is mediated bodily. Most poetry is encountered visually. If we agree that a line of poetry is a rhythmic construct of written language, whether we be traditional or non-traditional versifiers, we might agree that the only control poets have over their words, once set, is how they are arranged within the line, how the sentences that contain them are broken across these lines, and what effect the whole has on a reader, cognitively and physically.

Consider this small, masterful poem, "Pink," by Terese Svoboda:

In China I remembered you only once:
the restaurant's speciality, chosen
from a braid of live varieties,
spiraled to the floor while the waiter
flayed it with a knife flicked

from his wrist. The snake made your initial
over and over the black tile.
What pain! Love's all touch
was the ideogram it made as it crossed
the hot stones to the table. (84)

An unrhymed, unmetered lyric poem with a clear narrative core and strong central image is literally flayed before our eyes by the stanza break, which slices the poem in half and offers to us the figure of the flailing snake. The lines can be said to break as violently as the poem itself: "chosen" at the end of line 2 highlighting both the misfortune and the individual nature of the doomed creature; "waiter" at the end of line 4 quite literally pausing before the swift and irrevocable flaying that opens line 5. The second stanza then begins with two half sentences that echo the gesture, the gasp/gap, of the stanza break. The next caesura-containing line, "What pain! Love's all touch," reads like an equation: pain = love. And the penultimate line, ending in "crossed," once again embodies the action of the poem, roasting and serving the memory of the once-beloved to the speaker.

The delectable "speciality" of line 2 prepares our ears for the exotic "varieties" and "ideogram" that follow, and allows Svoboda's monosyllables, varied vowel sounds, and alliterative moves to generate much of the poem's suspense, pacing, and strangeness.

Aside from Chinese culinary practices, this poem's drama arises from the purposefulness of its shaping, from its artifice, albeit the artifice of "free" verse. The poem might succeed as a short prose piece, but its horrors and delights would be diminished without its lineation. Without a commitment to aggressive enjambment, for instance, the mirrored stanzas, so expertly embodying the split form, might not have suggested themselves to the poet. And the creepy reserve we hear in the poem, the kind of cool diction that raises the hair on the backs of our necks, might not have been achieved without the halved figure of the poem and all it evokes. Just as champagne is best enjoyed in a fluted glass and coffee in a stout cup, Svoboda's vessel serves her poem up artfully and satisfyingly.

WORKS CITED

Longenbach, James. *The Art of the Poetic Line*. Saint Paul: Graywolf Press, 2008.
Svoboda, Terese. "Pink." *Laughing Africa*. Iowa City: University of Iowa Press, 1990. 84.

Grails and Legacies: Thoughts on the Line

Annie Finch

The line, the
line,
the
line—oh holy
grail of the free
verse work-
shop!

Now that I write the majority of my poetry in meter, I have a slightly different relation to the line than I did during my first couple of decades when a large part of writing meant fiddling obsessively with line-breaks. Now, I tend to put more energy into what comes in the middle of lines. In essence, every foot in a line of metrical poetry has its own little line-break at the end—not to mention the longer pause, the caesura, which falls once or twice within most lines of metrical poetry.

The lines that haunt me most, those that sound in my head literally for years as I try to encompass and fathom their waves, are lines in meter, such as the solemnly counted-out beats of Robert Hayden's famous opening line, ringing with their hollow echo, as if they know ahead of time how their initial trochees will continue to sound with a stubbornly unforgettable shudder through the rest of that iambic poem: "Sundays too my father got up early . . ." The break at the end of the line is the least of it; the center of gravity of a metrical line can be anywhere, and usually is.

Williams and the other high modernists were passionately interested in expanding the metrical vocabulary of verse beyond the iambic pentameter (Pound's dactyls are among his most beautiful free-verse effects) but, as Timothy Steele shows in his book *Missing Measures*, their goal was not to jettison meter altogether. Deeply schooled in meter, these poets handled the line beautifully:

> so much depends
> upon (Williams 224)

The p's here are a wonderful sight, and the visual pun (with the second line seeming to "depend"—literally, to "hang"—from its predecessor) memorable. But without the symmetry between two iambs and one iamb, this line-break would lack its signature bounce; it's the rhythmic conversation that lends this iconic bit of free verse such ineffable and iconic energy.

Poets like to muse about the free-verse line—how and whether a particular line has "weight," a "justification," an "identity," or any one of the numerous quasi-mystical terms we use for that indescribable quality of "thisness" that a good line of free verse exudes. But the next time you hear someone in a workshop remarking on how good a particular free-verse line or passage sounds, scan it. The odds are that it will fall into a regular metrical pattern. If free-verse poets were educated about meter again (as the great free-verse poets of the early twentieth century always were) and meter became a more conscious part of such discussions, the mysticism would sound less subjective and futile and the quest for the true essence of "the line" would likely become, if not more fun, at least quite a bit less stressful.

No matter what other factors go into a successful free-verse line—imagery, syntax, a center of meaning or wit—rhythmic energy is the *sine qua non*. Most good free-verse passages have a metrical (by which I mean a regularly and predictably rhythmical) subtext. The best free verse is alert and conscious of this energy, able to keep its head above the rhythmical water—a feat which takes a certain amount of ear-training in meter (not only iambic meter). For example, this rhythmically fluent passage by Audre Lorde segues a dactylic rhythm at the opening of the first line into a trochaic rhythm, which continues through the second line and into the third line, which then emerges as a headless iambic pentameter:

> Some words are open like a diamond
> on glass windows
> singing out within the crash of sun (163)

This kind of tension against other meters is crucial when using iambic pentameter in a free-verse poem; iambic pentameter is so hackneyed and familiar-sounding that, inserted into prosey free verse without strong counterbalancing rhythms, its presence (especially in the final line of a poem, where it is most likely to appear) can add a smug, flaccid, or pedestrian quality to otherwise good free verse.

So the skillful and conscious wielding of meter is a key aspect of strong free-verse lines. Yet still, yet still, there is something else to say. There is stillness as well as bounce in Williams's line-breaks. Just when I feel that the nub of the whole question is the need to apprehend a fluent diversity of meters, I suddenly feel my eyes. Raised as I was on the visual feast of the line-break, it is not only my ears I need to feed.

I distinguish five basic kinds of free verse, the first three essentially oral-based and the other two essentially visual-based. There is the performative long line of the Bible and Ginsberg, which is closely tied to oral performance and to the ear's pleasure in accentual and in dactylic verse—"angelheaded hipsters burning for the ancient heavenly connection to the starry dynamo in the machinery of night" (Ginsberg 9). There is the medium-length, literature-based line of poets such as Hass and Olds, which plays off of and is always flirting with centuries of metrical verse, mostly iambic pentameter—"All the new thinking is about loss. / In this it resembles all the old thinking" (Hass 4). And there is the more irregular, jazz-inspired variable-lined free verse of Brooks and Lorde, which moves between short and long lines with a kinetic, oral drive—"A mistake. / A cliff. / A hymn, a snare, and an exceeding sun" (Brooks 439). The two main kinds of visual-based free verse are the open field of Duncan and Howe, where the visual energy of the page's whiteness is an essential and constant partner ("holes in a cloud are minutes passing / which is / which / view odds of images swept rag-tag" (Howe 36); and the contemplative short-lined free verse of Williams and H. D., of "red wheel / barrow" fame (Williams 30).

This last, of course, really drove free verse to be the central mode of mainstream twentieth-century poetry. And, as Paul Lake points out in his essay "Verse That Print Bred," it couldn't have happened without the typewriter opening up the field of the page to poets as a site of visual control. It is true that, as Dana Gioia has suggested, the red wheelbarrow can be scanned as two lines of iambic pentameter (with a few uncommon, but imaginable, metrical variations). But, of course, that is not the whole story; the wheelbarrow-like sight of the jolting stanzas is still essential to the poem, as Fran Quinn has pointed out. In the end, the free-verse line-break holds an irreducible visual power, like that of the Chinese ideograms that attended its birth. This visual identity is, it seems to me, the essential legacy of free verse.

So there are two basically different motivations for poetic lines: aural and visual (and also the possibility of a counterpoint or dialogue between them).

Different in etiology and in effect, in the ways they reach us and perhaps in the parts of us they reach, both are, still, called lines. What is the shared quality that reaches deeper than their significant differences? Simply this, that they repeat. This is part of what James Longenbach means when he writes that "in the end, line doesn't exist as a principle in itself. Line has a meaningful identity only when we begin to hear its relationship to other elements in the poem" (5).

Lines, in themselves, lend the words of poems a weight, a reality that no other kind of language implies. They do this through repeating—the dignity of that physical structure which precedes and underlies words. They have the ability to weave us back over and over through their cycling and turning: ourselves hearing or ourselves seeing. They can bring us back over and over to the same place in a different way, and the words we are hearing or reading along with us. This is not a small thing to do. Just as the repetition of breaths or of seasons can create and sustain life, so can the repetition of lines.

WORKS CITED

Brooks, Gwendolyn. "Boy Breaking Glass." *Blacks*. Chicago: Third World Press, 1987.

Ginsberg, Allen. *Howl*. San Francisco: City Lights, 1992.

Hass, Robert. "Meditation at Lagunitas." *Praise*. New York: Harper Collins, 1979.

Hayden, Robert. "Those Winter Sundays." *Robert Hayden: Collected Poems*. Ed. Frederick Glaysher. New York: Liveright, 1985.

Howe, Susan. "Pythagorean Silence." *The Europe of Trusts*. New York: New Directions, 1990.

Lake, Paul. "Verse That Print Bred." *After New Formalism: Poets on Form, Narrative, and Tradition*. Ed. Annie Finch. Ashland, OR: Story Line Press, 1997. 25–30.

Longenbach, James. *The Art of the Poetic Line*. St. Paul, MN: Graywolf Press, 2008.

Lorde, Audre. "Coal." *The Collected Poems of Audre Lorde*. New York: W. W. Norton, 2000.

Williams, William Carlos. *The Collected Poems of William Carlos Williams*. Vol. 1. New York: New Directions, 1967.

Only the Broken Breathe

Graham Foust

"To be conscious," writes Roberto Unger, "is to have the experience of being cut off from that about which one reflects: it is to be a subject that stands over against its objects" (200). According to Unger, this odd division between the thinking subject and thought-about object is made possible by the subject's ability to "defin[e] its relationship to its object as a question to which different answers might be given." Here, reflection is figured as kind of renunciation, that "piercing Virtue" Emily Dickinson calls "The letting go / A Presence—for an Expectation—" (365–366).

But what happens when the subject becomes conscious of herself? That is, what happens when the subject is the object of her own reflection? Dickinson's poem is helpful here, too, ending as it does by reframing renunciation—previously figured as a "letting go"—as a kind of reaching out:

Renunciation—is the Choosing
Against itself—
Itself to justify
Unto itself—

If the self is "over against" itself when it selects itself as the object of reflection, it must also in some way align with (i.e., "justify") itself, which may be to say that moments of self-reflection involve alternately calling for and renouncing one's own wholeness, an oscillation we might liken to inhaling and exhaling.

Because they are spoken language—and because they are broken language— poems are places (and times) in which we are able to hear ourselves enact this process. Tell me where in the poem the reader is, and I will tell you of what she is or is not conscious. If she is in the poem, taking it at its words by speaking and hearing them, then she is also in some way rendered unconscious, put under by the sound of her voice as she gives away her breath to the poem. If she is hovering outside the poem, however briefly, in that place we call the line-break—figured there as breathless by the poem's placement on the page—she then regains her consciousness. Strangely, though, this waking comes by way of her sudden removal from the very process (breathing) that makes consciousness possible.

In common parlance, to "take a break" is to take "a breather." This is not so in the uncommon parlance of poems. In a poem—or, rather, just outside of it—we breathe just after we break, electing to then return to unconsciousness in order to say the poem's next line.

WORKS CITED

Dickinson, Emily. *The Complete Poems of Emily Dickinson*. Ed. Thomas H. Johnson. New York: Little, Brown and Company, 1961.
Unger, Roberto Mangabeira. *Knowledge and Politics*. New York: Free Press, 1976.

As a Means, Shaped by Its Container

Alice Fulton

A poem's unity is never simple. The line frames a linguistic gesture in uninscribed space, encouraging us to contemplate it as a discrete entity and a contributor to the whole. There's a structural reciprocity, a nesting of each in each. For readers, the line encourages a lingering that is also a reveling in words. For poets, it's an invitation to play rather than tell.

Prose seldom highlights language: the words tend to dissolve into meaning as soon as they're read. Poetry combats this transparency, asking us to experience rather than ignore the materiality of language, as if the poem were a linguistic wall that gradually and lusciously dawns into window. By surrounding words with a blazing frame of blank, the line underscores the *stuff* the poem's made of. The surface becomes part of the subject: we read on two levels.

Fiction depends on narrative conflict, but a poem's tension arises from its connotative richness. It never says one thing only, and its wiliness is abetted by the line. As fiction has its unreliable narrators, poetry has its unreliable denotators. The end word in a line can change its part of speech when it's enjambed, an effect Cristanne Miller has called "syntactic doubling" (37). This helpful term describes a word's slippage at the line-break, the instant when a poem can swerve and become manifold, as in these subtle lines from Emily Rosko's "Aquatic":

If I think of any beginning I think water
down to the taproot, cell base, underground

aquifers that stretch Nebraska's ends: the stillness (3)

When the second line is decontexualized and read alone, the end word "underground" seems a noun. But when the line's enjambed, "underground" morphs to an adjective modifying "aquifers." The lineation both severs and retains syntactic continuity.

Narrative is about what happens next; poetry is about what happens now. The line contributes to this immediacy. Warped by enjambments, it complicates the forward momentum of the poem. It's a gesture of resistance, counterpointing and countervailing the current, thwarting an unimpeded passage through language, turning language to plunge pool rather than racing lane. There's a meditative pause, a beat—sometimes even a recursive push backwards—at the end of a line. We find ourselves gazing farther into the page instead of moving onward. Its depth detains us.

Shifty, volatile, full of subterfuge and intelligence, lineation gives rise to sudden reconceptions of content:

. . . Clouds
releasing the first skeptical drops, next sheets

to overfill land: torrents, then torrents
not for years. The sea's upwelling cold gone

warm . . . (Rosko 3)

"Torrents, then torrents." What a downpour. But the phrase implodes upon enjambment, becoming "torrents / not for years." In another reversal, "The sea's upwelling cold gone" at first describes a vanishing and is followed by a stanza space mimetic of absence. Yet when carried over, the phrase evolves into a description of temperature: "The sea's upwelling cold gone // warm."

The line is a way of denaturalizing language. It stages words as spectacle and footlights meter. Lines governed by "natural" syntactical patterns often end with nouns or verbs and begin with function words—conjunctions, articles, prepositions, the sizing of language. If you scrutinize the left margin of poems, you'll usually see several lines beginning with "of," "in," or other prepositions. Poets often break lines on the noun preceding a prepositional phrase because there's a small surprise when the phrase is completed. A countersyntactical lineation might break on function words to emphasize the semantic seams. Ending on these small parts of speech tends to frontload lines with nouns and verbs, weight and muscle—while the right margin, composed of linguistic nonentities, feathers into flimsiness, deckle-edged and ragged. If this effect is repeated throughout, the entire poem can seem seductively hesitant, off-kilter, rather than classically poised. Function words placed at the end of a line, a position of power, draw attention to the invisible glue of language. What is the effect of *of*? And *and*? Or *or*? Where is *to* going to? In the following excerpt, the first line hangs suspended, enacting the transformation it describes:

Adaptation among organisms: salt to fresh to
in between. Uptake in the xylem, circulation

in the vein: miracle, madness, exit: water
as a means, shaped by its container . . . (Rosko 3)

Prose is all figure: it regards the ground as immaterial. Only lineated poetry turns negative into positive space, constantly renegotiating absence and presence. The page becomes a visual field where stanzas can have the regular elegance of crystals or the irregular beauty of a brook over bedrock. While prose relies on punctuation marks to modify tempo, lineated poetry uses space to slow or speed the eye. The poem is punctuated by snow: areas of reticence vibrant with nuance. The line works the blizzard till the uninscribed page resonates with implication, haunted by the words around it. What a commotion! The blanks of poetry are its loudest moments. They are silence amplified, shaking the bars of language.

And as we read, we become the space where lines fibrillate and multiply. As poetry incarnates thought into matter—paper, ink, the materiality of words—readers excarnate the matter of poetry into mind and spirit. The lines continue imperiously within us, packed in their important snow.

WORKS CITED

Miller, Cristanne. *Emily Dickinson: A Poet's Grammar*. Cambridge: Harvard University Press, 1987.
Rosko, Emily. *Raw Goods Inventory*. Iowa City: University of Iowa Press, 2006.

A Line Is a Hesitation, Not a World

John Gallaher

Poems invent time down a page, and the line paces the poem. If line-breaks are meaningless, as some assert, try taking the line-breaks out of a Rae Armantrout poem and see what you get. So line-breaks aren't meaningless.

But then again, when people take this point into talking about the "music" of the line, I've no idea what they're talking about. I dislike hearing someone mention the "music" of the line just about as much as I dislike hearing someone speak of the "poetry" of things that aren't poems. I think this idea of "music" is what's behind so many people reading with such strongly affected "poet" voices, a kind of forced lilt. I'm much more comfortable thinking about sentences in poetry unfolding as sentences. But then I'm up against the obvious non-poetry moments of chopping prose sentences into lengths, and I don't think poetry is that, either. So poetry is neither, in my reading of it, music nor prose. And then I come back to a square close to square one, but a nuanced square one, where poetry doesn't have the same intentions as regular prose, and lines and their breakages assist in enacting that difference.

If new form equals new content, as has been asserted many times over the last century, one's use of the line has to be of some primary importance to that new content. So what is the nature of that importance?

For me, beyond a gestural definition of the line as somehow indicating the hesitations of the voice down the page, any concept of the line seems a before-the-fact definition of the poem, so I become anxious. Except for the fact that one's poems tend to resemble each other over time (ah, the glories of "finding your voice" [a conversation I like to avoid])—and they resemble each other in some enacting of the line, the kind of words one chooses, the sorts of sentences, punctuation, as well as the pacing of the line; though I can think of examples where the kinds of words chosen, and the types of sentences structured, are more dominant than the way the lines unfold, some theory of the line as a compositional unit is at play, no matter how subterranean.

A word is a collecting. A line is a collecting. As are sentence, stanza, and poem. The parts part and return. It's how the attention makes a focusing.

And we all can agree that line-breaks interrupt sentence "logic." But if a line enacts a propelling force toward a hesitation, what about ending a line with a period or comma, where the hesitations of grammar and line-break coincide? And what happens in that empty space between stanzas? These things have meaning, but I'm beginning to think the meaning is not languageable outside of the act of the poem itself, so that the poem becomes a one-time use definition of line-break, line, stanza, and so forth. And so I fade out of attention until I come across a poem where the use of line-breaks grates on my nerves. There has to be some elegance to it, as there is elegance in the body, the breath of the body expelling the poem.

My difficulty in talking about the line in American poetry is that a theory of the line is a poetics, and therefore it is like a theory of ethics; at some point it posits one "ought" to do something. Being an absolute, it can have no experiential basis, and is destroyed by examples. It becomes a lens that sits between the reader and the poem. It, in the end, only describes the lens itself. As well, a poetics is a form of therapy. It purports that through its enacting, thoughts are put in order in the poem, are at peace, are a stable economy.

For me, "cause and effect" is less useful a proposition in describing what is the case with the line than is "chance," because life as I've lived it feels highly ambiguous and chancy, so art that does not exhibit a knowledge of this does not exist contemporaneously with life. The way the arbitrary is a kind of thinking. The way chance is a form of knowledge. If a poem yields itself to a rational reading, it isn't a very successful art object for me, because the things I find in the world that are the most important aren't explainable, so why should the creation of poetry be finally explainable?

Poets of differing moods live in different worlds; as they see through the lens of differing moods, so they will fundamentally misunderstand each other. But a misreading is still a reading, reading across each other's lines, reading against each other's content. At the same time, the fact of grammar makes talk of differing poetics problematic, as grammar demands a similarity to all sentences. Which is, single lines from wildly different poets (Lyn Hejinian and Billy Collins perhaps) can often seem indistinguishable, even as their poems are radically at odds with each other. The poem can neither be outside of language (really in the world), nor remove itself from being tied to the mutually agreed-upon referent. Those who step outside of this economy do not really step outside of this economy. The attempt only produces elegies of the poet's inability to do so. Perhaps this is the hidden final subject of all poems. Poetry, then, as I see it, is a family of cases: as poetry does not have uncoverable foundations or distinct borders, all poems bear family resemblances. A poetics of a group tendency is half an artificial difference, and half an artificial unity. A poetics, then, or a movement or a school, to some degree, is nothing more than brand loyalty, or at last they are more about an artistic stance toward content than they are about the smallest levels of that content.

Thoughts are not in language. So intentionality does not produce what the thinker was thinking, only how the thinker formed the thinking on the page, and having an idea for the poem is not something that the poem can accomplish. What a poet meant in writing a poem is interesting, but no more interesting, or helpful, than what a reader receives from the poem.

As the poem is languaged, it is a game, an imagined space, as is any use of language (at its base). But the poem heightens this as it purports to foreground its otherness, its distance from unconscious taken-for-granted language games. In this way, poetry is a movement into consciousness, in both world and world-of-language, and meaning is not something that can be fixed in place, either through denotation or connotation, as each new application recontextualizes the space of language's habitation.

As a writer of poems, one goes on nerve, then; yes, but more, one goes by continuing to go. In going, one finds one's way. Art objects, on some level, are therefore unplannable, though they can and should be studied toward and practiced for. What will happen in the next line is unknowable, as what will occur is beyond a poetics, in the swirl of further texts. If a poetics were to be predictive, all poems would disappear.

Four Allegories of the Line

Noah Eli Gordon

> They cry O Spider spread thy web! Enlarge thy bones & fill'd
> With marrow. sinews & flesh Exalt thyself attain a voice
> —WILLIAM BLAKE, "THE FOUR ZOAS"

1

In the first allegory I am a small child. I mark my height on the wall in green pen, challenging my smallness. Slowly, the marks rise. A spider deposits itself underneath a thick leaf in the backyard. I tell no one my discovery, as I told no one about the tooth I'd lost before placing it beneath a pillow, where it remained well into the following afternoon. My discovery is not the spider, but the compulsion to experience the fear that it elicits. What frightens me is the certainty of its color, jet-black made all the more so against the soft green of the large leaf. For weeks, I check daily on the spider. It hasn't moved from its tiny canopy. In solidarity, I change the color of my marks, which continue to rise, well after the morning of the spider's disappearance. Once granted, one can only observe the agency of the line.

2

Like you, I am reading, but unlike you, I am faced with an awful dilemma. If I move from my current position—flat on my stomach, chest propped up by two pillows, arms bent at the elbows, book in hand—if I move at all, succumb to the overwhelming impulse to cringe and recoil in disgust, I risk a fate even worse. That I know this is the only thing granting me stillness. Like you, I am reading. A spider the size of an acorn sits on the inner cuff of my shirtsleeve, staring outward, nearly touching my wrist. A few seconds pass. I'm frozen. A few more, a full minute, two, three. I'm transfixed. There are laws to consider, laws of gravity, geometry, physics, but I am reading *Fools Crow*, a novel permeated by a communal understanding and respect between humans and the animals moving through their lives. Somehow, with a single, instantaneous motion, I contort my body in such a way that the spider flips from my sleeve onto the bedroom floor. Immediately, I crush it beneath the book. The line is autonomous but doesn't believe in autonomy.

3

In an hour, I have a job interview at Acme Surplus, a discount store in the basement of Thornes Marketplace. I want to look decent, pick out a shirt barely worn from the back of the closet, straighten myself, and step on the porch for a smoke before making the trek downtown. Something stings me, a few ashes I think. No, this is worse, continuous. Like someone's stubbing hundreds of cigarettes on my wrist. I unbutton the shirt, pull it off, twisting the sleeves inside out. There's a small grey clump, pulsating like a miniature heart. For a moment, I'm baffled, then I see twin mandibles extending outward from the mess. The spider has barricaded itself in silk and is striking frantically at whatever monstrosity invaded its home. In comparing those who turn from God to a spider building its house, the Koran calls the spider's the frailest of all houses. As punishment for her ambition, Arachne, who dared consider her skill with weaving as something other than a gift from the gods, was turned into a spider. I get the job, work there fresh out of college at near minimum wage for a year. Mostly, I hide in the backroom, reading. The line fears its love of tradition and loves its fear of innovation.

4

I was on my way out the front door when morning light caught the first anchoring volleys of a spiderweb, making it glisten and clearly visible. Normally, I'd have just pushed the threads aside and continued on, but seeing the little thing hard at work was too intriguing, its systematic creation too stunning. I stood in the doorway for an hour. I loved how it weaved back and forth, leaving behind tiny boxes, which, on its next pass, were subdivided even further. A previously unarticulated understanding of form was beginning to emerge. At the time, I lived with several housemates, and left them a note asking that they not use the front door that day. After leaving out the back, I returned home several hours later, and, having forgotten entirely the spider and my note, burst through the front door to find two of my housemates laughing at my transgression—the sincerity of my note and my own forgetfulness. The line is equal parts diligent exactitude and explosive, ebullient destruction.

The Hyperextension of the Line

Arielle Greenberg

One important thing I've noticed happening to the line in poetry lately I first spotted in the work of my contemporary Rachel Zucker. Her work is out of the postmodern tradition of the fragmented line, and clearly pays homage to innovative women poets like Jorie Graham and Brenda Hillman, and, before them, Barbara Guest, as seen in this, from the poem "Garment" in Guest's *Quill, Solitary Apparition*:

> Model stranger
>
>   this hiding
> of "hiding"
>   (a necessary evocation
>
>   and thee),   intuition.   (338)

But rather than use the line-fragment to *cut off* before the completion of thought or narrative, Zucker does something I've been calling the *hyperextension* of the line, pushing the line past the point of sentence unit into something that feels at once fragmented and stretched. To my mind, the hyperextended line can present itself in a number of ways—enjambed, lineated, making visual use of the whole page, etc.—but the effect is always one of muchness, of multitude: the hyperextended line feels pushed beyond what would be considered a "normal" length for the unit of the poetic line, either grammatically or content-wise or both. The hyperextended line has a voluble, almost manic energy to it, as if the speaker is hurrying to catch up to or capture all of his or her thoughts, and the result is something that feels honest and modern in its messiness, its ability to cop to confusion and contradiction. Poets who employ this mode often seem to be trying to challenge themselves to write what is just past the acceptable or beautiful or epiphanic.

The effect on narrative is, in some ways, the same as in the work of the predecessors I mentioned. There is an uncanny resonance with narrative or confession that swerves deliciously off course, but by pushing the line beyond its normal capacity or load, Zucker's hyperextended line allows for greater vulnerability, greater emotional risk, on the part of the poet, and thus can have a different, more visceral impact on the reader. Zucker's recent poem, "Hey Allen Ginsberg Where Have You Gone and What Would You Think of My Drugs?" which itself exemplifies the hyperextended line, makes explicit one of the sources for this kind of use of the line, and, in referencing Ginsberg, also nods toward Whitman and his contradictions and multitudes.

The hyperextended line appears vividly in Zucker's recent collection, *The Bad Wife Handbook*. Here's a sample from "The Rise and Fall of the Central Dogma":

> <in the language the real way I feel
> but not *separable* or *explain*, and if I
> felt otherwise, outside articulate,
> I would not, like a bad wife,
> go tearing around in constant *where is the o o o of my belief?* (74)

In these lines—which are not themselves particularly lengthy; again, the hyperextended line can happen even when lineated—the speaker qualifies her statements as she goes, building both contradiction and specifications along the way, in a tone that feels at once casual and conversational as well as rhetorical and argumentative. The effect is a sort of anti-stream-of-consciousness: a careful but cluttered working-through of a complex thought. It's a postmodern Henry Jamesian construction, allowing for ambiguity and clarity to occur in equal measure.

There are a number of other younger poets working with hyperextension as well. Noelle Kocot's book *Poem for the End of Time and Other Poems* comes to mind, as in these lines from "Lithium":

> I know what it is to mourn,
> And to breathe bliss into the wormhole of the senses,
> And that I must disabuse myself of the lion's share of who-knows-where
> And the whirring of new grasses on the rainy side of spring. (2)

In this example, the effect is less discursive and more cumulative: rather than cutting off or separating out the experience of mourning from that of bliss, or of self-knowledge or the joy of spring, Kocot piles one on top of another, allowing the seemingly disparate moods and tones to "whir" together in an emotional heap. If we consider Kocot and Zucker as poets who might be referred to as "post-confessional" or "elliptical," we can see how they break and borrow from two ends of the aesthetic spectrum upon which this gestalt lies: the fragmented, nonlinear lyric and the linear narrative. Zucker and Kocot do not cut emotional content or descriptive narrative short for the sake of mystery or metonym, nor do they seek to clarify a linear epiphany. Rather, their hyperextended lines, even when lineated, illustrate a complicated and layered way of thinking and being.

Perhaps the most obvious trend among younger American poets of the "elliptical" aesthetic mentioned above (which, it could be argued, has become the dominant contemporary mode among young American poets, as evidenced in the *Legitimate Dangers* anthology) is an anti-lyrical move toward a purposefully flat or deadpan line-break that denies or effaces the beautiful, musical, or epiphanic moments that happen elsewhere in the poem: a kind of shrug or "whatever" gesture through short or prosaic lines (though also through tone and diction). In this kind of poem, a line-break serves to show how the text contradicts or second-guesses that of the previous line. This seems to me a Generation-X move, one of irony and cynicism but also of a grudging admission of the urge toward lyric and epiphany. Here's an example from Spencer Short's book *Tremolo*, from the poem "Four Meals a Day":

As one buys before
the amalgamated & steel-gated
storefront of empty shelves (read:
Closed [Electronics] Forever)
a square red hat & wears it for
just one day—because one is
in love & believes love is
like a square red hat—

It turns out that it is— (67)

In addition to poets like Kocot and Zucker, whose use of fragment and the hyperextended line have been somewhat present throughout their books, there are younger poets who began their careers writing poems that made liberal use of moves such as the ones in the Short poem above, but who have seemed to be moving away from such use in subsequent projects. One could theorize that as the Generation-X poets mature and age, the risk of sounding glib or closed-off in poems that use a deadpan, abridged sensibility holds less appeal than poems that allow for fuller and more complex expression and feeling, albeit expression that retains a postmodern questioning, an assemblage of thought and senti-ment. The hyperextended line carries with it the potential for emotional raw-ness and depth, with its sweeping Whitmanian or Ginsbergian gesture toward communality and ecstasy, one that is unafraid of bigness or beauty, one that risks a lovely messiness both emotional and syntactic.

WORKS CITED

Guest, Barbara. *The Collected Poems of Barbara Guest*. Middletown, CT: Wesleyan University Press, 2008.
Kocot, Noelle. *Poem for the End of Time and Other Poems*. New York: Wave Books, 2006.
Short, Spencer. *Tremolo*. New York: Harper Perennial, 2001.
Zucker, Rachel. *The Bad Wife Handbook*. Middletown, CT: Wesleyan University Press, 2007.

Slash

Sarah Gridley

Delivered April 18, 1968. *One, if by land, and two, if by sea; and I on the opposite shore will be.*

A corruption of "self-edge": *selvage*, word for the edge of a woven cloth, the outside warp-ends around which the filling wraps to keep the fabric from unraveling. In Dutch, *zelfkant*, or "self-border."

Brocade floats on top of ground-weave—like embroidery, is a line of no utility.[1]

In short, the form of an object is a "diagram of forces," in this sense, at least, that from it we can judge of or deduce the forces that are acting or have acted upon it . . .

To interrogate poetic form, Valéry cast his mind over seashells: *. . . we can never, in our object, arrive at the happy union of substance and shape that is achieved by the inarticulate creature which makes nothing, but whose work, little by little is differentiated from its flesh, progressively moving away from the living state as though passing from one state of balance to another.*

The ocean, consummate line-breaker, comes in verse. That we might step into the same ocean twice.

As Robert Duncan knew: *There is a woman who resembles the sentence.*

[who]

    has a place in memory that moves language.

[whose]
> *voice comes across the waters*

from a shore I don't know   to a shore I know . . .

Broken could be the matter with a decomposed poet. What would you break, from all the borders of yourself?

If I knew when or where to begin, I would break into the Grand Canyon.

In terms of lines, I have a tactile memory. For instance, the weight on my knees of an Etch A Sketch, my girlhood attention's penitentiary.

Two white knobs: one for the vertical, and one for the horizontal. Erratic swoops of working both knobs at once.

For erasure—shake the red frame.

The erotic swoop is something else. I think it lives in interruption, out on the *zelfkant*, on the wind-strutted isthmus. Red of Sappho's highest apple, the one the picker left to hang—no, the one the picker couldn't reach.

L'Ecran Magique—The Magic Screen. Invention of a Frenchman, discovered at a European toy fair in 1959.

A slit in a garment, an open tract in a forest, the cutting stroke of a weapon . . .

In the toy reviving lineography: in the line that brooks no interruption. In the line whose pressure never lifts.

Wittgenstein, on the Etch A Sketch: *One thinks one is tracing the outline of the thing's nature over and over again, and one is merely tracing round the frame through which we look at it.*

[the red frame, the plaything]

Moby Dick, Chapter 60, "The Line": *The whale-line is only two thirds of an inch in thickness. At first sight, you would not think it so strong as it really is. By experiment its* one and fifty yarns will each suspend a weight of one hundred and twenty pounds; so that the whole rope will bear a strain nearly equal to three tons.

Foucault, like a brain between selvage and selvage: The limit and transgression depend on each other for whatever density of being they possess: a limit could not exist if it were absolutely uncrossable and, reciprocally, transgression would be pointless if it merely crossed a limit composed of illusions and shadows.

For its density of being, a line-break I love: Bavarian gentians, big and dark, only dark / darkening the daytime, torch-like, with the smoking blueness of Pluto's gloom . . .

dark slash darkening—what happens to broad daylight

ombré: in weaving, stripes that are mindfully graduated from one tone to another

and by a sleep to say we end / The heart-ache and the thousand natural shocks / That flesh is heir to

Eiffel studied the oak. Not so lofty as the pine, but able to bear more weight.

A girdle of the great whale's back / was in the shapely Crane-Bag: / I tell thee without harm, / it used to be carried in it. / / When the sea was full, / its treasures were visible in its middle; / when the fierce sea was in ebb, the Crane-Bag / in turn was empty.

Oh to be one with what one is doing.

Where knowledge, as W. C. Williams knew, is not at the end of deduction, is in each phase of it and everywhere—

because more pressing than deductions we are making would be the deductions being made of us.

So that the Indians in spearing a fish allow for refraction by the water and aim not at the false image but at the spot where the fish will be

The truth (from Wikipedia) about the Etch A Sketch: The "black" line merely exposes the darkness inside of the toy.

Of the prose poem, ocean ensorcelled, the darkroom voices (hear miracle as the French hear miracle), *supple and resistant enough to adapt itself to the lyrical stirrings of the soul, the wave motions of dreaming, the shocks of consciousness*, think Baudelaire, the swordsman, parrying his way forward.

That we might seize each other's substance by refraction. At the shared boundary of glass and ray the waves the waves are changing speed

Out flew the web and floated wide;   SLASH   *The mirror crack'd from side to side*

After the planking, a boat would have its seams caulked with oakum, hemp or jute fiber "impregnated" with tar, a pitch made of molten pine resin. This was known as "paying the seams." Known as the boatyard "rhythm section," caulkers were likely to go deaf.

Before the blueberries are out / we are lost on the barrens / in search of a lake, a pine-rigged rope-swing

The *weft* is crosswise, horizontal. A strand of weft is called a *pick*. The *loft* is the springiness of the yarn, or of the woven fabric as a whole.

quarrel: a cut glass pane

Dead William James, are you substantive, or transitive? The passerines are quarreling over flights and perches. There are many bounces to branch. There is friable syntax. A festival called "The Terminalia." A stuffed peregrine called "Zenith." Divination from the heat-induced stress cracks of tortoise shell.

Call it a "dump" or a "transfer station." Could the line-break be this: the *inverse materiality* Bergson spoke of? *Creative of matter by its interruption alone?*

Rimbaud: *Je me suis allongé dans la boue:*   *I laid myself down in the mud.*

When the caulkers are paying the seams

When *aquiden* might mean "it floats" in Algonquian—

From the weaving glossary of Azalea Stuart Thorpe & Jack Lenor Larsen:

Thrums are the lengths of warp ends that remain unwoven after the cloth has been brought to completion.

1. Sources in order of appearance: Thorpe and Larsen, *Elements of Weaving: A Complete Introduction to the Art and Techniques*; Thompson, *On Growth and Form: The Complete Revised Edition*; Valéry, *Sea Shells* (illustrations by Henri Mondor); Duncan, "The Structure of Rime I"; Wikipedia, all information pertaining to Etch A Sketch; *Moby Dick*; Foucault, *Language, Counter-Memory, Practice: Selected Essays & Interviews*; D. H. Lawrence, "Bavarian Gentians"; *Hamlet*; *Duanaire Finn*, ("crane-bag" section) translated by E. MacNeill, Irish Texts Society, 1908; Williams, *The Embodiment of Knowledge*; Baudelaire, from his dedication of *Spleen de Paris* to Arsène Houssaye; "the darkroom voices" is a nod (and a thanks) to Noah Eli Gordon and Joshua Marie Wilkinson, who, on the occasion of their reading in Cleveland, put into my hands a copy of their collaboration *Figures for a Darkroom Voice*, a book that has been filtering and fibering my blood ever since. Hooray for the ecstasies of collaborations. Why do we not "ex-author" more of them?; Tennyson, "The Lady of Shalott"; Maine Maritime Museum, all information pertaining to caulking; Henri Bergson, *Creative Evolution*.

The Line as Fetish and Fascist Reliquary

Gabriel Gudding

The line is not a feature of poetry.

The line is basically a disciplinary fiction, a fantasy of technique, an imaginary feature upon which to render pronouncements and leverage arbitrary distinctions for the purposes of acquiring or wielding social and disciplinary power.

The history of the line, as something ostensibly worth making distinctions about, is the history of poetry both as a fetishized cultural commodity and, since the modernist moment, as part of a broader system of belief that has helped lead to the disenchantment of everyday cultural life in an advanced, industrial world. This history of the line, then, is, in its latest iteration, in great part a holdover from the history of the right-wing modernist fetish of form, which marked the removal of poetry fully from the office of humility.

So the line is, in one sense, a gendered and fascist reliquary containing the careers of Pound, Eliot, Olson, William Logan, LangPo, and the dismal tantrums of the neoformalists—groups and personalities defined by the genre of conviction and pronouncement. In another sense, the line is a verbal machine, or a machinic talisman, that marks a fetish of music and voice and wax over content, context, flesh, ethical inspiration and political struggle—often, on the one hand, in the name of archetypal, transcendental, universal, colonial, ostensibly transcultural values, and, on the other, in the name of provisional resistance and socio-aesthetic struggle against late-capitalist hegemonies, authoritarianism, and consumerism.

The line is a vomito-aesthetic concrescence of a larger, mystifying ideology known both as "official art" and its false rival "avant-garde art" whose purposes are both to entrench administrative culture and delimit the range of experiences we call "human" as a broader push continually to establish, disenchant, and rationalize advanced, industrial society. It's a trumped up vomitnothing about which and around which belief and conviction and argument are purposefully constructed in spasms of pseudo-activity—the purpose of which is to mobilize collective narcissistic excitement in a genre characterized by ethical inaction.

So, yeah. Our world is in peril. We don't have time for the line, except against a backdrop of those cosmologies positing (a) an eternal realm, (b) an impending apocalypse followed by redemption for true believers, (c) a viable suburbia. Basically, we live in a time in which poetry has to resist itself and its own unsustainable habits in favor of facing reality. The line is one such conceptual habit; an iterative fraud. Renounce it quickly.

This necessary renunciation will inevitably extend to poetry's other most favored myths: that song destroys illusion; that dysraphic poetry also destroys illusion and, unlike song, also destroys capitalist hegemony; that messing with syntax is somehow in itself politically radical; that formalism is really exhaustively open to content; that close reading isn't textual fetishism; that craft isn't technical fetishism; that imagination is somehow by itself salutary; that poetry is precious speech uttered by special beings or by necessarily radical people.

In short, the line is an ideological device masquerading as an aesthetic element. Which would in itself not be a bad thing, except for the fact that the current effect of what gets called "art" in our world, or what gets called "poetry" in our life, is in fact to limit the number and categories of experience in which, by which, and through which one can become what one is and work toward justice and develop a truly loving heart. If we are to stop the professional suppression of joy that we call literature, and if we are to cease manufacturing false needs through poetry, if in short we are to stop treating poetry as both a kind of country music and a hipster cagefight, we'll need at some point to wake up and stop ritualizing literature, stop valorizing its sacred heresies, and stop attributing inherent value to technique (both belletristic technique and dysraphic technique—as they are two sides of the same coin). Breaking the habit of obeisance to the religion of literature would especially mean renouncing poetry's fetishes, sublanguages, arguments, battles—especially its purportedly liberational ones—in favor of poetry's fundamental ethical argument, pragmatic kosmophilia, and not confusing that renunciation as further invitation to bicker. Why climb pebbles?

And let's maybe instead spend that time and energy in sacralizing our relationships to one another, to our Selves, to other animals, to plants, to sunlight, to rivers, to lakes, to soil, to compost, to seas, to air.

A Personal Response to the Line

Kimiko Hahn

When I cannot find my way—*feel my way*—to the line, I open William Carlos Williams's "Asphodel, That Greeny Flower" and read aloud. Here are the opening lines:

> Of asphodel, that greeny flower,
>> like a buttercup
>>> upon its branching stem—
> save that it's green and wooden—
>> I come, my sweet,
>>> to sing to you. (310)

I turn to Williams not so much because I believe in the variable foot but because, put simply, his lines feel good. They cradle an American cadence. And this is the cadence I experienced when I was stepping into it all. It was the mid-seventies. I was nineteen.

In childhood, poetry was Poe or Longfellow with their era's songlike qualities. In high school, poetry was a hip list containing e. e. cummings and Gertrude Stein. Here were radically different lines, if there were lines or even words. Plus, I read some Eliot on the side, although I had no idea what was going on but meaning didn't seem to matter outside final exams. In college, I was moving into two worlds: classical Japanese literature and, in workshop, poems by Theodore Roethke and Denise Levertov.

I recall Levertov's work making a particular impression: I could lift out just about any line and it became a startling fragment that had its own integrity. A few isolated lines from "A Common Ground":

> grown in grit or fine
> [. . .]

new green, of coppery
[...]
crumpled wax-paper, cartons
[...]
curved, green-centered, falling (16–18)

These fragments spot-lit language the way cummings or Stein did. Adding poems by Charles Wright and Adrienne Rich to the mix, I experienced in their lines a language under pressure; this dynamic became an essential combination. Diction was paramount for me—more so than cadence.

Then came Williams's *Paterson* and *Pictures from Brueghel*—the first with its radical disorganization as organization, the latter with its variable foot. I was in love! Even so, in spite of adoring "Asphodel," my own writing still exhibited little regard for cadence. Not absent, I hope, but haphazard. Over the course of early work, I began to feel that my own play with diction and imagery was sometimes at the expense of the ear. So I returned to "Asphodel." I began a more conscious attention to the *feel* of the line.

Fast forward to *Toxic Flora*. In this new collection, I combine cadence a little better with my earlier preoccupations. I make use of an informal structure that utilizes one- and two-line stanzas to highlight diction and that allows each stanza an integrity of its own. As always, I test the poems aloud, but with more attention to cadence. Here are a few lines where I steal language from *Science Times* articles:

in the Oort Cloud, *a hypothetical region*
of icy objects that become comets
[...]
a resistance to the larval infection,
[...]
(*everts its pharynx*)

A simultaneous interest is tangent to these Western concerns: I have become fascinated with the monostich—especially as exemplified by recent translations of the tanka which are conventionally translated into five lines. Although my academic studies were heavily weighted in Japanese literature, until ten years ago I did not know that even today "the established view [is that] the tanka is a one-line poem" (27). This quote is from a collection that has made a major impression on me: Hiroaki Sato's set of translations, *String of Beads: Complete Poems of Princess Shikishi*. Examples:

Night cold, I awake and listen: a wood duck cries, unable to brush off the frost formed on it.

[...]

The sky as a flock rises grows snowy, lucid, dark; in my icy bedroom a wood duck cries.

Sato reaffirms this provocative decision in his volume *Japanese Women Poets*, quoting the contemporary poet Ishii Tatsuhiko: "*Tanka wa ichigyoo no shi de aru* (tanka is a one-line poem)" (xxxix). To my own thinking, the customary syllabic break into 5–7–5–7–7 may be impressed in the Japanese body. The pivot between the first three and the last two "lines" are physically anticipated so that the progression is intuited without obvious lineation. Western readers might know this intuited movement from the sonnet. The end of the line is anticipated because we expect pentameter. Also, depending on whether a sonnet is Petrarchan or Shakespearean, the material itself progresses to the *volta* differently—and the closure varies accordingly. All this movement is very physical.

This interest in a single line poem—the monostich—probably stems from my fascination with isolating the diction in a Levertov line. And, too, I felt challenged by the definition of monostich: an early edition of *The Princeton Encyclopedia of Poetry and Poetics* suggests that the monostich is not possible in Western poetry. What prompted them to make such a pronouncement? Was such a bias against one-line poems really a disapproval of fragmentary experiments, a clinging to traditional poetics?

Friends know that I have been mixing these Western and Eastern poetics all along. And I know that while I work on cadence in more conventional-looking pieces, it is still lacking in my tanka. I do imagine that my various interests in the line will increasingly merge: perhaps my "ear" is catching up with my "eye," i.e., cadence with diction and imagery. The following poem, from my recent book *Toxic Flora*, may be an ordinary lyric to most readers. Fair enough. But in my mind, the short stanzas and the amount of white space on the page suggest both the monostich as well as a *sequence* of Japanese poems. They suggest, to borrow this poem's metaphor, "the shifting // and colliding and breaking apart alone. // The drifting. The sadness—/ that marks the opening of a quest // only to discover estrangement." Here's the poem in full:

Just Walk Away Renée

The mite harvestman, a daddy longlegs

found in 400-million-year-old fossils,

has wandered between several continents
without so much as a swim. A conundrum

if it weren't for plate tectonics,

a notion only realized in 1911
when a scientist matched up fossils

on either side of the Atlantic.
I think about this discovery and try to tease out a simile

but really it's better just to leave
the first land animals alone. The shifting

and colliding and breaking apart alone.

The drifting. The sadness—
that marks the opening of a quest

only to discover estrangement. (27)

WORKS CITED

Hahn, Kimiko. "Just Walk Away Renée." *Toxic Flora*. New York: W. W. Norton, 2010.
Levertov, Denise. *Selected Poems*. New York: New Directions, 2002.
Sato, Hiroaki. *Japanese Women Poets*. Armonk, NY: M. E. Sharpe, 2008.
———. *String of Beads: Complete Poems of Princess Shikishi*. Honolulu: University of Hawaii
    Press, 1993.
Williams, William Carlos. *The Collected Poems of William Carlos Williams*. Vol. 2. New York:
    New Directions, 1967.

The Uncompressing of the Line

Raza Ali Hasan

George T. Wright declares in *Shakespeare's Metrical Art* that "Chaucer could handle the marriage of meter and phrasing with a masterly touch" (26). Even if we— master and novice—possessed the "masterly touch," most of us living in the poetry world in the aftermath of the acrimonious divorce of meter and phrasing do not have the choice to employ it anymore. In this fallen poetry world, what the novice as well as the master have to deal with is the immeasurable line, the free-verse line—the broken thing.

It was this broken line that I first encountered and still continue to struggle with. The free-verse line's inner workings can seem as opaque and mysterious as its outer parameters. Writing a poem by putting together a bunch of broken things leaves me feeling like a master mason who, having built an arch with uncut stones of arbitrary sizes and varying shapes, is told to stand under this new arch with its scaffolding removed.

The regulated environment in which the traditional line and its phrases used to perform their tasks has disappeared along with the meter. The phrasing has been decoupled from its metrical grid, and the individual line's relationship with the preceding line and following line has become much more indeterminate. Thus, the difficulties inherent in writing a line of verse have been compounded immeasurably.

With metered poetry, one did not know why a line "To be, or not to be—that is the question," or a group of lines:

I hear him coming. Let's withdraw, my lord.
To be, or not to be—that is the question:
Whether 'tis nobler in the mind to suffer
The slings and arrows of outrageous fortune (3.1.54–57)

were so successful, but one could confidently say certain things about the probable causes for their success.

For instance, the success of the line "To be, or not to be—that is the question" could be explained by the pent up energy exhibited by the phrases "to be" or "not to be" when paradoxically they are shackled down by the iambic metrical grid.

Furthermore, in the regulated environment, this line is preceded by the extremely humdrum, perfectly iambic line (no variations whatsoever) containing absolutely humdrum phrases (given to Polonius to deliver): "I hear him coming. Let's withdraw, my lord." Therefore, the reader when he comes to the famous opening line of Hamlet's famous soliloquy can only be startled. The famous line's effectiveness and power are then carefully heightened by making the following line begin with an inverted first foot, which puts the stress on the opening syllable as if the following, second line of the soliloquy is answering the rhetorical question put forth by the first line. The second line itself is not end-stopped but propels the reader to the third line via the urgency of an enjambment, and the third line also reverts back to normal iambic pattern (with no variations except for the feminine ending it shares with the other two lines). These were the kinds of observation a poet could depend on when evaluating his work.

Now let us suppose a free-verse poet who has never seen these lines before is given these four lines (without line-breaks, in a paragraph) and told to rearrange them, to make them into a short poem in whatsoever way she wants. She can only go by intuition and dim memory of all the poems and their lines which she has cumulatively read, for she has neither the metrical grid nor the understanding of the relationship between the grid and the phrases to guide her. Our free-verse poet could end up with the following chopped-up arrangement of lines:

I hear him coming.
Let's withdraw, my lord.

To be, or not
to be—
that is the question:
Whether 'tis nobler in the mind
to suffer the slings and arrows
of outrageous fortune

The success of these new lines depends completely on the intuitive dexterity of the free-verse poet. Without the metrical grid to compare this new arrangement of lines, one is at a loss to say why this particular arrangement of lines is better than another. Decoupled from their iambic pentameter, extra white space seems to be randomly placed between the phrases creating extra pauses. One could say that previously taut lines and phrases seem to have gone limp, or maybe not. And that exactly is the point: the nature of the relationship between the new set of lines and phrases in them becomes largely indeterminable—the fate of a free-verse poem.

It is, then, doubly remarkable that given this state of affairs so many successful lines of free verse have been written. For one thing, the readers (mostly other poets) are looking for different cues (that they have internalized) than readers schooled in the metrical tradition. Second, the specter of the measured line still haunts the practice of the free-verse poet, serendipitously intervening with her tasks and practices, allowing for ghostly yet apt demarcations.

So why did we ditch the sure thing, the metered line? Why did we take on all the uncertainties that come with the free-verse line? The simple answer is: change in taste—away from abstraction and conciseness and toward the concrete and the expansive. Think of Whitman, not Dickinson.

This general uncompressing of the line can also be seen in modern Urdu poetry. The contemporary Urdu poet does not use the super-compressed, highly abstract lines that can be found in the classical Urdu poetry of, for instance, Iqbal or Ghalib. In fact, the traditional line from the classical Urdu poetry is so hyper-compressed that in contemporary English translations it can experience a doubling or tripling of length, as can be seen in the English language versions of Ghalib's poetry in *Ghazals of Ghalib* by poets as diverse as W. S. Merwin, Adrienne Rich, and Mark Strand, who worked from the still highly abstract, compressed literal English translations provided by Aijaz Ahmad.

In short, what we gain from this broken thing is our ability to overload the line, and, if need be, go almost to the right margin. What we lose is the peace of mind, the assurance that we know what we are doing—but that might just have been an illusion in the first place.

WORKS CITED

Ahmad, Aijaz. *Ghazals of Ghalib: Versions from the Urdu*. New York: Columbia University Press, 1971.
Shakespeare, William. *Hamlet*. Ed. Susanne L. Wofford. Boston: Bedford Books, 1994.
Wright, George T. *Shakespeare's Metrical Art*. Berkeley: University of California Press, 1988.

Line of Inquiry

H. L. Hix

It's amusing to add "in bed" to the end of one's fortune-cookie fortune because changing the referent of a revelation makes it a different revelation. I wonder if something analogous happens when one takes colloquial and technical uses of "line" as if they referred to the poetic line. Do they tell us anything about the (poetic) line we didn't know already? Do they raise questions we hadn't thought to ask? Does their juxtaposition prompt associations and ideas we might not otherwise find?

For example, I feel provoked lately by matters of orthodoxy/heterodoxy, conformity/dissent, obedience/disobedience, and so on. Such a range of concerns laid over my practice of poetry leads to questions such as these: Is poetry (can poetry be) a uniquely effective tool for recusancy and other modes of civil nonconformity? Does poetry (or can poetry) offer refuge for the scapegoat, the exile, the dissident, the refusnik? A complex of questions related to those seems to me to be suggested by reading—as referring to poetry—such locutions as "stay in line" and "you're outta line." The questions might be reformulated to follow the suggestive locutions. Is it possible through lineation to step out of line? According to what order of things is this poem in line? According to what order of things is it out of line? And so on.

I take it, then, as an ongoing obligation of a poet to interrogate—if we have a tragic or martial sensibility—or play with—if we prefer the comic and ludic—(mis)uses of "line." Line up. Line out. Give him some line. Outline. Straight line. Broken line. Line drive. I walk the line. Draw a line. Draw the line. Toe the line. Underline. Borderline. One toke over the line. Fine line. Line of work. Line of fire. Drop me a line. Sign on the dotted line. Line of least resistance. Line of questioning. She kept me on the line. I know my lines. A line in the sand. He fed me a line. Line your pockets. Down the line. Up the line. Enemy lines. Hold the line.

You understand my line of thought.

Out of Joint: An Ir/reverent Meditation on the Line

Cynthia Hogue

"The line, for a poet, locates the gesture of longing brought into language."

—KATHLEEN FRASER

The line as used in contemporary American poetry is a joint as well as building block, tensile and flexible, active and affective, distilling great feeling into a form of endless variance—sometimes a sentence, sometimes part of a sentence, or a series of words or fragments—all strung across a page (not always the whole page, and not always horizontally). Sometimes the line is working visually. Sometimes, still, it rhymes aslant. The line both contains and releases emotional energy, and makes the syntactic and synaptic leaps and connections that fret and construct the poem today. The line is telling, not only in what it says but what it doesn't say. As Kathleen Fraser observes, the line is "a *gesture* of longing" (emphasis added). There it is. The visible tethering of emotion (*longing*), creative and performative act (*gesture*), and the poetic materiality that puts the "long" in "longing"!

In thinking about the way poets today stretch and torque the free-verse line, I time-travel back to when it all was new and the modernist avant-garde first pushed the envelope in giddy, gaudy ways. The witty wordplay that makes the end of William Carlos Williams's poem "The Right of Way" also artful has to do with the cross-linguistic pun, which works as forceful enjambment:

I saw a girl with one leg
over the rail of a balcony. (206)

The first line in the couplet is whole, but contains an image that is both partial and disfigured (at least temporarily). The speaker's erotic longing is a perverse moment that shocks us, when we follow the image with the gaze over the edge of the line and there we are, just like the girl who has thrown her leg over the railing in a balancing act. Reading the whole couplet, we're still surprised to be misled: the girl only *looks* one-legged because the other leg isn't visible to the speaker. The line enacts the very pun with which the image is playing (*jambe* being French for leg). It's mean fun, and it allows Williams to explore what an enjambed line can do to stretch meaning. It's a wry, sly move that still has bite today.[1]

In stark contrast, Leslie Scalapino's postmodern sequence "DeLay Rose" stretches the line to house not simply perception but acute scrutiny. In a passage that revises Williams's couplet, Scalapino trenchantly transfigures it to confront our times. The lines envisioning the results of stepping on a landmine explode across the page:

> simply there
> a   left
>   leg   (196)

These lines comprise one observation, broken into individual words in spatial patterning on the page: "left" and "leg" justified with each other, neither right nor left justified, the indefinite article cast off from the rest of the lines. They complete a statement (if not a sentence), but all else is scrubbed away, nothing descriptive, all grave. The missing body is an absent presence in the spaces among the words. The lines resist going past their own speech act: the single word made flesh. To say more, Scalapino says less. She revises Williams's punning line, heartbreakingly, by literalizing it.

In order to extrapolate the viscerality of Scalapino's torquing of "the line," however, I want briefly to explore how she concentrates profound emotion—grief, outrage, and despair—into analytic focus. Lines fissure along the literally "on-the-ground" consequences of removed and abstract decisions. Scalapino's lines think past or beyond, we might say, a postmodern, abstract dematerialization. The shattering of the lines is meaningful in particular ways. She terms this method "decomposition" and "dismantling" in "DeLay Rose" (198), which the poem enacts by moving among dislocated or unlocatable subjects in seamed passages of lines that fracture the real.

There is a conceptual level to Scalapino's use of the line as well, which is worth noting. The figure of Tom DeLay in the poetic sequence works metonymically, a part representing a whole that her poem investigates. As a metonym, "DeLay" is drawn along the same lines as the other metonyms circulating in the poem—an inundated New Orleans and the Iraq War—by means of the concept of the "isobath," an "imaginary line" which connects points of equal depth. Scalapino renders visible the isobathic connections among "DeLay," "New Orleans," and the "Iraq War"—the visible effects of a system-wide corruption—by de/composing the fissuring lines. The following passage, for example, traverses the Battle of Fallujah and Hurricane Katrina, ending by referring to an infamous remark made by Barbara Bush after the evacuation of New Orleans. American soldiers, ordered to execute prisoners rather than bring them back to base, followed the chain of command "until Fallujah filled // with":

> [. . .] naked Iraqi corpses tied as a deer on a Hum
>   vee's hood,
> sport *Occur's first* a corpse killed driven on the hood through
> the streets dome floating ours penned starving, moved—The
> worst thing is—of the flooded poor here, left corpses swimming
> —some of these people (will) want to *stay* in Texas, as if they
> already do will want, the mother
> of 'our' president says who's from Texas [. . .] (169–170)

The passage constitutes an isobathic line that reveals (and ravels together) what has occurred first as unconnected, on the surface of a "Hum" (literally, white noise?) / "vee's hood" (V for victory or victim?) and the watery surface of an inundated New Orleans. The lines are jointed: both drawing connections and also seamed to join the seemingly disconnected. The lineation "hums" with the crackle of insight along moral and military fault lines.

To close, consider the way Juliana Spahr has literalized Olson's notion of the prosodic line as marked by breath. Sandra Gilbert reminds us that for Olson, a "new breath" created a "new line" (43). The new line marks where another breath starts. Spahr thinks *through* breath in a poem written after 9/11, collected in *This Connection of Everyone with Lungs*, contemplating not how breath separates lines but how it actually connects human beings (otherwise so invested in marking differences among us). Measured, long lines in verse paragraphs in the poem repeat what came before and incrementally add new elements. These paragraphs give imaginative space to what breath touches:

> Everyone with lungs breathes the space in and out
> [. . .]
> as everyone with lungs breathes the space between the hands and the space

around the hands and the space of the room and the space of the building
that surrounds the room in and out
[. . .]
as everyone with lungs breathes the space between the hands and the space
around the hands and the space of the room and the space of the building
that surrounds the room and the space of the neighborhoods nearby and
the space of the cities in and out. (4–5)

And so the poem continues, short paragraphs building in length through the
repeated units until finally cities, nations, continents, oceans are connected
through breath, the images yoked by coordinating conjunctions and enjambed
lines pursuing analytical investigation of the tragic through the mechanism of
the line. There's a cumulative force that the repeated lines gather into contemporary insight, heartfelt and palpable: everyone around the world is connected
because eventually we will all have breathed the same air from the collapse of
the WTC on 9/11: "nitrogen and oxygen and water vapor and / . . . titanium and
nickel and minute silicon particles from pulverized / glass and concrete" (9–10).
If there is emphasis at the line-break, it's incidental. If there's enjambment, it's
because the page ends. We're alert to our shock, however, to how the lines mark
specific events, how we are breathing with the lines, making us conscious of our
unconscious breathing apparatus: *this connection of everthing with lines.*

Song lines of longing. *These fragments we have gathered.* The poetic line today may be a "glass joint" (Gilbert's phrase), but it is also a titanium hinge,
mechanically strong, to absorb shock, concentrate feeling, radiate insight: a
crystal prism through which the poem's light is captured and refracted into the
radiantly radio/active.

1. On this moment in Williams's *Spring and All* "Poem XI" (titled in *Selected Poems* "The
   Right of Way") as a "literalized enjambment" that links the "erotic image" of the
   one-legged girl with Williams's "revolution in the conception of the poetic foot,"
   see Susan McCabe (128).

WORKS CITED

Fraser, Kathleen. "Line. On the Line. Lining up. Lined with. Between the Lines. Bottom
   Line." *The Line in Postmodern Poetry.* Ed. Robert Frank and Henry M. Sayre. Urbana:
   University of Illinois Press, 1988. 152–174.

Gilbert, Sandra. "Glass Joints: A Meditation on the Line." *The Line in Postmodern Poetry.* Ed. Robert Frank and Henry M. Sayre. Urbana: University of Illinois Press, 1988. 41–50.

McCabe, Susan. *Cinematic Modernism: Modernist Poetry and Film.* New York: Cambridge University Press, 2005.

Scalapino, Leslie. *Day Ocean State of Stars' Night: Poems & Writings.* Los Angeles: Green Integer, 2007.

Spahr, Juliana. *This Connection of Everyone with Lungs.* Berkeley: University of California Press, 2005.

Williams, William Carlos. *The Collected Poems of William Carlos Williams.* Vol. 1. New York: New Directions, 1986.

The Virtues of Verse

Fanny Howe

In response to the literacy problem
in this country
the poetic line
might need to come
to the rescue of the children.

The children might learn
to understand syntax
and the reasons for it
by writing all their papers
in short lines.

These would include
book reports, compositions
and every form
of creative prose.
Each would look like a poem.

If the children could see
the points where breath
and length come together
they might decipher
the necessity of syntax.

Finally while writing
they might feel the stirrings
of love for harmony
and complexity
that exists in grammar.

Metaphors, imagery,
action, conversation,
plot, theme, and timing
might emerge as games
in the use of short lines.

I truly believe
every American child
could learn the meaning
of the sentence, painlessly,
through very plain poetry.

Case on the Line

Christine Hume

Remember rotating a journal sideways for the first time to read the Mei-mei Berssenbrugge line?

Askewed by its constant reorientations and communality, I lost my place.

The dilating precision of Berssenbrugge's line required my most bionic patience when I first came to it in the early 1990s.

If she wants to make an abstraction, I thought, let her; if she wants to make a scene, let her: this blurs the two.

Dangling in utopian auras of accommodation, then comes tenderness.

Berssenbrugge's line teases mediation into multiplicities.

Her line walks circuits among rabbit holes. I am hurrying to catch up.

Enjambment, from the French *enjamb(er)*, to stride, to stride over, to encroach, derived of *jambe*, leg. The continuation beyond the end or edge. The extension beyond limits.

That is, between her lines is made "of radio waves trying to locate you. She is only moving" (37).

I follow her community of moods and sensitivities.

The Berssenbrugge line leads to the gutter and the margin. Double-edged or an arrow pointing every-which-way.

Slipping me off. Slips me off the path and onto another and another, pushes me past known horizons, undermines my footing, and misleads.

A giddy vertiginous line that runs across the footbridge, daring me to look thundering down, urging me to cruel inclines.

I walk in another's footsteps trying not to make sounds.

In her line, hear a bipedal gait organizing the distance, pacing an inner life. Steps seed experiences. Steps isolated and replayed and delayed and skipped and expansive and reversed and mother-may-Ied and distorted and discontinuous and forward and.

Leslie Scalapino: "I've changed my mind and I'd still be able to walk around after I've / died."

A vibrating line like a scent trail. A kinesthetic line perceived through entire bodies.

Yoko Ono: "Stir inside of your brains with a penis until things are mixed well. Take a walk."

A walking line gathers me in it, strives outside me.

A riposte to my taste for speed, the Berssenbrugge line curates sonic marvels through abstractions.

With a persuasive prehensile awareness her line hits the subconscious direct.

Reading it simulates car crash or orgasm: simultaneously experiencing its felt time—a protracted moment of everything coming into play—and real time—the quicksilver flash toward void—the scene is too fast to control and too slow to avoid the sharp pleasure of understanding.

With it comes the terror of compassion, comes continually.

Her line leads me into the inscribed space of continual displacement.

When I come to its end, I have given up definitive knowledge in favor of inspiration.

"At night, inspiration fell on her like rain, penetrating the subject at the germ-line, like a navel" (87).

Her line cuts me out—asks me to wander, animates my lust for clairvoyance.

These lines invite me to think along with them. They imitate internal cadences and synaptic movements so closely, in them perceiving smartens the thinking-and-feeling complex.

Madeline Gins: "A natural affinity exists between perceiving and anything that even resembles a line. That perceiving occurs consecutively or sequentially gives it an air of linearity" (194).

Part of the giddiness her line imparts is a kind of imagistic and narrative oxygen deprivation.

Her line is a "chain of oxidation" (125) that offers sensual apprehension unbeholden to visual coherence.

"Cast oxygen across the line, a person walking toward a mountain across water routes north to south, z's of run off, taking the interrupted line (of walker A) across voids" (139).

Looking into a Berssenbrugge line stirs gliding sensations—I tumble slow-mo into its scales, its phantasmagorical topography of surfaces.

It offers a panoramic view, by which destruction of linear perspective gets at the subliminal.

Vistas of textual sublime open up a many-horizoned outlook.

A series of ground-surfaces, each with its own vanishing point.

As in Chinese landscape painting, there are many paths I could follow out of the fantasy of Western objectivism.

"There is the line of a wall in the mist. I go in and out of the fog on the rim trail, and the mountains rise in fog among yellow leaves" (39).

A web of lines telescope infinite fields of inscription that I cannot look through (*per specter*), but inhabit, dehabitualized.

Her calligraphic approach to perspective allows a social, less eye/I-dominant attitude.

Its inclusivity unsettles normalized alienation and the oppositional version of foreignness.

Between Berssenbrugge lines, "double-touch" (Coleridge) and "double-consciousness" (Du Bois) reverberate.

Unfolding in tidal intervals, an undercurrent of devotion moves me to receptivity.

In them, presence doesn't replace distance. Detachment and investment symbiotically embrace each other, they take on the undifferentiated "direction of diversity" (Darragh), at once sensual and remote.

Here objectivity is a conduit through which subjectivities course, often out of line.

Their electric equivalencies organize relations around an omniscient subjectivity.

The expansions of her lines extend my perceptual limits as they front the limits of my comprehension.

To extract the tale while savoring the leisurely delectations of her lines is like watching a game only to keep score.

"Join lineation and surface of her body by voice and hearing, small animals, fragments swept away, lost colors of refractions inside cells, feathers, albino, crepe de Chine" (120).

Her lines are separate yet linked like the organs of a body, like veins.

Lines become internalized, and their language becomes a nervous system that packs memory around it.

I take her lines in from a distance like a landscape; I take her lines in intimately like a portrait.

She suggested the line is a frontier, full of fervent dangers and desires, alive with swarming pluralities. The underfoot textures, the dust kicking up accompaniment.

A frontier is a holding environment, a line is a holding ecology.

A pioneering line refers openly and opens up endlessly.

Piled high prepositional phrases, subordinate clauses, passive constructions track the contours of individuals, narratives, and environments.

That flat language could induce a stomach-churning and vision-blurring emotional intensity; this was a revelation to me.

For me, Berssenbrugge was the first keeper of a radiant spectrum beyond the caged line.

WORKS CITED

Berssenbrugge, Mei-mei. I Love Artists: New and Selected Poems. Berkeley: University of California Press, 2006.

Coleridge, Samuel Taylor. The Notebooks of Samuel Taylor Coleridge: 1827–1834. Ed. Kathleen Coburn, Merton Christensen, and Anthony John Harding. Princeton, NJ: Princeton University Press, 2002.

Darragh, Tina. a(gain)²st the odds. Elmwood, CT: Potes and Poets Press, 1989.

Du Bois, W. E. B. The Souls of Black Folk. 1897. Avenel, NJ: Gramercy Books, 1994.

Gins, Madeline. "Arakawa's Line in Helen Keller's Signature." *Imagining Language: An Anthology*. Ed. Jed Rasula and Steve McCaffery. Cambridge, MA: MIT Press, 1998. 194–195.

Scalapino, Leslie. *Considering How Exaggerated Music Is*. San Francisco: North Point Press, 1982.

Lines and Spaces

Catherine Imbriglio

The notion of "line" entered my awareness early, through acquaintance with the musical staff, on which lines and spaces were inseparable—lines created spaces, with both being used for material notation of the temporal. I've never quite gotten over my childhood attachment to the multiplicity of tonalities that could be represented on the musical staff, or the visual beauty of musical notations themselves, away from any instrument. Though grounded in music, I subsequently became more absorbed by the line/space entanglements of poetry: the line played with space so it could pull itself out of silence or suspend itself momentarily before falling into the abyss. I always knew there would be a rescue by the first word in the next line—wherever it managed to appear. Mid-poem, end-stopped lines could be particularly treacherous, requiring a deliberate leap into the unknown when you could have turned back instead of continuing. And the last line, a real pressure point: did it resonate back up through the poem or did it resist its own closure? The best rescues were from lines that ran off with you in a direction you least expected. An especially well-executed line—from Donne, Stevens, Dickinson—could induce an exquisite moment of linguistic suspense akin to cognitive or emotional panic: What next? Would you be losing your breath or catching it?

But I found myself growing tired of thinking about the poetic line solely in this way—that is, as single-voiced encounters playing with expectation and the ephemeral. Though lineation conveniently provides instant recognition, it seemed too restrictive for what a poem could do and be. I started to think of the entire line, not just beginning and end words, as setting up tensions between the temporal and the spatial, with *each* line having a hard-core relation with *every other line and every space* in the poem, not just the ones before and after it. Poems could play with the prose sentence too, interrogating the "poetic" and taking risks with their own identity as poems, rather than limiting themselves yet again to well-rehearsed correspondences between phrasal units and silence, or phrasal units and emphasis. What words could go in such prose-lined poems? All words, any words, even if they rubbed conventional musicality the wrong way. Collage was a way of bringing in other voices and discourses, including the scientific, the philosophical, and the informational, with condensation giving a poem a density that complicated linearity. Collaged lines could radiate multi-dimensionality; outwardly and inwardly, they could entertain and submit to multivocal pressures, implicitly or explicitly. Useful too was Jack Spicer's proposal that we should think about poems in relation to one another. For Spicer, single poems were "one-night stands"; poems should operate serially for them to really make sense as poems. What if we started thinking about lines this way too, paying attention to them across poems, rather than just within the poem? A poem could then function as a chord, a series of poems chord progressions, and across poems, lines—repeated or parallel—would sustain a poetic sequence via a resonance that would continually reconstitute poetic meaning and emphasis. A line or a portion of a line introduced in an early poem and repeated in a later one could be helpful in developing or resolving subsequent poems or it could subversively disrupt them. And lines not seemingly related initially could suddenly make a poetic sequence seem cumulative.

But even that seems not to be enough—not enough to recharge poetry for our times. What if you saw the words on your line first as syntactical rather than semantic notations? What if you saw larger semiotic units first instead of words, as if you were looking at a poem on the page from across a room? What if you overran or otherwise violated the containment inherent in the line, but still called it "line"? Would any of these moves make you better prepared to comprehend the pent-up music in the poem, the formal and acoustic elements without which there might be semantic meaning but probably not much poetry? And what if you started thinking about an utter inseparability between poetic lines and spaces, but put space first in the line/space binary? What if you made some of your lines "larger than lines," filled them up with word-notes across so much territory that they no longer looked like lines but resembled prose? And then balanced these overrun spaces against normal-sized lines? What if you thought of poetic space as having its notation and being it too? In these ways you could read space as key in coordinating and distributing poetic distance, order, regularity, irregularity, and weight, with space playing single lines against one another, playing one line against different-sized groupings of lines, playing breaks against no breaks, groups against no groups, space filling itself up with semiotic meaning and emptying itself of it too. Space is necessary for the sound-shape of the line, fleshed-out or slim, and there may be myriad ways of exploiting this. But it may also be that giving more attention to the visual space-shapes of the entire poem will make comprehensible how intricately dependent the musicality of a poem is upon the reciprocity of its lines and spaces. Spatial arrangement seems to me essential to the tuning of a poem, a poem which can really only be well-tempered in relation to spatial-temporal arrangement within its lines and among its lines, as well as to the arrangements it makes with those of its neighboring poems. If the overall effect of a poem depends on its pace, the way it builds its highs and lows, then this comes from the way the poem distributes its musical energy through its formal configuration of lines and spaces. It's space pressuring the poetic line into a mutually seductive relationship that helps ensure the contemporary poem won't be tamed to a tired, overly familiar music that bestows on the poem a larger-than-poem visual-acoustic beauty too.

Lineation in the Land of the New Sentence

Karla Kelsey

Rereading Ron Silliman's essay on the new sentence—first published in 1980 and a poetics staple ever since—remains a breathtaking event. There is the thrill of reading a theoretical articulation of what I feel in my bones and blood: poetic language has the capacity to absorb us in images, ideas, and narrative while drawing attention to the fact that such elements are created in language. This attentive absorption brings us to question and investigate the very system that we are, while we are reading, engaged in creating. Not only does Silliman articulate this concept, but he also delineates the way in which the structure of new-sentence work causes this conflux of absorption and reflection. The new sentence achieves this feat by playing with the expectations of syllogistic logic. The connections between sentences are loosened so that, while pathways between sentences can still be created, movements through sentences are not restricted to a particular path. In this way the reader comes to reflect upon the connections he or she makes between sentences, considering the structures and expectations embedded in language. All of this happens simultaneously with an engagement of the images, ideas, and narratives created in the mind's eye.

After the thrilling sensation of recognition, the conclusion at which I arrive after each reading always shocks me: everything for which I depend upon the line-as-formal-instrument, the new sentence has already done. This, I whisper to myself, perhaps renders the line irrelevant for all poets writing work structured by the new sentence. At this point, the volume of my thought rises as I think about the possibility of having used the line when it is not necessary, as if it were a decoration. Perhaps the line is now decadent—a formal signifier that has been extended beyond its time.

Allow me to detail the thought process leading to this sensation of inevitability by citing four of the eight specific qualities of the new sentence as listed by Silliman:

1. Sentence length is a unit of measure;
2. Sentence structure is altered for torque, or increased polysemy/ambiguity;
3. Syllogistic movement is: (a) limited; (b) controlled;
4. The limiting of syllogistic movement keeps the reader's attention at or very close to the level of language, that is, most often at the sentence level or below. (91)

In application of the above, the new sentence does the work that I want to require of the line in the following ways. First, I want the line to be a unit of measure. Second, I want the line to launch possibility into blank space, rendering a singular meaning impossible. Third, I want line-breaks to both join and break free of connections. Fourth, I want the line to draw the reader's attention to language, lest the poem be read as a transparent window. And finally, I want the silence and pause of space that the line breaks into. The new sentence even provides for the latter, for Silliman introduces us to the pause of space created between sentences via a "limited" and "controlled" syllogistic movement. He tells us that the new sentence's effect occurs "as much between, as within, sentences. Thus it reveals that the blank space, between words or sentences, is much more than the 27th letter of the alphabet" (92). Thus we find that the space of the page beyond the line denses down into space between sentences, black holes that fold into alternate universes.

At times I become so entranced with this line of thought that I make plans to de-lineate all new sentence-based verse that I meet. At this point, a more discriminating sensibility usually chimes in with the assertion that the line, nevertheless, can still perform a unique and specific function. Even if a poet is composing poems made of new sentences, strategic line-breaks can do two marvelous things that extend the capacity of new-sentence work. First, if one lineates a poem composed of new sentences, the structure and relations of the line can be crafted so as to be homologous to the structure and relations of the new sentence that makes up the very fabric of the line. This creates, at the torque of each line-break, another opportunity for space, for polysemy, and for the reader to think through the acts of connection performed as one reads. Line-breaks require the reader to consider the relation of part to whole, the connection between line and sentence and stanza.

The second marvelous thing that a lineated new sentence can achieve is due to this act of consideration and connection. We can most readily appreciate the achievement within the context of what Gertrude Stein tells us about the limits of the sentence. According to Stein in How to Write, "A Sentence is not emotional a paragraph is" (23). Sentences cannot be emotional because they do not require the reader to perform acts of integration and combination, which are the actions of mind that provide the complexity necessary for emotional investment. However, the lineated sentence requires the reader to integrate and connect each line with the lines that come before and after it, engaging the meat of the poem in the very substance of emotion: connection.

This is not to say that new-sentence work is devoid of emotion—the connective action of emotion happens in the work between sentences and on the level of the paragraph. This is to say that lineation is still relevant to writers working with the new sentence, for lineation is a tool that can increase and concentrate the emotion-act of mind. I will leave you with an example of such increase and concentration, such texture of emotion in thought, by Martha Ronk, a writer whose grip and intensity is due, in no small part, to her lineated sentences.

Compared to examples of the new sentence pulled from Language writing, the movement from sentence to sentence in Ronk's ten-line poem "A memory of the pond," from Why/Why Not, has much more continuity and offers a subtle version of Silliman's ideas. The poem is constructed of three long, serpentine sentences that all have a similar mood of introspection and share some landscape details—"hills" are mentioned in the first two sentences; "clouds" and "storms" are mentioned throughout. Undermining this continuity, however, are pronoun shifts between and within sentences, disrupting the reader's path through the poem. The poem begins with "I" swerves to "she" moves back to "I" and then "she" and then ends with "we" and "you." This disruption dislocates the reader as much as shifts highlighted by more typical examples of new-sentence work—shifts in tone, subject matter, sentence structure, etc. Like these kinds of dislocations, Ronk's work with pronouns causes the reader to question some of the basic assumptions of reading a poem. Here, we wonder at the relationship between the speaker of the poem and the pronouns populating it.

This dislocation happens not only on the level of the poem's movement from sentence to sentence, but also within the sentences themselves. This is where lineation comes in to heighten the effect found between sentences. Since lineation allows a reader to see only a fragment of the sentence at a time, we meet the shifts in pronouns when we round the corner of a line-break—and they come as quite a surprise.

For example, the first sentence begins with what feels like a first-person statement:

If the slightly wet air in the skin is the hillside
is wherever I have to forgive what I have forgotten (53)

In the next two lines, we follow the speaker for another line and a half, listening to what appears to be a first-person meditation on forgiveness, error, and forgetting:

is error unretrieved from clouds over ponds
is we're going swimming she said.

At the end of line four, the sentence comes to completion with that disorienting phrase: "she said." *She* said? But I thought I was listening to the poem's I?

Each time I read this poem, upon hitting the phrase "she said," I feel the shock of being unsure about what I had been listening to all along. Was what I had taken to be "a meditation on forgiveness, error, and forgetting" actually some "she's" recounting of someone else's thought? Or did the speaker change elsewhere in the sentence, somewhere, perhaps, between the third and fourth lines? Absent any quotation marks, it is impossible to tell where any given speaker begins and ends. The sensation of this dislocation is similar to eavesdropping on a conversation wherein you are sure you know who is talking, only to find yourself face-to-face with strangers when you enter the room.

Granted, the "she said" surprise ending of this sentence would have had similar impact if the poem was in prose poem form, but the impact would have been lighter. The impact would have been more along the lines of finding out after dessert that your blind date is actually witty: the poet has played fast and loose with her pronouns and isn't it funny that we fall for it again and again. However, by lineating her poem, Ronk gives us dramatic corners that heighten the suspension of the surprise. The line-breaks slow me down so that I am more deeply submerged in the voice that I assume to be speaking the line at hand. Because of this absorption, and the natural blind caused by the verse's turnings, the surprise ending resonates. Instead of a moment of wit, the lineation of the poem gives us the kind of slap of confusion and betrayal that happens when one realizes that a person one thought one knew so very intimately is actually not such a person at all.

WORKS CITED

Ronk, Martha. *Why/Why Not*. Berkeley: University of California Press, 2003.
Silliman, Ron. *The New Sentence*. New York: Roof Books, 1989.
Stein, Gertrude. *How to Write*. Mineola, NY: Dover, 1975.

The Invisible Tether: Some Thoughts on the Line

Sarah Kennedy

Leaving the grocery store one recent afternoon, I was making my way through the lot when I saw, several lanes over, a large glossy hound standing in the back of a pickup. The truck was empty and the dog was untied, but the day was sunny and cool and all seemed tranquil. That is, it did until another customer strolled by with his cart, closer than I was to the animal's territory. The dog growled, howled, and clawed, her huge paws on, almost over, the tailgate. The hair mountain-ranged on her thick neck and her jaws foamed. We humans both recoiled, sure that an attack was coming, but the dog, which seemed savage, delirious with the prospect of blood, remained in the bed. The other shopper stopped, stared, and then slipped on past, looking over his shoulder now and then to make sure the dog was staying where she belonged. She was, though her barking continued to sound across the lanes of parked cars.

When I have fears that I may cease to be

The poetic line: a big dog in a truck. The image of that animal haunted me for the rest of the day, an instantly memorable visual and auditory refrain. A line in a poem has always seemed to me a string of words in conversation—or perhaps in a flyting match—with the sentence. Perhaps, I was thinking, it's also a unit of language trained into control. Most poets I know—and I realize that the exceptions to this are many and complex—usually write in sentences, if the sentence can be defined to include sensible and frequent violations, such as the fragment. We try to vary our structure (count how many recent poems do *not* contain either a question or an exclamation), but we still tend to rely on recognizable grammar: subject, verb, and surrounding modifiers and subordinates. And that dog can be fenced in. Passersby can relax a little, fairly sure that they're safe.

After such knowledge, what forgiveness? Think now

The line, however, lowers the railing, and whatever principle governs lineation—meter, phrase, syllable count—the images and tropes speed to the end, with all that white space tempting a leap into . . . what? Chaos? Possibly, but, no, the words lean into the void, then they stop, and the poem demands that the reader make a turn, move toward the bottom of the page. The margin helps to set the words off. Their potential for multiple meanings, including frenzy and violence, is unleashed by the approach of a reader but is kept in check by training (the poet's skill in choice) and confined space. When lineation is working, it brings image and metaphor right up to the edge of each margin, where they can snarl and snap and make that reader move on down.

—Even losing you (the joking voice, a gesture

So the eye drops to the next line, with a moment of lingering if the ending word is a concrete noun or verb (especially monosyllables or final-syllable accents), with a screeching turn if the line stops on a preposition, article, or hyphenation. If the line also ends a stanza, that choice is even more crucial, as a reader may assume a temporary closure is coming and find herself dangling dangerously, without semantic or syntactic footing. Leaping that white space, the reader will speed to the next word, making a link, somehow, between the previous line/stanza and what follows. To make sure that the animal is a dog, is domestic, is restrained. Or maybe to recognize the possibility that even the most well-trained beast can get away from its owner.

She had decided he should have left the doves
their beloved sky, for she would not be won. ·

Now, I like a lazy, lie-by-the-fire pet as much as the next dog lover. But what got my attention in the parking lot that day was the adrenaline rush of sudden danger and its equally sudden—and almost simultaneous—relief. Lines of poetry are musical in their rhythmic cadences, yes, and they make meaning(s), yes, and they are often beautiful, yes, but what makes a line of words a poetic line, for me, rather than just part of a sentence broken halfway across the page is that tensive moment at the last word, when the entire animal rushes to the boundary in full gorgeous fury—

to Mississippi, state that made a crime

of me—mulatto, half-breed—native

—and then obeys the silent command that all readers and writers of poetry
hear: down.

WORKS CITED (IN ORDER OF APPEARANCE)

Keats, John. "When I Have Fears That I May Cease to Be." *The Norton Anthology of English
Literature: The Romantic Period.* Eighth Edition. Ed. Stephen Greenblatt. New York:
W. W. Norton, 2006. 888.

Eliot, T. S. *Poems.* New York: Knopf, 1920.

Bishop, Elizabeth. "One Art." *The Seagull Reader: Poems.* Ed. Joseph Kelly. New York:
Norton, 2001. 22.

Emerson, Claudia. "The Admirer." *Shenandoah* 50.2 (Summer 2000): 22–23.

Trethewey, Natasha. "South." *Native Guard.* New York: Houghton Mifflin Harcourt, 2006.
45–46.

"What I cannot say is / Is at the vertex": Some Working Notes on Failure and the Line

Ben Lerner

I'm increasingly interested in how poetry can track failures of representation—hesitation, doubling back, fragmentation—in a manner that more accurately measures the experience of speaking and thinking in time than any sort of polished resolution. I think here of Robert Creeley's "For Love," how the speaker's failure to figure his emotional state becomes a compelling figure *for* his emotional state, an expressive failure of expression. And I mention "For Love" because my new book is in part a love poem, or a poem about the possibility of writing a contemporary love poem. When I speak of measuring, the ruler is the line.

The book is entitled *Mean Free Path*. In physics, the mean free path of a particle is the average distance it travels between collisions with other particles. The poems are full of little collisions: lines break off, reappear, or recombine throughout the book. And the way these units of composition get sucked up into the recombinatory machinery of the sequences dramatizes my struggle to insist on the particularity of my love for a particular person, to keep her from becoming one more interchangeable unit in the formal system. So I'm trying to represent the struggle to represent particularity in an era of what Adorno described as universal fungibility. I fail, but my hope is that the failure itself figures an affection I cannot express directly.

Let me mention a few other little formal features that register failure in *Mean Free Path*, failures I'd like to think enable a kind of experience unavailable in the poetry of mere description, failures that only exist as a felt effect of lineation. First, the stutter. There is frequent repetition of words across the right margin. Second, false starts. Many lines are abandoned but not deleted. Dead ends are part of reading the poem the way they're part of navigating cities. Third, interruptions. There are quick changes of direction between lines producing some unlikely juxtapositions, but these aren't surrealist chance meetings so much as records of distraction or shifts of perspective. These techniques focus attention on the activity of thinking over the finished thought. They track the constant reorientations—reorientations that take place at line-breaks—necessary in order to avoid the twin traps of incoherence and some kind of falsifying heroic expression.

Another failure: the lines are often out of order or belong to several possible orders simultaneously. In a given stanza, what might seem like an abandoned false start might be picked up later in the stanza (or in the next stanza, a later page, even a later section). Or a line might have a variety of possible continuations, might link up with more than one subsequent or previous line, and the reader has to select an order, or linger among a plurality of orders. If nothing else, I hope the reader is forced to read her reading: to experience her participation in the construction of meaning, to collaborate in the articulation of the stanzaic space.

I'll try to describe one way this technique—one might call it braiding lines—is thematized. One section of the book involves an elegy for a friend; or, again, a poem about the possibility of elegy: how to arrive at a form responsive to that occasion that neither amounts to a lyric subject congratulating himself on the depth of his feeling or a total abdication of the communicative capacity of the medium. One thing braiding does is make the poem nearly impossible to coherently vocalize. While the stutters and interruptions seem to privilege the spoken, the braid makes speaking the poems in a linear fashion exceedingly difficult. Unreadable, the poems become a kind of moment of silence held in memory of a friend, and that silence measures the incommensurability of elegy and its object. I hope the failure to speak speaks.

From *Mean Free Path*:

I know it's full of flowers, music, stars, but
But the pressures under which it fails
How it falls apart if read aloud, or falls
What we might call its physics
Together like applause, a false totality
Scales. The words are just there to confuse
The censors, like mock eyes on the wing
Except for Ari. No energy is lost if they collide
The censors inside me, and that's love

[. . .]

And that's elegy. I know I am a felt
This is the form where my friend is buried
Effect of the things that I take personally
A gentle rippling across the social body
I know that I can't touch her with the hand
That has touched money, I mean without
Several competing forms of closure
Irony, now warm and capable of
Decay on strings as we descend (56)

The poem moves from a stuttering apology for its romantic vocabulary to a description of its own procedures. One can hear, although it is much easier to see, how the lines can belong to various orders. "Several competing forms of closure" initially seems to be a continuation of the two preceding lines: "I know that I can't touch her with the hand / That has touched money, I mean without . . ." But the next line, beginning with "Irony," disrupts this linear reading: now it seems that the most coherent sequence is: "I know that I can't touch her with the hand / That has touched money, I mean without / Irony, now warm and capable of." The reference to Keats's "This Living Hand" also focuses attention on that linkage. Meanwhile, "Several competing forms of closure" now appears to connect with "Decay on strings as we descend." But the last line can also link up with the penultimate line (and thus the fifth line): "the hand . . . now warm and capable of / Decay . . ." However, the penultimate line could also be read as a fragment, as breaking off (which happens elsewhere in the sequence). And these multiple orders also compete with the stanza's sonic organization, a long *e* that ripples across the stanza—*elegy, buried, personally, rippling, body, money, competing, irony*—a musical ordering: like standing waves decaying on vibrating strings, another kind of line that expresses through tension and oscillation.

WORK CITED

Lerner, Ben. *Mean Free Path*. Port Townsend, WA: Copper Canyon Press, 2010.

Where It Breaks: Drama, Silence, Speed, and Accrual

Dana Levin

I am not interested in the line as much as where it breaks. I am interested in drama.

Eliot's Prufrock's "Do I dare": the pregnant hesitation.

Of course, to link breakage and drama is to lend enjambment the weight of content: white space as communicative pause.

Rises and falls in tension, the pauses that accompany a draw of breath during a cry or rant, a loss for words due to a struggle to articulate, express or understand, the sensation of being overwhelmed by feeling or epiphany. A physical blacking out.

I want the line-break to tell me something about how a poem feels: where a speaker butts up against silence.

We are made silent by awe, shock, doubt, bliss, rage, fear, grief, shame, tristesse. We are made silent by confusion.

When William Carlos Williams says of Elsie:

> voluptuous water
> expressing with broken
>
> brain the truth about us— (218)

He's not, for a minute, sure how he feels. How he feels percolates in white space.

Enjambment enacts the drama, and pace, of *feeling* or *thinking through*.

⁓

Because I am interested in drama, I am interested in how fast a line moves.

When Ginsberg says:

> who were burned alive in their innocent flannel suits on Madison Avenue amid blasts of leaden verse & the tanked-up clatter of the iron regiments of fashion & the nitroglycerine shrieks of the fairies of advertising & the mustard gas of sinister intelligent editors, or were run down by the drunken taxicabs of Absolute Reality

we hurtle towards a wall. Stop short, rear back, and hurl ourselves again:

> who sang out of their windows in despair, fell out of the subway window, jumped in the filthy Passaic, leaped on negroes, cried all over the street, danced on broken wineglasses barefoot smashed phonograph records of nostalgic European 1930s German jazz finished the whiskey and threw up groaning into the bloody toilet, moans in their ears and the blast of colossal steamwhistles (14)

like an animal trapped—slam!
with its howl.

⁓

Ginsberg's barely containable line (for that's what each who-beginning stanza-looking thing is, one long line meeting the iron edge of a page too small for it) was unique to the poetry of the 1950s; the 2000s have offered us a bounty of square books and prose blocks: lines streaming from margin to margin, often morphing mind/feeling/locale/subject/self as they flow, channel-surfing, flipping the dial, dazzled and weary, dazzling and wearying, driven on by engines of hope and worry: lines that well-capture that feeling of brakes-off acceleration, inundation (desperate, terrifying, exhilarating), that characterizes so much of our age.

Under such conditions, heavy enjambment arrests me.

> I'm not dead but I am
> standing very still
> in the backyard
> staring up at the maple
> thirty years ago
> a tiny kid waiting on the ground
> alone in heaven
> in the world
> in white sneakers (51–52)

I could meditate for quite some time on "I'm not dead but I am."

Admittedly, the narrative relayed above in Michael Dickman's "We Did Not Make Ourselves" is fairly pedestrian, and the word-choice lacks the lexical exuberance that is another marker of the contemporary moment—which offers an interesting kind of relief and novelty to this reader. But ultimately, it's the *pace* at which I am asked to move through this narrative that so entices: Dickman (like Williams and Creeley and Guest and a host of other white-spacers before and with him) invites me to participate in the construction of memory, of perception, in something that feels like real time; as the lines descend down the page, I literally drop down into experience: from thought ("I'm not dead but I am") to sneakered feet.

Accrual is what is at work here, not today's familiar roll of successive, loosely connected impressions. Dickman tends to build a scene or thought slowly (short lines) and then extend in a rush, as in this funny and rather gorgeous escalation:

> We did not make ourselves is one thing
> I keep singing into my hands
> while falling
> asleep
>
> for just a second

before I have to get up and turn on all the lights in the house, one
  after the other, like opening
  an Advent calendar (51)

The processional pace of meditative thought, the nod off into the stanza break
(for just a second) before the leap out of bed and the sort-of-spooked/sort-
of-slapstick socks-slipping-along-the-wood-floor-of-that-very-long-line that
brings in the Light: I'm not just thinking with the speaker of this poem, I am
moving like him; the enjambments and the sudden line extension across the
page teach me how.

Drama, from the Greek meaning "action," derived from "to do."

  ～

When my students read poems aloud, I insist they "read" the line-breaks (this
is not very popular).

Feeling speaks where the line is silenced.

  Do I dare
  Disturb the universe?

  In a minute there is time
  For decisions and revisions which a minute will reverse. (Eliot 4–5)

The line is a unit of experience.

WORKS CITED

Dickman, Michael. *The End of the West*. Port Townsend, WA: Copper Canyon Press, 2009.
Eliot, T. S. *The Complete Poems and Plays, 1909–1950*. New York: Harcourt Brace, 1950.
Ginsberg, Allen. *Howl and Other Poems*. San Francisco: City Lights Books, 1973.
Levin, Dana. "From Thought to Sneakered Feet." Review of *The End of the West*, by Michael
  Dickman. *Poetry* 195, no. 1 (October 2009): 71.
Williams, William Carlos. *The Collected Poems of William Carlos Williams*. Vol. 1. New York:
  New Directions, 1986.

This Is Just to Say That So Much Depends Upon

Timothy Liu

Some years ago, I was invited to a pre-reading dinner at the Iowa Writers' Workshop, the guest of honor being Sam Hamill. At some point between the main course and dessert, the poets around the table, one by one, each began reciting William Carlos Williams's poem, "This Is Just to Say," perhaps in anticipation of the plums we would not be getting served since we were, alas, in the wrong season. Those seated around the table included Marvin Bell, James Galvin, Jorie Graham, and others—and all of us, it turned out, knew the poem by heart! To up the ante, Jorie began to pass out paper napkins and asked if any of us knew how to write the poem out, line by line, stanza by stanza, our communal recitation quickly turning into a parlor game if not a contest of wills. This occurred at a time when cell phones were still a novelty, for I remember when we were all finished Jorie whipped hers out and called up Jan Weismiller at Prairie Lights Bookstore who proceeded to verify the Williams as printed on the page. Only one of us got it right, and that poet became the evening's toast.

Here are the twenty-eight words (sans line or stanza breaks) of "This Is Just to Say": "I have eaten the plums that were in the icebox and which you were probably saving for breakfast forgive me they were delicious so sweet and so cold."

In the intervening years since, in most every intro level workshop I've led, I have my students read and discuss this poem for a good fifteen minutes before asking them to close their books. Then I relate the anecdote above before writing the words on the board, issuing the challenge. Invariably, someone gets it right:

> I have eaten
> the plums
> that were in
> the icebox

and which
you were probably
saving
for breakfast

Forgive me
they were delicious
so sweet
and so cold (372)

We spend the remainder of our time looking at Williams's enjambments, his grouping of three quatrains. In particular, we look at the 3–2 word pattern of the first stanza followed by a 2–3 reversal in the second. Then we consider how midway through the second stanza, Williams switches things up to a 2–3 syllabic pattern (thereby "saving" one word from each line in lines seven and eight) before restoring the final stanza to a 2–3 word pattern, thereby completing his chiastic structure. We go on to discuss the different parts of speech that terminate the lines (past participle, plural noun, preposition, noun, etc.) and the effect of concluding his final three lines with three adjectives in a row (delicious, sweet, cold). We discuss numerical symbolism (the meaning of one versus two versus three versus four) before moving onto issues like the absence of punctuation or why only one other word besides the opening "I" is capitalized. It was Williams who said that a poem is "a little machine made out of words," so it seems fitting to take his poem apart to see how it works. I often teach the sixteen-word "Red Wheelbarrow" in tandem with this exercise in enjambment.

Sometimes, I'll present another variation. I like to hand out a poem—say, the eponymous opening poem of Louise Glück's The Wild Iris—as a block of prose before instructing the class to break it up into twenty-three lines, and to hazard a guess at its stanzaic structure. Of course, I've never had anyone get it right. In fact, someone would be lucky to get even two or three lines exactly right. After sufficient time, I hand out a copy of the poem as it appears in her book, and we spend the rest of the time talking about her verse-libre choices, how much intellect comes into play versus, say, intuition. Or rhythm. Or how the thing ends up looking on the page. Or what is lost when the poem is presented as an unlineated prose poem. Lately, I've been going the other way, asking my students to take a prose poem (something from Gertrude Stein's Tender Buttons or, say, Lydia Davis's "Men") and lineate it. In what ways is the poem augmented or diminished by such an exercise?

For what it's worth, James Galvin was the one that night who got Williams's poem right; but maybe getting it wrong was more the point, something worth remembering.

WORK CITED

Williams, William Carlos. *The Collected Poems of William Carlos Williams*. Vol. 1. New York: New Directions, 1967.

The Line

Thomas Lux

The only inarguable difference between prose and poetry: poets write sentences broken up into lines, the basic unit of poetry. Everything that occurs in poetry— metaphor, simile, imagery, rhythms, oxymoron, synesthesia, even meter (usually accidentally)—occurs in prose. So, the line, and therefore the line-break, is a quintessential poetic tool. Roethke says somewhere that one of the tests of a good poem is this: isolate any individual line and that line should stand, by itself, as a poem. Tough standard, but shouldn't every line of a good poem have something particularly fresh or reverberant in it? Good image, good simile, good dance, good verbs, good word couplings? Shouldn't each line earn the distinction of being called a line?

The line is one of the ways you teach readers to hear the poem exactly as you want them to hear it, which, of course, has as much to do with the line's (and the poem's) ulteriority as anything. Tone, attitude, making body language implicit through regular language, saying one thing and meaning another and making that understood—a tough, rip-tooth job.

Line-breaks: my ear was taught, somehow, that the last word of each line gets a little more emphasis than other words in the line. Want a little emphasis on a word? Break a line on it. Avoid passive verb line-breaks, conjunctions, prepositions, articles. Avoid too many feminine endings (which make lines trail off). Most lines will be broken—if you're trying to make the reader hear the poem, out loud, either literally or using the wonderful acoustics inside his/her skull—at places of normal pauses in breath. Maybe you change those normal places a bit, when you have reason to. That's fine. In fact, those (either normal or not-normal-with-a-reason) almost have to be the dominant kinds of line-breaks. A few others: (1) What I call a "suspense" line-break. Ending a line, for example, with a particularly strong adjective and beginning the next with an unexpected (but right) noun. (2) A kind of double entendre line-break—you read the line to its end and get one whiff of the poem's inner life, and then you read on and also get the grammatical meaning. They both have to contribute. This kind of line-break must be used sparingly, I believe, because any tool that calls attention to itself begins to seem gimmicky. Hart Crane, Robert Lowell, Bill Knott, and Heather McHugh all strike me as masters of this kind of line-break.

I think Keats was thinking of the line when he offered his injunction to "Load every rift with ore." I also assume he meant the line should be loaded with gold ore and not, say, lead.

"And then a Plank in Reason, Broke"

Joanie Mackowski

The line is contemporary poetry's definitive feature, even for prose poems, as what defines a prose poem is its lack of lineation.

However, the contemporary poetic line has no concrete definition: as poetry has drifted away from its metric anchor, and the conventional poem is now a free-verse poem, the line's no longer necessarily a rhythmic measure—i.e., it's no longer a pentameter line, a hexameter line, etc. Rather, the length, function, or shape of today's line is a variable: $x(y) = a$ line of poetry, and x is the shape of the line, and y is all available linguistic resources: denotation, connotation, syntax, figure, trope, rhythm, rhyme. So, the poetic line, having no inherent definition, achieves definition and energy in individual poems via its interaction with all definable aspects of language.

In *How to Read a Poem*, Terry Eagleton suggests that a poem is distinct from other forms of writing in part because "it is the author, rather than the printer or word processor, who decides where the lines should end" (25). While I feel that Eagleton's assertion is usefully open-ended, I'd like to pause on his choice of the word "decides" and consider the complexities of the decision process.

For when writing metrical verse, the nature of this decision changes. Let's say, for example, one has decided to write a poem in a pentameter line, and then (if one is Theodore Roethke), one writes:

The elm tree is our highest mountain peak;
A five-foot drop a valley, so to speak . . . (12)

Decision isn't the right word to describe how line-breaks such as Roethke's came to be (and those are the opening two lines of "In Praise of Prairie"). Rather, the line-break in metrical poems is more an observance, a compliance: the writer's not imposing a decision on individual lines but responding to a dynamic structure. And while the compromised, tangential nature of the writer's active deciding may be most obvious when considering metrical poems, I feel that these notions of *observance* (watching carefully, and taking cues from the writing-in-progress regarding where to break the line) and *compliance* (I'm no Latinist, but my etymology for this is *bending together*) can productively inform the practice of free verse.

When teaching introductory poetry courses, I've often come across fledgling writers who conceive of the poetic line as a tool for destabilization. I wonder if this conception has been egged on by popularizations of Stanley Fish's ideas seeping into high school English classes—with each line-break plunging the reader into an abyss of free-fall uncertainty. But a young student who wields line-breaks merely to unsettle, to make the reader have to "work" to get at the "deep meaning" of the poem, might come up with something like this:

> a very small bull
> snake coiled
> over mother's face
> of her wristwatch. ("Bull")

Lines such as these aren't productive of meaning; they're merely obstacles to whatever image or sense is at hand, or not at hand, and they help the writer to fake-out and escape the reader (or make her seasick). The incomplete conception leading to this approach is that a poem, by definition, is hard to grasp. Many of us first experience poems as dazzlingly elusive, so it's understandable that one might try to write one as an exercise in evasion. But the *decision* in these fledgling cases rests squarely with a writer who regards the line-break as something to inflict or impose on the poem, as a means to divert the reader from an indomitable progress of sense. More productive line-breaks, however, develop in conversation with the poem taking shape on the page: as one observes the developing images and structures and bends with them to yield multiple resonances.

I'd like to show some productively destabilizing free-verse lines: they're from the opening to Forrest Gander's "Burning Towers, Standing Wall." The poem's nine-line opening description generates extreme instability: reading this passage is like falling through a series of awnings (as in "Project A," when Jackie Chan hangs from the big hand on a clock tower, lets go, and then falls through three awnings to land safely on the ground [and, by the way, Chan's feat is an homage to Harold Lloyd's]). So, reading these lines by Gander isn't like a free fall; rather, the lines enact a series of careful ruptures and tenuous landings.

Describing ruins in Tabasco Province, Mexico, and interweaving images of the ruins today with reflections on their complicated history, the poem constructs a meditative speaker without using the pronoun "I." Indeed, an "us," appearing twenty-five lines into the poem, is the first overt index of subjectivity. However, "Burning Towers" reads nothing like cool objective description; rather, it opens, if you will, in the midst of a subjective sublime. Sublimity is, in part, what overpowers us, erasing our distinct boundaries as individual beings, as when Longinus writes, "sublimity flashing forth . . . and scattering everything before it like a thunderbolt" (77). From the get-go, the speaker merges thoughtfully, ecstatically, with the ruins and their history. In the first lines, a wall among the ruins "gleams gold gleaming" and seems "swelling forward to meet the light / or the gaze of the visitor" (5). This is the first inversion, the first suggestion we'll be knocked off our feet: that the ruin moves forward, not the looker. Next, the poem introduces "locals"—as tour guides, or trinket vendors, who:

> show what they mean
> to sell in a mixed language of numbers and night
> disperses everyone but insects crawling into fissures (5)

The break after the first line introduces a tension between visitors and locals. After turning the corner of this line, one thinks, Oh, *the locals don't show what they mean, but they show what they mean to sell*. To show what one means is to be direct and unambiguous; this line-break *unwrites* that first connotation, however, and introduces another that contrasts directly with the first: "selling" evokes ploy, strategy. So, this line-break establishes tension between subject and object, actor and acted upon: those who *show what they mean* let themselves be "read" by the speaker; those who *mean to sell* may be implicitly understood to "read" the speaker (and others) as the objects of their sales pitch. And one might also read this to suggest that whatever the locals "mean" (i.e., their perspectives, their culture) perhaps has been subverted by tourism.

Next, no punctuation stops one from reading that the locals speak a language mixed "of numbers and night." This mysterious phrase presents itself to the reader first—a language that's part numerical clarity and part untranslatable "night," dark to the understanding. And this mystery, this hint of information withheld, reverberates with that latent echo of what the locals really "mean." But that's not it. The line-break again *unwrites* the assertion that "night" is part of the "mixed language" once one again turns the corner and realizes that "night" is not the object of the preposition "of"; instead, it's the subject of a new clause: *night disperses.*

And, in the mind's eye, for a split second, the reader sees shadows, a darkening sky filtering through the ruins, night scattering itself through the scene. Yet this is wrong too, for "disperses" is transitive here, and "night" pulls itself together to a coherent force and *causes* "everyone but insects" to disperse.

While these are highly slippery line-breaks, the destabilization is productive: it's not a hindrance to meaning but a source of meaning, of significance. This writer has worked this medium, developing these breaks in conjunction with bends in the language. *Conjunction:* perhaps that's a better term for line-break—a *line conjunction.* But anyway, the lineation here energizes this poem to question relationships between looker and looked-at, actor and acted-upon, ruin and whole, past and future. It creates dynamic conversations among the images, phrasings, subjects, and objects. The line, then, is a means whereby a writer may organize what's flat and void as words on a page to create the illusion of an animate, thinking, conflicted humanity.

WORKS CITED

Eagleton, Terry. *How to Read a Poem.* Oxford: Blackwell, 2007.
Gander, Forrest. *Eye Against Eye.* New York: New Directions, 2005.
Mackowski, Joanie. "Bull."
Roethke, Theodore. "In Praise of Prairie." *The Collected Poems of Theodore Roethke.* Garden City, NY: Doubleday/Anchor, 1966.
Longinus. "On the Sublime." *Critical Theory Since Plato.* Ed. Hazard Adams. New York: Harcourt Brace Jovanovich, 1971. 77–102.

The Free-Verse Line: Rhythm and Voice

Shara McCallum

The free-verse line holds sway over me through its orality. Rhetorical and visual imperatives for the line-break have some appeal; but, in excess—or relied upon as the guiding principle—they feel gimmicky, distracting from, and often overpowering, other aspects of the poem. I come back to the idea that the line in free verse is first and foremost a unit of sound, more specifically a sonic device that establishes the poem's rhythm and contributes to voice.

Assigning the word "rhythm" to a free-verse poem is tricky business; but we know that rhythm exists in language separate from meter. Prose writers rely on rhythms inherent to the sentence—created through syntax and conventions of grammar and idiom, fine-tuned on the page by punctuation. Poets have all of these same tools at their disposal, and also the line, as it works with or against the sentence. As a teacher of poetry, I find myself saying over and over to my students that a line of poetry is almost always in relationship to the sentence, evidenced by the fact that we describe poems as either enjambed or end-stopped. In either case, a poet's line-breaks, where and how he or she "turns the line," dictates the rhythm of the poem, or the lack thereof in poems that show poor attention to such matters. A poet's conscious control of the line is, for me, one marker of the poem's success—as important to free verse as it is to formal verse, if not more so since the logic behind the free-verse line is not as immediately identifiable.

Gwendolyn Brooks demonstrates how the relationship between line and sentence establishes the poem's rhythm most famously in "We Real Cool":

We real cool. We
Left school. We

Lurk late. We
Strike straight. We

Sing sin. We
Thin gin. We

Jazz June. We
Die soon. (315)

While Brooks makes use of many elements of sound in this poem (assonance,
alliteration, and end-rhyme), anyone reading the poem quickly realizes that the
tension between Brooks's line-breaks and the natural syntactical breaks of the
sentences are primarily responsible for the poem's rhythm. If we mistakenly
read according to the poem's sentences—marking pauses only by syntax and
punctuation rather than by those pauses created by Brooks's line-breaks—we
lose the kinetic energy of the poem, and we fail to hear the voice that emerges
out of the poem's emphasis on syncopation. Syncopation, a term most often
applied to jazz, is useful for describing the rhythm not only of "We Real Cool"
but of a good many contemporary free-verse poems by black writers and others who lean on this device. Brooks herself often discussed the influence of
jazz on her writing of "We Real Cool," in particular on her development of the
collective, disaffected-and-brimming-with-anger voice of the pool players she
renders in the poem.

When I lived in Memphis several years ago, I visited the Civil Rights Museum
several times. On one occasion, I came across the lyrics of a protest song whose
linguistic structure bore striking similarity to Brooks's poem. Taken together,
Brooks's connection of her poem to jazz and my stumbling across this other text
heighten my sense that there exists a vibrant link between the rhythms found
in black speech, black music, and black poetry.

Yusef Komunyakaa is one contemporary black poet whose body of work
is notably influenced by jazz. His poem "Ode to the Maggot" offers another
example of the way the line-break governs the rhythm of a poem. In lines such
as, "Yes, you / Go to the root of all things," and, "Jesus Christ, you're merciless /
With the truth," enjambment emphasizes the off-beat, creating the poem's
syncopated, jazz-like feel (10). It also helps to establish voice, as the rhythm
(along with diction) lends the poem linguistic specificity and character. Finally,
Komunyakaa's line-breaks control the way the poem unfolds as it moves down
the page. In a sixteen-line poem, ten lines are enjambed, pitting the poet and
reader's desire to hold onto the line's individual utterance against the compulsion to rush forward to complete the logic of the sentence.

As a reader, writer, and teacher of poetry, I'm interested in how the line in free verse, chafing against or in concert with the sentence, creates a rhythm that corresponds to the inflections of an actual, human voice. This is the primary reason I insist that my students working in free verse read according to their line-breaks and that they read their poems aloud as they compose them. Even in "free" verse, I tell them, where sound patterns in the line are less predictable and quantifiable, rhythm can and should exist. The elasticity of the free-verse line does not imply that it lacks integrity, but rather that each poet, sometimes poem by poem, must determine the function of the line as part of his or her craft.

WORKS CITED

Brooks, Gwendolyn. The World of Gwendolyn Brooks. New York: Harper and Row, 1971.
Komunyakaa, Yusef. Talking Dirty to the Gods. New York: Farrar, Straus and Giroux, 2000.

Tiny Étude on the Poetic Line

Heather McHugh

John Donne's "The Triple Fool" characterizes the lines of a poem (especially their breaking and turning) as a contrivance for taking away pain, of which love supplies such an abundance. I'll second that, and generalize it a bit: the poetic line is an advertency constructed to contend with a world of inadvertencies— inadvertencies that, otherwise, could swamp us.

~

To my mind, Creeley is the masterful modern inquirer into the varying valences and vertencies of the poetic line—both its leanings and its turnings (for which verse is named). One might study long and lovingly the delicacy with which (in poems like "The Window" and "The Language") he uses the reader's inclination to "think along certain lines"—uses that inclination in order, precisely, to avert or advert it, sidestep the predictable, and undermine inclining.

Lineated poetry, given its contexts of prescription and subscription, works to re-scribe and to de-scribe. Its course is far more significantly a matter of underminings than of underlinings.

~

The line is where the wish to go forth in words (along one axis of a journey) encounters the need to break off—or fall out—with words (along the other axis, a vertical).

~

A poem can be construed as a drama of a sort, set not merely against a vacuum or vacancy or space of emptiness (the white page's wings), but also against a great babble of presumption, anticipation, commonplace, chatter, twitter, and byte—a deafening background noise brought to the poem by the audience, by the very nature of its conventions, its automatons of memory and mind.

The world of common expectations (the fabric of our sense of the "usual"—a prefabrication, really, of habits of mind, laid down in neural loops and imprinted with clichés) supplies the circumstantial volume: it is brought by every reader to every act of language. Poetic acts *contend* with that circumstance, that source material, its overdose of underwriting.

~

The poet is a reader, too, of course—both of the world and of the work. So the poet's own mind has to be chastened in the act. (The act of revision changes the vision. One starts over and winds up under. That's why Thomas Mann says a writer is someone for whom writing is *harder* than it is for other people.)

~

Each writer/reader, pausing on the page before the poem begins, is a roar of mundanities. But then the words themselves, figured into syntax and line, bring quiet to the world.

Dickinson's Dashes and the Free-Verse Line

Wayne Miller

Whitman's contribution to free verse is clear. His capacious, often Biblically cadenced lines suspend the poems in *Leaves of Grass* somewhere between the essay and the kind of regularly metered work a nineteenth-century reader might have more immediately identified as verse. (Notice that Emerson, in his famous letter, described the book as an "extraordinary piece of wit and wisdom," not, specifically, as poetry.) Whitman's lines foreground plain, common speech and replace, as a guiding principle, metrics with Whitman's own intuitive sense of rhythm.

Yet, despite free verse's dominance in twentieth-century and contemporary American poetry, Whitman's long, unwieldy lines have few direct descendants. Sure, there's Ginsberg and Kenneth Fearing, there's C. K. Williams and the occasional poem by Jorie Graham, and one could make a case for Richard Siken and D. A. Powell among others. But if I were to pick up five poetry journals at random from the shelf, I would be hard pressed to find all that many poems with lines that even begin to approach the right-hand margin, let alone wrap it. Whitman's sense of the line as a thing that holds an extraordinary amount of information before it breaks—a thing that, by its very capaciousness, pulls lists of details and characters and places into the mesh of the poem—has had relatively few takers.

What about Dickinson? The majority of her lines are built on the meters of ballads and hymns. There's no question that Dickinson's primary lineating principle is that of patterned metrics, not free verse. But, within those "traditional" lines, we encounter her dashes. It is my contention that Dickinson's dashes often work like the line-breaks we frequently come across in contemporary free verse; that is, rather than building metrical patterns, as her actual lines do, her dashes serve to control the arrival of ideas within the unfolding of the poem. In the process, they often disrupt and/or complicate the meanings of her sentences, constructing subordinate, fragmentary meanings within those sentences, and even building indeterminacies (or multiplicities) inside them.

Take, for example, the last line of "I felt a Funeral, in my Brain." When we read the line, "And Finished knowing—then—" (128), we have to decide if Dickinson means *and finished knowing then*, end stop, or if she means, *and finished knowing, then*, where we are left waiting after an elliptical conditional. In this first possibility, the speaker's death becomes the definitive end to her knowing, and thus her living. In the second, after the end of her limited, earthly knowledge, the speaker encounters a kind of knowing that can't be communicated, one that can be hinted at only by an open ending. In *The Art of the Poetic Line*, James Longenbach draws a distinction between what he calls "parsing" and "annotating" lines—the first essentially used to clarify meaning, the second used to complicate meaning. Here, we find Dickinson's dashes doing the work of the "annotating" line.

Another example: in the first stanza of "I heard a Fly buzz—when I died—" we encounter the famous opening lines:

I heard a Fly buzz—when I died—
The Stillness in the Room
Was like the Stillness in the Air—
Between the Heaves of Storm— (223)

Here, the reader must decide with what piece of language "when I died" belongs. Do we read those lines as "I heard a fly buzz. When I died, the stillness in the room was like the stillness in the air"? Or do we read them, "I heard a fly buzz when I died. The stillness in the room was like the stillness in the air"? Again, the dashes are disruptively "annotating."

What happens if we lineate those opening stanzas according to their dashes, instead of their line-breaks? We get something like this:

I heard a fly buzz
When I died
The stillness in the room was like the stillness in the air
Between the heaves of storm
The eyes around
Had wrung them dry

And breaths were gathering firm for the last onset
When the King be witnessed
In the room
I willed my keepsakes . . .

Suddenly those lines look like W. S. Merwin's; they have the same slipperiness of line created by his controlled lack of punctuation, where the line-breaks disruptively take the place of punctuation, requiring a repeated negotiation of multiple possibilities of interpretation. In other words, they play the same punctuating role as Dickinson's dashes in the above example from "I felt a Funeral, in my Brain"—they suggest punctuation without entirely determining what punctuation should be there.

And what if we punctuate the poem while still attempting to maintain Dickinson's disruptions and ambiguities:

I heard a fly buzz. When I died,
the stillness in the room

was like the stillness in the air.
Between the heaves of storm,

the eyes around
had wrung them dry,

and breaths were gathering firm
for the last onset,

when the King be witnessed.
In the room,

I willed my keepsakes . . .

Here, many of the lines are "annotating." Just as in the original, "When I died" belongs with "I heard a fly buzz" because it sits on the same line with it. Yet, it also belongs with "the stillness in the room" because it exists in a sentence with it. This version of the poem looks and operates like so many contemporary American poems; that is, it uses lineation to organize the poem's language into complex and often multiply suggestive units of meaning that cut across the more overt meanings of the sentences. The overall effect is that of several meanings coexisting within the poem—as created and determined by the poet's formal choices regarding the line. We could play these games with Dickinson's dashes all day.

WORKS CITED

Dickinson, Emily. *The Complete Poems of Emily Dickinson*. Ed. Thomas H. Johnson. New York: Little, Brown and Company, 1961.
Longenbach, James. *The Art of the Poetic Line*. Saint Paul: Graywolf Press, 2008.

Minding the Gaps

Jenny Mueller

The experimental line comes in witless. Like any baldness, it lacks memory. Its purpose is *free*, not mnemonic. It springs up along the road to the contagious hospital and falls, a wild child, into the custody of Dr. Williams, for he could best tend to its ferocities.

The free line will flourish or fail alongside the modern mind's leaky memory. Of course poetry hadn't required meter as a means of memorization for a while, but it wanted loosening, not only from the habits of poetic tradition but from the habit of memory itself. As James Scully has emphasized (the italics are his), "free verse needs *and assumes* a memory that may be consigned to memory banks such as books and notebooks, not to mention their electronic extensions" (126–127). Or, as Stevens wrote in "On Modern Poetry," it need not repeat "what was in the script" and this released its new quality of thinking (218). Consigning memory to memory banks allowed the poet to pay a new kind of attention to attention itself.

But what does one make of this wild child so many years on, now that it is bald not in birth but in dotage? Writing with this line today, we rarely associate it with the shock of the new—if by "new" we also mean youthful. In fact, the modern line feels quite old, bearing, as it does, the freight of modernism's appalled hopes. (And those "electronic extensions" of Scully's keep proliferating, so much that we can feel as if they're now replacing attention, rather than enabling it.) The feeling that one's shackled to the same old modern line can be frustrating, since no writer wants to work with stale techniques, and because to the extent that American poetry still takes an interest in its history of antagonistic movements and schools, it continues to honor a rhetoric by which making a poem *good* also entails "making it new."

Yet the face one turns toward experiment need not be dewy. The line still lends itself to encounter with mysteries, including some urgent questions of age: Is the self who can no longer speak "reasonably" still a self? What's left to "suffice" when memory and words, and the power to shape a meaning, are lost? With its built-in poor memory and lengthening life span, the modern free-verse line may be consciously turned to these questions—because, in being released of a need to bear memorizable features, the modern line has been bound to engage more freely with silence, to develop new capacities for silence as it finds its new definition. And this also allows it to remain innovative, because in silence it traffics with unassigned potential, with undesignated freedoms and limits. The silence of the page: where the reader meets it as her own time. The silence of white space, breaking in with a wildness: in the line-break; in the "open field" (as the poem, like Williams's field in "Queen-Anne's-Lace," goes over to whiteness, contagiously) that overwhelms the grid in which the line lays its horizontal track; in the gaps and spans of various sizes occurring between words within single lines (as practiced by Williams in "The Sound of Waves"); in the standard caesura and in standard punctuation (because there are so many nonstandard options). Within such silences, poems may make revolutionary turns, searches, and strange propulsions. The line "breaks" not simply because it ends, but because its sense may be smashed, amazed, or thrown in all directions.

Scriptless, experimental, wild: for all their heroic force, I think we have grown too familiar with these ways of speaking of "modern" poetry and have tired of their association with the new, not to mention with the American. A natural reaction is to feel jaded, tempted to ironize, beyond bothering with such concerns—in other words, to feel old. But this, I would argue, is a most vital aspect of the modern line: it speaks faithfully of age, and with no loss of innovative relevance. In giving sensuous form to the ongoing *now* of apperception, the line may encounter such wildnesses as aphasia, folly, the strangest of dreams. Riddled by silence, stowing memory poorly, "the poem of the mind in the act" searches among gaps and fathoms, finds itself to be *composed* of gaps and fathoms.

This is surely terrifying, if also thrilling. But in poetry terrors serve to transform. They approach in relation to what Rilke called beauty and Edmund Burke termed the sublime. It seems to me that our times talk nonstop (though lately somewhat numbly) of sublimity, yet we still lock away our age, and this last, always unfinished experiment of our humanity waits to astonish us in our lines.

WORKS CITED

Scully, James. *Line Break: Poetry as Social Practice*. Seattle: Bay Press, 1988.

Stevens, Wallace. *Collected Poetry and Prose*. New York: Library of America, 1997.

Line / Break

Laura Mullen

"What does not change / is the will to change"
—CHARLES OLSON, "THE KINGFISHERS"

"If you read a poet's line-breaks correctly," I recall Robert Hass saying, "you'll be breathing as the poet breathed." Lyric poetry's magical promise: to be in the other's inspiration (reinvented there, aloft and steadied). Charles Olson's announcement, my epigraph, enacts an intensity of thought and feeling in breath over time—its marked internal line-break and isolation on the field of the page open the space to inhale stasis, and exhale variation. Sentences are not emotional, Gertrude Stein famously noticed, paragraphs are—but the line discovers or creates emotion in the sentence. "Wait for it," a gone love laughed, enticing a sharpened attention to the arriving connection: *you're going to like this*. The line has always been, for me, a mode of inquiry, the *venture*: into shared time, and its end—that flash of white. Wake for—morning and mourning—the presence of the "unseen," as Amiri Baraka wrote (382), or "death" (Graham 409). Silence is partner and part of the music. Historically, of course, the free-verse line is the end of the line for a regulated musical phrase (marked out by the metronome, whose tyranny Ezra Pound bemoaned). One story of the line (described through the haze of a distrust for—and love of—stories) involves just this movement: from measure and number (meant to help memorization) to a musical phrase based in the breath. This is Olson's contention: the line gets out from under meter's feet, freeing itself to find the heart. But when Vladimir Mayakovsky links his walk to poetic composition (beat . . . beat) meter lingers as ghost motor, and you can hear it ticking over in Sylvia Plath's "Morning Song": "Love set you going like a fat gold watch" (5). My line-breaks began as a negotiation between a heard music (coming to me) and a (careful) camera work controlling what came into view and when. At first, the work of (revised) lines seemed to be *surprise*, making use of time to delight a ("wait for it") Reader Response critic, alive to possibilities that flower in hesitations of sense. Here's an early line-break from a poem called "Greed": "The greed of the gaping mouth / Of the grave." That *gotcha* was a skill I got fast and made much of: the turn (hole in the face becoming hole in the earth) came easily, if not naturally. Now my youthful rage for inherited ideas of order (tight, fairly short lines, clear and clearly controlled images) seems gendered in overdetermined ways as well as dated. Then I thought I was getting it (poetry) right. One night not long ago, a little drunk in a restaurant restroom, I watched a young woman repairing her ornate makeup, took in the perfection of her outfit, and sighed, "We women work *so* hard." "I know," the reflected blond winced, "*all* the time." "And the men," I laughed, "they don't work like this." "No," she answered, capping the mascara, "it wouldn't be worth it if it weren't for . . ." (wait for it) "diamonds." "So," I suggested when I got my breath back, "get a job and get your own?" "Oh I don't know," she smiled, waving the rock on her left hand at the mirror, glitter to glitter. The urge to appear a certain way—a pressure so severe it often threatened to preclude any appearance at all—is no longer in control for me, nor is it clear that recognized good behavior is worth its limited rewards. "Poetry is a way of happening," as W. H. Auden famously put it (82), and what all else it is, "I," as Cecilia Vicuña memorably said (at Naropa), "write to find out." I'm interested in traced alternatives that remain available, where accomplishment (meant to be admired) moves—through attention to the medium—into vulnerability. As in the line (from "Story for Reproduction"): "Pane of glass / 'pain of.'" Incorporating a remarked break, not made but cited, it's as if what was written had been read, while another double exposure is troubled in the subject matter ("pane" is to look through but "pain" can't be seen). Stein said that genius consists in talking and listening at the same time: I take her to mean that we need to stay on/with the changing edge between inside and outside as we write, and to leave that edge open and alive. I'm interested in how a piece remarks its own making, hears a line-break already heard, breaks in where a mishearing moves the speaker away from and yet further into the situation which motivated speech, making the line a stanza, resonant in apparent isolation (connections come back): "And then outside" (outside the line? the poem? The imagined window?). There's a return to the effort to be *part of* something, to understand without letting the life out: to apprehend how apprehension might work in that space, a loose grasp, not a clutch. Say a very aviary? An uncertainty principle in action, engaged with the vagaries of subject and object: that's my line now in an ongoing effort to know, and I'm interested in how spooky that widening space is perceived to be. *I'm not sure I got what you wanted me to is*—to my ears—the cry of the damaged (or abused) reader, controlled by the teacher (and perhaps the poet?): forced to "get" something out of the poem—something stilled, presentable as a brace of dead birds. I recall, in high school, dropping—as commanded—the "two most important lines of 'The Love Song of J. Alfred Prufrock'" at my teacher's feet. His authority was unquestioned, and I . . . ? "And I," as Robert Duncan puts it, "would fly to bring back / from the blue of the sky [. . .], bleeding, a prize" (88). (But whose breath is it? Whose desire?) At one point, in that long study which is called teaching, I brought a stopwatch to workshop to see the tiny but acute differences between students' sense of line-breaks: enjambed and end-stopped (how long each flash of white translated into a pause in speech). What do you believe (in your body) the line (break) to be? Listening to the way Claude Royet-Journoud reads the silence in his work (how we waited for the next word or phrase) was revelatory. The break in a line freed from meter is not only the ghost of our own sensed breath and an invitation to a later other to breathe with or even *as* — it's an acknowledgment that what does not change (*pace* editors, and natural or unnatural disasters) is the page. What will not stay: readings, breathings, performances, bodies, love, a particular will to change. Line / break as if to say read this aloud, read this this way ("wait for it"): open a space. Memorable, whether or not memorized, the line's a scored portion of shared sky: a cloud study, unsteady (to be studied), an aspect of an always already changing event, ending (as something else begins) mid-

WORKS CITED

Auden, W. H. *Selected Poems*. First Vintage International Edition. New York: Vintage, 1989.
Baraka, Amiri. "Hunting Is Not Those Heads on the Wall." *The Poetics of the New American Poetry*. Ed. Donald M. Allen and Warren Tallman. New York: Grove, 1973. 378–382.
Creeley, Robert. *Selected Poems*. Berkeley: University of California Press, 1991.
Duncan, Robert. *Selected Poems*. Ed. Robert J. Bertholf. New York: New Directions, 1993.
Graham, Jorie. "Some Notes on Silence." *19 New American Poets of the Golden Gate*. Ed. Philip Dow. San Diego: Harcourt Brace Jovanovich, 1984. 409–415.
Mullen, Laura. *Subject*. Berkeley: University of California Press, 2005.
———. *The Surface*. Urbana: University of Illinois Press, 1991.
Olson, Charles. *Selected Poems*. Berkeley: University of California Press, 1997.
Plath, Sylvia. *Ariel*. Restored Edition. New York: Harper Collins, 2004.

Rhyme and the Line

Molly Peacock

To the workshop dogmatists I ran around with, the line was only good for one thing—to be broken. All the emphasis was on the end. What about the middle? I began to paw over some of my favorite lines, looking for the secrets of their remarkably still sense of wholeness, yet their simultaneous ability to catapult the poem forward. Even simple lines—Howard Nemerov's "People are putting up storm windows now" (56); Edna St. Vincent Millay's "and rise and sink and rise and sink again" (659); or Shelley's "Ozymandias" barking, "Look on my Works, ye Mighty, and despair!" (375)—had a rhythmic and syntactic integrity that thrilled me. The weight of these lines was centered, not shifted precariously toward the end.

What if some ideologue in a workshop had told Nemerov to break the line between "putting" and "up"? Or instructed Millay to break her line after the third "and"? Or tried to con Shelley into believing that the sentence should govern his flow—break it after the second comma! I abandoned the line-busters and went home with Paul Fussell's *Poetic Meter and Poetic Form*.

Later, I found myself at my grandparents' breakfast table. I adored the way they spoke. My favorite word was "green," which they pronounced with two syllables (gree-un); second was the astonishing two-syllable pronunciation of "film" (fil-um). Curiously, this brought me back to the ends of lines and to rhyme.

I realized I could lock in the line with a rhyme, weighting the center with that end sound, even if I hid the sound behind some very ordinary phrase that would rhyme for me personally, if not for the rest of the world. For instance, the stuttering utterance, "Do I agree? Um, yes," to my grandparent-trained ear off-rhymes with, "Are they green? Yes." A loose rhyme scheme of conversational words, seemingly emphasizing the ends of lines, threw cargo into the middles, the way stevedores standing at the edges of ships' decks throw goods into the holds. I marveled at how this helped the energy of a poem both backwards and forwards. If I could hide a rhyme scheme (as I hid my lust for formal verse), the poems would have the structure without the fancy ear veneer that would mark them as old-fashioned. But it wasn't only rhyme that balanced the line. Next port: meter.

WORKS CITED

Millay, Edna St. Vincent. "Love is not all." *Collected Poems*. Ed. Norma Millay. New York: Harper, 1956.

Nemerov, Howard. "Storm Windows." *Contemporary American Poetry*. Ed. Donald Hall. Baltimore: Penguin, 1962.

Shelley, Percy Bysshe. "Ozymandias." *Selected Poetry and Prose of Shelley*. Ed. Carlos Baker. New York: Modern Library, 1951.

Enter the Line

V. Penelope Pelizzon

Conversation about the free-verse line often focuses on the break. How do breaks create tension syntactically? What auditory possibilities do enjambed or end-stopped lines offer a particular poem? This is not surprising, of course, given how free verse depends on the break for rhythmic drama and variation.

All well and good. But in our attention to its terminus, are we neglecting the rest of the line? The modernists complained that the Victorians padded their verses with syllables just to get to the end-rhyme's chime. Is our break fixation a version of the same narrow attention to the right margin? What if we focus equally on the rhythms of the line's *entrance*?

Frank Bidart has talked about the prosodic methods—including breaks, double punctuation, and typography—he uses to "fasten" a speaking voice to the page (*Western* 223). He's also a master of what we might call *strong* and *soft* *entrances*, modulating the rhythms of his line openings to create drama. Here's the first stanza of his "Song" from *Star Dust*, scanned to indicate heavier and lighter stresses:

You know that it is there, lair
where the bear ceases
for a time even to exist. (34)

The stanza's quiet intimacy stems not only from the second person address, internal rhymes, and images of animal hibernation. Bidart also establishes the lulling rhythm by opening each line with syllables of lighter stress before introducing a heavier accent. The third line's entrance is buffered even further by the feminine ending of the preceding line; our ear registers three gentler syllables before the downbeat of "time."

But this soothing quality changes in the second stanza, which enters with a spondaic imperative: [1]

Cráwl ín. Yŏu hăve ăt lást killed
ĕnoúgh ănd eáten ĕnoúgh tŏ bĕ fát
ĕnoúgh tŏ ceáse fŏr ă tíme tŏ exíst.

That first line is an auditory powerhouse, framing the syntactical demand and the notion of killing with paired rhythmic slaps at either end. The stanza then loosens with the next two lines' lighter syllable entrances, their mirrored double-iamb/double-anapest rhythms, and the repetition—like a voice calming itself—of "enough."

The next stanza, the third, amplifies rhythmic tension by increasing the number of lines with strong entrances; two of the three step off with heavily stressed syllables. And finally, by stanza four, all the lines enter on downbeats:

Cráwl ín. Whătévĕr fŏr góod ŏr íll
gróws wĭthín yŏu neéds
yóu fŏr ă tíme tŏ ceáse tŏ exíst.

Now we understand that the poem's "you" is a human maker. Only from the hibernation of "crawling in" can this maker bring forth a new work. Such dormancy is necessary but fearsome: the creation is as likely to turn out "ill" as "good"; it requires self-annihilation. By shortening the lines and opening them all on stresses that torque against the heavily accented end syllables, Bidart rhythmically enacts the trauma of this willed passivity. (This torquing strategy isn't reserved for free verse, of course; the most common variation in iambic pentameter is the first foot trochaic inversion, giving the line a snap at both ends.)

Obviously, line entrances aren't divorced from line-breaks. Rather, each entrance is a point where the poet can amplify, counterpoint, or redirect the energy of the preceding break. The last stanza of "Song" exemplifies such redirection. The stanza contains only two lines, both entering on light syllables. "It is not raining inside / tonight"; the lines whisper in the ear. And yet, this is an invitation one cannot refuse, as the poem's final line concludes with the now inevitable demand to "crawl in."

Part of the pleasure in attending to line entrances is discerning the varied strategies available. I want to turn quickly to Louise Glück, another master of the entrance. One of Glück's characteristic rhythmic tactics is to build a sequence of lines with soft openings, create a dramatic syntactical break, and then conclude the passage on a line with a heavily accented opening. Here, for example, is the start of "Formaggio," from *Vita Nova*:

> The world
> was whole because
> it shattered. When it shattered,
> then we knew what it was. (13)

The syntactical pause after "shattered" is heightened by the next line's opening stress. Glück is as likely to use this technique as a closing gesture. Here's the ending of one of the "Matins" from *The Wild Iris*, in which a human speaks to God:

> We never thought of you
> whom we were learning to worship.
> We merely knew it wasn't human nature to love
> only what returns love. (3)

This passage's poignance comes from the syntactically complete statement of line three—perhaps love is not what we do best—whose meaning is changed by the enjambment. The radical shift in meaning in the fourth line—it is God who does not love—is rhythmically amplified by the assertive downstroke of "only."

Bidart and Glück use pattern and meaningful variation to shape their free-verse line entrances. The line's end, clearly, is not the only end.

---

1. It's reasonable to ask whether we should really use metrical foot names when talking about verse in which there's no regularly established foot. That said, I'm relying on the old names here along with scansion as the simplest way to make rhythms clear.

WORKS CITED

Bidart, Frank. *In the Western Night: Poems 1965–90*. New York: Farrar, Straus and Giroux, 1990.

————. *Star Dust*. New York: New York: Farrar, Straus and Giroux, 2005.
Glück, Louise. *Vita Nova*. New York: HarperCollins, 1999.
————. *The Wild Iris*. Hopewell, NJ: Ecco Press, 1992.

Healing and the Poetic Line

Emmy Pérez

María Sabina didn't think about line-breaks or a written poem on the page during the veladas, her healing chants and ceremonies in Oaxaca:

> I am a woman who shouts
> I am a woman who whistles
> I am a woman who lightnings, says (93)

Did she think about the effect of the ceremonial pause or was it a needed breath
before the next language invention?

If "I am a woman who lightnings" were a line of its own, it would allow more
time for the extraordinary image to form in our minds. But right away we have
"says" after a brief pause with the comma that continues to build a cumulative
list, not privileging one line, one breath, one discovery over another.

~

U.S. American poets claim the poetic line can be a site for equality, for removal
of the capitalist ideology embedded in our unexamined rhetoric. Many U.S.
American poets want a language and poetic lines that examine and attempt to heal
social class injustices. U.S. American poets are slaves to their blogs, Facebook,
computers, and poetry. Many American poets often give the impression that
poetry [aesthetics] is the only subject of their poetry. I am guilty of that pleasure
as well at times, read poems as poetics statements. Maybe we secretly want poetry
manifestos to be statements on how to live life. But few will admit to this desire.
The poet divided from the streets. Many joining bureaucracy, willingly.

We know that a poetic line is not a thesis, a contract, a treaty. I am under the impression that most readers of non-literary prose in the U.S. believe more firmly in the solid U.S. American handshake. In Navajo country, the gentle handshake, skin touching skin, is the most genuine greeting I've ever experienced. None of these New York, European-inspired greeting kisses that can become obligatory expectations. And none of the U.S. American confidence and masculinity in business handshakes that suggest, *We promise to respect our treaty. I will look you in the eye and share my confidence with you to build trust.*

Lawmakers examine concrete and abstract words and phrases for openings that will allow them to better serve the interests of their clients. Line as justice; line as ambiguity; line as manipulation.

I am trying to remember my love
Of the poetic line, of poetic breaks
And the border patrol
Van hasn't moved in an hour
On the new "levee" at the Old Hidalgo Pumphouse
World Birding Center where la migra
Looks across and down into México
U.S. side a concrete wall "levee" disguised with dirt
Dirt piled up to form a mountain
The Mexican side
A sheer 18 foot white concrete wall

Who's patrolling, who's crossing
The line

The river's invisible line—by eye?—
Water momentarily Bravo then Grande
Then Bravo. Always Río or Rio.

~

I can't build poems faster
Than the wall's construction

We can't write poems to halt
The wall's construction

~

The poetic line of social justice will not be improved until more poets get up from their computers. Poetic line as picket line. Poetic line as hands without weapons. Hands. Want to kiss the hands of our lover before moving elsewhere on the body. Poets as lovers, not only with each other.

~

The line is the beloved. Again and again and again. Your prose is poetry. Your ends of sentences do not trail off; you fight for them, that space for additional meaning, that breath dying and not wanting to end. Your ends of sentences expand my mind, qucrid@, create openings instead of endings. When can I see you to kiss you or meet you, again, in person and on the page?

~

"*(Tal vez | tuve que olvidar cómo)*" — Dolores Dorantes (6)

"*(May be | I had to forget how)*"

May be I had to forget how to write an essay, how to craft a poetic line, how to not use a pen to write it, how to speak love and desire while riding a bike on a paved road through the monte near the Rio Grande-Bravo. *May be I had to forget how* to express bitterness, how to stop pointing to the bad qualities in humans in preparation for them hurting me someday. *May be I had to forget how* to address the new concrete border wall. Its supporters. Its burial disguised as a levee.

~

How to teach about the poetic line, about desire and syntax, about a poem's formal considerations as equally significant to the exploration of content, as a search for social justice and possibility, when students and I are standing in Hidalgo, Texas, touching the new concrete border wall? It's February 2009. There is so much content and so little time. Many of our graduate students have full-time jobs and attend class at night. I was here in Hidalgo at this World Birding Center a few months ago and there were no walls. Hummingbirds, black bees, mariposas, path to the Rio Grande-Bravo. When I arrive late January, I curse our former and current president. February. Men continue driving the construction trucks. They wave as they pass by us, as if to say, with guilt, so sorry, we need to eat too. One student, a visual artist-poet, says not only did the federal government order the wall's existence, "but they are making our people build it to keep our people out" (Z.). The two students who show up know about work—one about working as a migrant farm laborer in the heat of harvests and another about the work of language, having Spanish shamed out of her in the schools. They don't consider themselves poets. There is no time to write a poem to help stop the construction (as if it could), there is no time for elegant poetry or lines or teaching of forms while these walls are quickly constructed before pumpkin time. Before *princesa güera* Cinderella turns back into ragged stepchild, before her elegant carriage turns back into gourd (indigenous to the Americas). But the horses have already turned to mice. The inauguration of our new president did not halt the building. It is now more than water, the distance from our mother, grandmother countries, depending on our generation. We later hear of news reports, of residents who live near the wall saying it is not stopping crossers. The wall is an abstraction for out-of-town haters. (The wall is a line-break not to create desire but to halt it.) If the line-break, if enjambment, creates desire, then the end-stopped concrete line is the concrete end where crosses must and will find openings further away in the desert, the concrete end where birds fly over, where turtles repeat walking into it, where we cannot see. The river still rushes past on its way to the mouth, Boca Chica–Playa Bagdad, Gulf of Mexico, from its long journey from the source in Colorado and mostly other waters, Río Conchos de México. The Hidalgo Pumphouse praised for bringing irrigation to the area in the early 1900s, helping form the "Magic Valley" of Texas, ruining nearly all the brushlands, the monte, for citrus growers. The river still rushes past and people still have the need to cross it. (Desire and need are different entities.)

~

"Language lies   across the barbed lines,
piles of its bodies   pierced y pinchados."

—BRENDA CÁRDENAS

~

"Jesus Christ
There is no resentment, there is no rancor, there is no insult, there is no
   anger
It is not a matter of insults, it is not a matter of lies
It is a matter of life and well-being, of lifting up, of restoring" (100)

—MARÍA SABINA

WORKS CITED

Cárdenas, Brenda. "Report from the Temple of Confessions in Old Chicano English."
   E-Poets Network., 26 Apr. 2002. Web. 2 May 2009. <http://voices.e-poets.net
   /CardenasB/poem-temple.shtml>.
Dorantes, Dolores. *sexoPUROsexoVELOZ and Septiembre*. Trans. Jen Hofer. Berkeley: Counter-
   path Press Kenning Editions, 2008.
Sabina, María. "The Folkways Chant." *María Sabina: Selections*. Ed. Jerome Rothenberg.
   Berkeley: University of California Press, 2003.
Z., Emi. Personal interview. 20 Feb. 2009.

Some of What's in a Line

Carl Phillips

At best, when the line is in meaningful tension with the sentence, meaning itself gets endowed with a physicality that I feel at once in the head and in the gut.

⌇

A sentence has any number of possibilities for grace, tension, seduction, force—the line is the poet's opportunity to send an extra ripple through all of these.

⌇

And there's the strange, undeniable pleasure both in controlling and in being controlled, yes, there was that . . .

⌇

Here is some prose:

> When I hit her on the head, it was good, and then I did it to her a couple of times. But it was funny: afterwards, it was as if somebody else did it—everything flat, without sharpness, richness or line.

And here's the same material, cast as poetry, from Frank Bidart's "Herbert White":

> When I hit her on the head, it was good,

and then I did it to her a couple of times,—
but it was funny,—afterwards,
it was as if somebody else did it . . .

Everything flat, without sharpness, richness or line. (3)

Bidart allows each of the first four lines to contain information that gets continually revised: hitting her "was good, // and then . . . / but . . . / it was as if somebody
else did it." In effect, the line enacts the particular way in which the commit-
ting of murder can estrange the murderer, psychologically, from himself. The
lineation controls the speed with which we receive the information, and at the
same time it isolates each piece of information, throwing it into greater relief
(visually, but also aurally, assuming—and I do—that there should always be a
pause at the end of a line). A prose sentence has only punctuation as a means
of doing this. Lines 1–4 make a complete sentence, though there's a grappling
feeling to it, as if we're watching the speaker stumble towards clarity. Clarity
may not emerge in line 5, but that line feels both complete and like arrival, even
though it's a fragment. This is the result of a tension between *types* of lines, I
believe. Lines 1–4 lineate a prose sentence; with line 5, Bidart employs a carefully modulated line of pentameter, in which two dactyls are followed by two
trochees, themselves followed by an iamb:

Everything FLAT, without SHARPness, RICHness, or LINE.

The effect, sonically, is of a gallop slowing to a canter—the final iamb becomes
the only foot that ends on a stressed syllable, and this moment of stress, co-
inciding with the line's end (itself endstopped), brings the horse (to continue
the metaphor) to a halt. The tension between the free-verse lines 1–4 and the
metered line 5 offers a release that feels like pleasure, albeit (given the context) a decidedly sinister one. It feels like the slipping of mere speech, briefly,
into song.

~

Or like the slipping from
mere speech, briefly,
into song?

It is precisely because poetry is not mere speech, even in the work of poets who ground their poems in demotic speech (Langston Hughes and William Carlos Williams for example), that the line is so important.

~

"I caught this morning morning's minion . . . " (Hopkins 69)

Yes, and the line seemed suddenly, to poetry, what waves are to the shore.

WORKS CITED

Bidart, Frank. "Herbert White." *Golden State*. New York: George Braziller, 1973. 3.
Hopkins, Gerard Manley. "The Windhover." *The Poems of Gerard Manley Hopkins*. Fourth edition. Ed. W. H. Gardner and N. H. MacKenzie. Oxford: Oxford University Press, 1970. 69.

Harold and the Purple Crayon:
The Line as a Generative Force

Patrick Phillips

Crockett Johnson's classic picture book *Harold and the Purple Crayon* begins: "One evening, after thinking it over for some time, Harold decided to go for a walk in the moonlight." Above these words, we see a pajama-clad boy clutching a crayon, at the end of a long and formless purple scribble. "There wasn't any moon, and Harold needed a moon for a walk in the moonlight," Johnson writes, as Harold reaches high up into the white space of the page, and draws a purple crescent. Then Harold stoops to draw the first lines of a purple sidewalk, because, of course, "he needed something to walk on."

Most theories of the line in poetry are concerned with the effect lines have on readers once a poem is finished, but I want to talk instead about the way unwritten lines—the empty containers of a poem in the making—help me to write. That is, I am interested in the pragmatic theory of "the line" in *Harold and the Purple Crayon*, where Harold, confronted with a blank page, draws a moon not because he thinks a moon will look good when he is finished, but because he needs one to go for a walk in the moonlight; where he draws a sidewalk not because readers of children's books like sidewalks, but so he'll have something to walk on; and where he makes a boat not because he has a thing for boats, but because he is drowning.

In Harold's world, the line is not ornamentation—not a way of gussying up his scribbles—but, rather, the ground beneath him: the conveyance that keeps him going where he has to go. On Harold's journey, as on the poet's, it is this inchoate, shape-shifting nature of the line that matters. Harold is not concerned with the overarching sense that his lines, taken together, will make once he is finished, for Harold doesn't know where he is going. Instead, each line he draws solves the immediate problem before him: the line that was an ocean becomes a boat he clings to, then a hill he climbs to look around, then a hot air balloon that stops his free fall, and, finally, a bed in which he can, exhausted, fall asleep. Were Harold to make his lines with no consideration for the situation in which he finds himself—that is, were he to fail as a *reader* of what he's written—he would surely drown, or be eaten by a dragon, or fall through thin air forever.

What does all this mean in practice? That when confronted with the blank page, I try to look only as far ahead as the empty, unwritten line racing out ahead of the one I just wrote. And I try to be an extremely attentive reader of the lines I *have* managed to write. While the line-breaks of a finished poem create a particular effect on the reader, it is worth stressing the simple notion that the best poems are composed with no preset destination, with no foreknowledge of what they will discover. Instead, for a poet in the moment of creating, the most important aspect of the line is that it cuts the white space down to size. The line divides the page's unbearable silence into smaller vessels that we have just enough strength to fill, and hopefully to carry.

Of course, each line in a new poem also establishes requirements for the unwritten ones that follow. On first setting pen to page, the poet can say anything. But the very act of writing a first line limits the range of what can be successfully added in the second, just as the third further narrows what utterance will "work" in the fourth. What I mean to underscore is that while this narrowing of possibilities as lines accrue is constraining, it is also, thank goodness, *generative*. It is a narrowing that shields us from the Medusa-head of infinite possibilities, and so helps us make our way.

In the middle of writing a poem, surely most of us feel much like Harold when he sees that his offhand squiggle has suddenly become a storm-tossed sea. What saves us from despair? What keeps our heads above the water? The small assignments of the empty line, which I sometimes chant to myself when returning from the coffeemaker: *One more line to make the stanza . . . Five more feet to make the line . . . Two more syllables to make the foot . . .* And suddenly, like Harold, I realize that salvation is in my hand, and that all I have to do is write the first few words that will become the line, which will become the craft I need to carry on. Like Harold's drawings, the lines I write cause endless problems (what next? where to from here?), but I also find that with a bearable amount of work, I can sail my trim little five-beat boat smoothly out of trouble, and into places I never imagined the poem could go. And, of course, like Harold, I barely have time to catch my breath and smile at my quick thinking before the next obstacle rises up from the abyss.

So what's a poet to do when facing that astonishing blankness of the page? Write the line that solves the *current* problem of the poem—the problem created by the line you just wrote, which solved the problem of the line before that. Embrace the limitations that accrue with each new line as both the source and the solution to poetry's difficulty. And keep the purple crayon moving until the lines that led you so far out to sea bring you, miraculously, home.

WORK CITED

Johnson, Crockett. *Harold and the Purple Crayon*. New York: Harper Collins, 1955.

On the Origin and Practice of a "Signature" Line

Donald Platt

For better or worse in my writing life, I have spent the last twenty years working almost exclusively in one form, with one approach to the poetic line. I wouldn't recommend it to anyone. Therefore, partly as a cautionary tale, I will describe here that "signature" line and its origin, as well as the seductions, riches, and impoverishments of composing poems in this form. Though I have been experimenting with other lines in the last five years, most of my poems look something like the opening of this new poem called "Der Streichholzhändler" (a German phrase meaning "the matchbox seller"):

> Where the guillotine precisely severed the cervical vertebrae
> of thirteen hundred people
> including Louis the Sixteenth, Marie-Antoinette, Danton,
>
> and Robespierre, where now
> small cars and motorcycles careen and carom around the gold-tipped
> Egyptian obelisk
>
> at the Place de la Concorde, we stroll past a beggar who has no
> arms and only
> stumps for legs. I cannot look him in the face
>
> and see only out
> of the corner of my eye how someone has propped him
> upon a black wool blanket
>
> against a stone pillar. . . .

This free-verse form or shape employs tercets that alternate long and short lines so that each stanza is the reverse of the preceding one. The long-short-long pattern of one stanza is turned inside out by the short-long-short lines of the next tercet. These long and short lines have always seemed to me to enable both narrative expansion and lyric contraction within one stanza. I can both tell an anecdote and isolate an image easily. Partly, of course, I like the look of the stanza on the page, so there's an aspect that appeals to a visual, even painterly, aesthetic. The stanza has "shapeliness," if you will. But, even though it's a free-verse structure, I'm counting beats, six to eight stresses usually in the longer lines, one to three in the shorter lines. I should say that some readers find the line-breaks completely arbitrary and private.

The first poem that I wrote in that shape was called "Untitled." It appears in my first book, *Fresh Peaches, Fireworks, & Guns,* and describes, among other things, the motion of surf against a shoreline. The ocean's repetitive in-and-out rhythms seemed to suggest this form. However, more importantly, I was reading closely C. K. Williams's poems in *Tar* at the time and liked the way that his long lines had to be printed with short, indented runovers because they wouldn't fit the usual trim size of poetry books. Those short "lines," which weren't technically lines, had for me great energy juxtaposed with the longer lines. I thought I'd try writing lines with runovers on purpose. I looked at the result, one large paragraph with zigzagging margins, liked it, but also found it too heavy and blocky. Then I thought I should try dividing the block into shorter stanzas, to aerate it. Couplets seemed dull. I still remember the thrill when I marked off tercets with a ruler and saw how that reversing form took over: long, short, long; then short, long, short. In *The Anxiety of Influence* (a much maligned book at present, I think), Bloom speaks of "creative misprision," a generative misreading of an older poet by a younger one (14). I hadn't yet read Bloom, but it seems in retrospect that my form came directly out of such a "creative misprision."

Soon afterwards, I discovered that James Schuyler uses an alternation of long and short lines within his forty-page poems "The Morning of the Poem" and "A Few Days." Though he does not divide his lines into tercets and keeps the poem in one long block stanza, I'd like to think that his rhythms are similar to my own. I was infatuated with him for many years; still am to some degree. Richard Howard, master of so many forms, uses reversing tercets in his book *Misgivings*, but there the shorter lines are longer than mine and the longer lines are shorter. Thus a form that at first seemed "my own" is anything but unique to me.

Why have I kept writing in this form, playing with it and (I hope) varying it for twenty years? First, I've grown to love spreading out a long sentence over the varying lengths of these lines, feeling the tensions between the sentence and the form, which tends to produce radical and asyntactic line-breaks. You might say that I've been seduced by perverse enjambment. Second, because of their plentiful white space, the poems jump associatively and/or digressively from one narrative moment or image to the next. I like that movement. Third, because of the staccato rhythm of long lines against short, there is, for me, always a "voiced" quality and urgency to the speech. The poems tend to be dramatic, not meditative, and I love that drama. Formally, I'm also reminded of the Pindaric ode's uneven lines, a device that seems to me to intensify their raptures. High emotion is rarely evenly measured, even when it's set into a regular meter.

When it comes down to it, I'd have to say that the rhythms of those long and short lines seem to capture the way I breathe, speak, and think. And the pitfalls of this "signature" form? They're contained in that next-to-last sentence. Naturally, I want to be able to capture other rhythms, tones, moods, and try narrative and lyric modes that are simply not possible in this highly inflected, idiosyncratic, run-on form. Sometimes too the form can seem stale or automatic, and I must push the poem to discover a new relation to its old breathing and speaking patterns. Sooner or later every poet, if he or she lives long enough, tires of the one music. But, however naively, I believe that I'll always keep returning to this form because it has sustained me as a writer and because it is where I still find pleasure.

WORKS CITED

Bloom, Harold. *The Anxiety of Influence: A Theory of Poetry*. Oxford: Oxford University Press, 1997.
Platt, Donald. "Der Streichholzhändler." *Agni* 72 (October 2010): 125–129.

Lines as Counterpoints

Kevin Prufer

The state of mind of the speaker in rhymed and metered verse is rarely tentative; the inevitability of the next line, the next weak or accented syllable, generally suggests to readers a voice that has figured out what it's going to say, that leads us always (though, ideally, with other complexities) to its concluding words, to its envoi, to that one-hundred-and-fortieth syllable of the sonnet. The traditional ballad doesn't often hem and haw, doesn't grind its heel in the dust, pause, scratch its head, and revise itself. The villanelle and the sestina may be obsessive, but they're rarely uncertain. The mind behind the limerick has worked out its punch line well in advance and delights in bringing us to it.

And I admire Denise Levertov's suggestion that much free-verse poetry, stripped of these formal inevitabilities, might be especially good at suggesting to readers a mind in flux. The freedom of free verse isn't, after all, the freedom to toss words about the page willy-nilly; but it may be a freedom to use the pauses of the line-break, the quickness of the long line against the tentative slowness of the short line, the complexities of rhythms unevenly applied to create for the reader the illusion of a mind working out a problem, wrestling with difficulty, asking questions, reaching for (often unattainable) solutions. The interiority of modernist anxiety, one might say, is also the interiority of free verse.

(Of course, these aren't hard and fast rules; they are tendencies. Only a fool would fail to recognize in the free verse of Whitman a declamatory style; and one feels even in many of the most formally predictable of Emily Dickinson's short poems a tentative mind at work on an unanswerable question.)

What I have come to admire recently, however, are sole strange hybrids that live between these two styles, the suggestiveness of the metered line in the free-verse poem or, contrariwise, the single line of unpredictable metrical variation in the middle of the otherwise traditionally formal poem.

Stevie Smith is, to my mind, one of the most underappreciated English-language poets of the twentieth century. Her often highly rhythmic free-verse poetry is versatile, disturbing, and complex—and generally falls neatly into that category described by Levertov, the short and long lines, the pauses at the breaks, creating the illusion of interiority, of the mind at work. But in the midst of this, Smith will often drop in a line of (superficially inappropriate) strictly metered verse, a ten- or twelve-syllable stretch of anapests, iambs, or dactyls, before returning to a more tentative mode in the next line. Take, for the sake of convenience, these two lines from her most famous poem, "Not Waving But Drowning," in which she describes simultaneously the plight of a man trying to get a crowd's attention as he drowns and, by extending the metaphor, the poem's speaker worrying about her own overwhelming psychic isolation:

> It must have been too cold for him his heart gave way,
> they said. (67)

The singular metrical playfulness of the first of these lines (and if you don't hear it, try clapping along to the beat) seems grossly inappropriate to the poem's subject matter. It's too chipper, too happy. And, of course, this is deliberate, throwing the horror of the rest of the poem into a stark sort of relief, the rictus smile of the upbeat iambs (against the mostly anapestic and dactylic free verse of the rest of the poem) suggesting by counterexample (or failing entirely to conceal) the terrible sadness beneath, the awful emotional distance of the happy crowd. And the curt line that follows not only draws the rollicking line up short but distances us from it, taking no responsibility for it, but applying it to others.

One sees something of the opposite approach in the work of Anne Bradstreet, who often interjects metrically looser lines into her otherwise strictly formal poetry. My favorite example comes at the end of her poem "In Memory of My Dear Grandchild, Elizabeth Bradstreet, Who Deceased August, 1665, Being a Year and a Half Old." In that rhymed, iambic poem, the speaker meditates on the loss of her grandchild (her "heart's too much content"), concluding, finally, that though she cannot escape her sadness, this very sadness is, in some ways, inappropriate. It is, after all, God who creates and guides the universe, and all elements of his plan must be for the good. Of course, this is a difficult truth to swallow in the midst of one's own mourning. Still, she ends the poem on an affirmation:

> But plants new set to be eradicate,
> And buds new blown to have so short a date,
> Is by His hand alone that guides nature and fate. (16)

The careful reader, however, will notice that, though the final line of the poem maintains the rhyme, it breaks somewhat with the meter, becoming mostly anapestic toward the end. And this break suggests to us the pain of the conclusion, the difficulty Bradstreet has in uttering what she knows to be true, her mind wrestling uncomfortably with the problem.

These are, of course, examples of individual lines pulling strongly against the dominant formal modes of the poems. I've found them instructive for my own writing, suggesting, first, that slavishly holding to one linear mode isn't always productive and, second, the importance of thinking of the poetic line as not just a useful envelope for words, but also as possible rhythmic counterpoints to the meanings of those words.

WORKS CITED

Bradstreet, Anne. *To My Husband and Other Poems*. Ed. Robert Hutchinson. Mineola, NY: Dover Publications, 2000.
Smith, Stevie. *New Selected Poems of Stevie Smith*. New York: New Directions, 1988.

Two Takes on Poetic Meaning and the Line

Paisley Rekdal

Novice poets tend to regard the line solely as a literal measure of breath, thus they unconsciously break lines according either to "normal" stops in syntax, or to an internal sense of rhythm, itself often based on the four-beat strong-stress rhythm of Anglo-Saxon meter. Rarely do they indent or break lines internally, nor do they break on words with multiple meanings, thus creating smaller moments of playfulness inside a larger work. And yet breaking according to breath/syntax or consistent rhythm creates monotony, and may even obscure a poem's meaning. The reimagined free-verse line can help the reader gain information about a poem that isn't—and maybe can't be—expressed in words itself.

I am particularly struck by this fact in Nick Flynn's poem "Ago." Here, the narrator, anxious about "the speed with which everything is replaced" eschews punctuation-induced lineation and blocky stanzas; instead, the poem splits into tercets and couplets and even single lines, and darts nervously away from the left-hand margin in fragmentary phrases that highlight the speaker's terror of the space that perpetually surrounds him, space that is often represented technologically but felt as existential confusion, as in the following lines:

> I don't even know
> how a telephone works, how your voice reached
> all the way from Iron River, fed
>
> across wires or satellites, transformed
>
> & returned. I don't understand
> the patience this takes, or anything
> about the light-years between stars. (15)

Flynn's lines break on phrases of disorientation that reinforce the speaker's psychic distress rather than the more mundane troubles that syntactically conclude his sentences. Thus, we "know" through the line-breaks that it is the speaker's subjective confusion which troubles him, not his inability to explain to us how a telephone works. And yet the line-breaks also reveal the ultimate reason for this confusion by the end of the poem, when the speaker writes:

> it's what

> I'm afraid of, the speed with which everything
> is replaced, these trees, your smile, my mother

> turning her back to me before work (16)

We understand by the break after "mother" that the mother has herself been "replaced," or, more aptly, that she has disappeared from the speaker's life. It is in the line-break that the speaker is able to pronounce his mother dead, while the breaks throughout the rest of the poem—hurried, frightened, surprisingly coherent non-utterances—register his nervousness at the temporal conditions of this world. Indeed, the final lines of the poem speed through people and images, making them weirdly equivalent in the quickness of their disappearance but not in their emotional impact on us. The poem is an elegy in which line-breaks—even more than words themselves—must do the emotional work.

Similarly crucial lineal disruptions occur in Myung Mi Kim's poem, "Food, Shelter, Clothing," a poem that explores the linguistic legacy of foreign imperialism in South Korea and its later effects on Korean immigration to America. Any country that occupies another, imposing on it its own politics and language, disrupts the identity and language of the occupied. Thus, Kim's fractured syntax—intensified by its increasingly fractured lineation—reminds us how the attempt to "own" one's own (or imposed) language can create great psychological disturbance in the (non-)native speaker. We see the poem begin with syntactically truncated but consistently rhythmic lines:

> In a gangplank thud and amplification take
> Spot of ground. Fended it might remain
> Republic and anthem, spot and same spot . . .
> Smear fear tyranny of attack
> Already the villages already the cities receding (23)

The poem then moves to lines in which the lineation ultimately mimics syntactic collapse:

allaying surge
　neighboring
Geographical trodden shelter

Locate deciphering

　　by force

as contour

Hurls

　　ga ga ga (27)

The poem itself linguistically and formally breaks down here, revealing a poetic identity (once grammatically "whole") as now childlike, fragmented, ultimately fragile. Lineation enforces this effect; the oppressive white space around the words "Hurls" and the nonsensical "ga ga ga" calls the reader's attention to what, ultimately, *cannot* be said, translated, or enforced in any language. To insist here upon a normative sense of lineation—one dependent on the effects of breath or rhythm and which itself would be dependent upon a regularized syntax— would argue against the poem's essence by trying to establish an undivided "I" able to process its many linguistic selves coherently. But take away any claim to rhythmic, syntactic, or visual coherency, and you have something much truer to the unrooted worlds this poet—like Flynn's own speaker—must occupy.

WORKS CITED

Flynn, Nick. *Some Ether*. Minneapolis: Graywolf Press, 2000.
Kim, Myung Mi. *Under Flag*. Berkeley: Kelsey Street Press, 1998.

The Line Is the Leaf

Donald Revell

Two books above all others have taught me to articulate (almost) exactly what I mean by a line of poetry. Rightly, happily, each is a travelogue, a journal. Line moves. And line happens to move in time. The first is Goethe's *Italian Journey*, and the other is Thoreau's *Journal: 1851*. (Sometimes, distances are very near—"I have traveled widely in Concord.") In each, the transfer of authority from language to the worldly lapse of time leads on to Transport—by which I mean that line is visionary always when the poet means to see and only *then* to say. Here is Goethe:

> While walking in the Public Gardens of Palermo, it came to me in a flash that in the organ of the plant which we are accustomed to call the *leaf* lies the true Proteus who can hide or reveal himself in all vegetal forms. From first to last, the plant is nothing but leaf, which is so inseparable from the future germ that one cannot think of one without the other. (366)

In the leaf, for Goethe, light becomes alive. In the line, vision finds its motive, motile shape and, from first to last, the poem is nothing but line. I often tell my students that all I do in editing their poems is to remove those words that lie, like wind-fallen debris, as obstacles between a given line and its immediate successor. And I use the word "immediate" in its entirety because both poet and poem are themselves debris unless their transfer of authority to the worldly lapse of lines is unmediated by intention, unobstructed by mere point of view. Vision goes. It is a godly Proteus whose shifts of shape are instantly prophetic.

In Thoreau's *Journal: 1851*, we read:

> . . . the oracular tree acquiring accumulating the prophetic fury. (231)

Oracles end where the oracular begins, where utterance enters time in the elapsing line. And it is wonderful here that acquisition yields to accumulation. Poems do not acquire meaning; they simply evidence meanings accumulated over time *as* and *through* the moving lines. Thoreau's "prophetic fury" is neither thesis nor conclusion; it is the acceleration of sheer presence approaching the speed of vision which is the velocity of light and time. The line is the leaf of poetry, a site and substance given over to action. When wholly given over, it is also true.

WORKS CITED

Goethe, Johann Wolfgang von. *Italian Journey*. Trans. W. H. Auden and Elizabeth Mayer. London: Penguin Books, 1970.

Thoreau, Henry David. *A Year in Thoreau's Journal: 1851*. Ed. H. Daniel Peck. New York: Penguin Books, 1993.

Writing Against Temperament: The Line

Martha Rhodes

I have a tense relationship with the right side of the page. As a poet, I tend to shy away from it. I am a short-lined poet who uses the left side of the page as launch pad, and the right side of the page as something to reach for, or something beyond reach. I work hard to inch away from the left. It is not impossible for me to venture out into the wilderness of the right side, but I must say that when I find myself out past right field, I don't much like it—the poem, that is. It may be that I have such a bad sense of direction, never knowing where I am on this planet, that I tend to count steps as I walk away from home, or walk up stairs, the poet in me coming out as I venture into the world. I like to be somewhere easy to navigate. Commercial Street in Provincetown, Massachusetts, for instance. It goes on for some miles. Ocean on one side, land on the other. Coffee, newspaper, post office, ATM, pizza, Kunitz's garden, then back again. I am firmly situated. But out on the whale boat, looking at the town, I have no idea where I am on the planet. Which way is which way?

When I push rightward, away from left margin, when I resist ending the particular line I am writing, when I force myself to continue, force more material out of myself before I end line and move left again, I feel, as I am resisting closure of the line, like I'm breaking through some kind of barrier. It can be exhilarating even if, ultimately, I bring the line in, executing often radical compression.

So, for a while I am excited to be out in right field. I feel like I am stretching my muscles, growing as a poet, trying something new. (I am.) Generally, I become adjectivally dependent, and chatty. Or I've entered the rant zone.

I long for the stretch and focus of C. K. Williams, the associative power of Whitman. What I tend to bring to the long line is clutter, though it may take me a while to discover that. A parking lot, a prostitute, a halogen lamp, a sex act, a box of donuts, a drive around Doylestown Pennsylvania, punctuated by a lot of commas, em dashes, and colons. And then I find myself paring down, down,

down, if only to add the donuts back in, or the halogen light. If only to take them away again. The long line gives me the liberty to *feel* expansive, to get it all out, to feel somewhat narrative even. Even if only during the drafting stage.

A large figure myself, I am, you see, at heart, a compressionist. I strive for much in a small amount of space. I love the short to short-ish line, but I have probably learned the most from the poems of mine that never see the light of day. Those are the poems that start out as fifteen-pagers, stretching boldly across the page. How the lines sustain themselves (or not) is through the syntax—for better or worse. Unlike the poets I admire who can pull the long line off, I lose focus, run out of steam, meander aimlessly. And yet. I encourage myself, my students, and my poet friends to work against temperament, to challenge every poem by producing interim drafts that grate against the poem's structural impulse. Why? Well, why not? We grow by building our muscles. By making choices. What stays in? What comes out? If we don't give ourselves the material with which to make these decisions, then how do we grow and dance around in our own work? Why not challenge the very structure of the poem—from the line to the stanza? Why not see what happens if we tuck our lines way in? What decisions are we forced to make by deciding what stays in, what gets put aside? And what changes are triggered by compression? What happens if we add? Are we adding narrative only? How is the poem impacted by these radical temperamental shifts and how does it ultimately help us, as writers, to go against our own grain? We learn, more and more, what it is that is essential to each poem. We learn, more and more, to gauge where our readers are as they make their way across our lines. We understand emphasis more. We understand pacing more completely. We understand the very vocabulary of the poem more deeply by adding words, by taking them away. By stretching the line out, if only to cut back.

We may never become strong right fielders. But we become stronger writers by trying different things. After all, why should all of our poems look alike? If we are angry, we might be breathless and monosyllabic. One word per line. We might slow down. Or, we might speed up and stack words on top of each other. The line might be a long angry slash, rushed and relentless. The line, in truth, follows our hearts. Our hearts are changeable. So should not, too, the line change as need be? I think so. I think we need to open our hearts and encourage our ears to listen to how the words want to position themselves on the page. And we must remind ourselves not to go by rules, the only rule being that we should distrust the rule. Never end a line on a preposition? Or conjunction? Or a this or that? My goodness! Each poem discovers its own needs. The line, that element that truly distinguishes poetry from prose, must always be challenged—if only to come back to our original impulse.

Ultimately, the more we challenge our lines, through exploration of vocabulary, syntax, punctuation, and length, the more we allow ourselves to become flexible writers. We loosen up and allow ourselves to explore. This doesn't always mean that our explorations reap great poems at the start. But exploration allows us to give up a preconceived notion of what our line should be, and the line then ceases to be contrived. "Look at me," our lines often say to our readers, "aren't I a brilliant line ending? Notice how I lead you to the next line, nay, stanza, so elegantly. Notice me. Appreciate me. Look at me. Look how well I am made." When I hear the gears cranking in my work, I push myself all the harder to go against temperament, to shake myself free, so that I can see where else I might stray.

Some Thoughts on the Integrity of the Single Line in Poetry

Alberto Ríos

The best line in a poem better be the line I'm reading.
This is an almost impossible standard, of course, but there is nothing wrong with that fierce ambition. I am an advocate—or rather, an appreciator—of the long line in poems, though by that I do not at all mean lines with simply more words. I mean instead lines that are long in their moment, that make me linger and give me the effect of having encountered something, something worth stopping for—the antithesis of our times, which seem to be all about getting somewhere else, and fast, and we're late already. The following are some thoughts on what might be your best line. They are not rules, of course, but they do stem from considerations likely important to you as a writer, whatever your decision in these matters.

1. A line is a moment, and a moment is intrinsically non-narrative. That is, a moment does not move forward, not readily, not right away. A moment stops, and stopping is the friendly nemesis of narrative. A line is a moment that has value right then, and which deserves some of our time. To go past a moment is to lose something. In our lives, finally, it is the moments we savor and it is the moments we savor in our reading as well.

2. The half line, or "poetic" line, goes something like this: *I went to the store and / bought some bread.* It breaks the line that otherwise would read: *I went to the store and bought some bread.* Which is more sincere? Is there anything to be gained by the break? Is there news in it, or insight? The break presents a moment of small melodrama, as if whatever follows the "and" is somehow more meaningful presented in this way. Inserting a line-break does not add to the poetic nature of the moment. If anything, this delay

keeps us in the commonplace longer, and even exacerbates the problem by giving the line drama that it cannot sustain and does not honestly own. At least the second version does not misrepresent itself.

3. Longer lines keep us in the moment, and out of the prose or story of the page. The story will take care of itself, and can claim the whole page, after all. The moment has only itself.

4. The line-break slows us as readers by making us wait until the next line to get whatever information follows. If that information is not something new, then perhaps it should in fact be on that immediate line, and not broken up at all. Think about television newscasts, with sound bites that give you a tantalizing bit—*This just in: the end of the world is at hand*—and then they say, *More at eleven*. In that moment, they cheat you. Similarly, a line-break should help, not hinder, the reader. Why wait until 11:00 P.M.? At that moment—withholding news on a news program—we believe the newscast less. It's the same with news in a poem. If it's worthy, say it now, and say it all. Use your words in service to the moment, not in place of it.

5. Complete lines help you discover your own line, your own intellectual unit, your pace. The length of the line is how long you take to say something. This is the size of your step. With this in mind, you must ask yourself how and if half-steps help you move forward in the ways that you want. Concurrently, you must ask yourself how they move the reader forward, who after all is following your lead.

6. Enjambment is often offered as the reason—and not simply the definition—for lines that keep moving down the page. Enjambment is cited as the way to keep readers moving forward. But why? Enjambment is a fine classification of what one might be doing, but it is not an explanation. As readers we move forward by default. Where else are we going? So, what is the greater necessity for enjambment? Forward movement needs to say something about the moment, finally.

7. A good line can find employment in any poem, whereas a good poem cannot employ just any line. The demand is squarely on the line. If every line

in a poem is good, chances are that the poem itself has little to worry about in this regard, and can put its shoulder to other things without having to make up for anything that the lines are not doing.

8. A line is an easy chair as well as a line—not half an easy chair. Another line is a lamp, another is a fireplace—not parts of each. Together they make the room you are describing, then the house, then the street, then the city. Whole lines make the city. Half lines do half the job. In the city, that will give you incomplete directions. In the kitchen, it will get you toast and. Stanza, as a point of information, means "room" in Italian.

9. Play no tricks on the readers, and exact no requirements. Readers do not *have* to do anything, which includes reading the next line in order to understand the line they are in. If you have to tell your reader, *just keep reading, it'll all get clear in a moment*, then you are writing prose, which is dependent on progressive clarification—a device called "plot"—rather than singular and memorable elucidation.

10. Integrity of the line as I am describing it suggests that the line is itself contained, though not necessarily complete. This is a lyric moment at its best, something on its own terms and part of a greater whole as well. It is the complete moment and part of a poem.

11. The line—the moment—is not subordinate to anything else. It does not need the other lines in a poem, though it clearly lives in their greater community. Still, a line does its own work. And in this way, it is a contributing member of that society.

12. A line suggests, for the moment, lateral, rather than linear, movement. It stays with something until the thing is done, or understood, or some understanding is gleaned. A line takes the time to listen to the words it holds, and asks the reader to do the same.

13. Lines are what distinguish poetry from all other art forms, and therefore they intrinsically mean something. They help us to see what makes a poem a poem. When they become simply part of something else, and not something on their own, they stop being lines of poetry.

14. A line-break is what defines a line. A line-break means something or it doesn't, but it can't sometimes mean one thing and sometimes another. In general, a line-break suggests a pause, however slight. Does what you are saying have a pause in it? If so, then this is the way to go—break your line there.

15. A preposition, by definition, expresses a relationship—in other words, it tells, rather than shows, breaking a foundational piece of advice in all creative classrooms. This does not mean you should stop using prepositions. But you should try to see if the juxtaposition of the two things you are relating might work just fine without the preposition. This is often the case.

There are, absolutely, other ways to think about a line. An argument can be made for the absolute opposite of everything that's said here, with unqualified historical backing. But the point is, every argument invariably suggests thinking about the line, not simply using it to make the writing "look like a poem," or simply to tell a story without regard for what a poem as a form might have to offer. Poems are not stories, after all. Poems are the fire that stories explain.

Comma Splice and Jump-Cut: On the Line

Dana Roeser

Recently, I had a dream in which I swallowed a pair of scissors. They lodged in my esophagus in the "wrong" position, that is, face (points) up. They were supposed to be inserted carefully face down, folded in the cylindrical compartment like a baby. Points up, the scissors would probably kill me. It happened by accident. They'd been on the brink, and I had dropped them.

It is hard to find a container for consciousness. It has sharp points and could cut us to ribbons. My friend Mary Leader, an adept formalist, says that my poetic "form" is a Hellman's jar, a democratic one-size-fits-all clear receptacle for my content. I like to think the helixes of the variously indented (usually short) lines of my couplets or tercets are more delicate, but I see her logic. To me, they are more like snakes, or the esophagus, compressing and equalizing the material that passes through.

When I finally learned to tame the details of my "stories" and make them bend to prerogatives of a larger design, to be open to what Aristotle called "probable impossibilities" rather than to what "really happened," there was room for other elements to come into play. I associated and jumped from strand to strand, story to story, element to element, and the form made sure that there were no topic sentences.

There were side stories, back stories, *in medias res* characters who weren't properly introduced, bits of dialogue, high diction, street talk, pop culture references, literary allusion, memories, dream, lyricism, flat-sounding journalese, one-word exclamations, pivots, high spirits, low spirits, bawdy humor, pathos, short sentences, long sentences, fragments, jagged enjambment, a full stop in the center of a line, a series not divided by commas; the poem devoid of commas altogether, the poem that takes or leaves periods, the temporary confusion of near-random association (within a line), pronoun ambiguity, tense inconsistency—many, many joys that riff off of those diagrammed sentences from ninth grade—and then I had to stick the landing.

I enjoy working this way—I feel like a painter, which was what I aspired to be at first. The material rubs and chafes and sometimes gives way to something beautiful. The voice of the speaker keeps the flights and incongruities glued to some essential unity. The lines norm around a certain number of stresses or sometimes words. The sentence does one thing; the line another.

In any line of mine there is always the pressure of where it came from and where it is going. Frank O'Hara, one of my beloved forebears, in his "Personism: A Manifesto" puts it this way: "I don't believe in god, so I don't have to make elaborately sounded structures. I hate Vachel Lindsay, always have; I don't even like rhythm, assonance, all that stuff. You just go on your nerve. If someone's chasing you down the street with a knife you just run, you don't turn around and shout, 'Give it up! I was a track star for Mineola Prep'" (xiii). Later, though, he makes a persuasive pitch for precision: "As for measure and other technical apparatus, that's just common sense: if you're going to buy a pair of pants you want them to be tight enough so everyone will want to go to bed with you." Speed and precision, then. Sequins, scissors, knife, river, wristwatch. Hum-colored cabs, dungarees, and snakespit. As my fourteen-year-old daughter Lucy would say, "Good luck with that!"

WORKS CITED

Aristotle. *Aristotle's Poetics*. Ed. Francis Fergusson. Trans. S. H. Butcher. New York: Hill and Wang, 1961. 109–110.

O'Hara, Frank. "Personism: A Manifesto." *The Selected Poems of Frank O'Hara*. Ed. Donald Allen. New York: Vintage Books, 1974. xiii–xiv.

Clarity and Mystery: Some Thoughts on the Line

Mary Ann Samyn

I've often thought that if I could live my life the way I write my poems I would be very calm and contented indeed. Because of whatever stroke of good luck, I am more patient, more confident, more trusting in my poems than in any other area of my life. Line has a lot to do with this. Line feels intuitive, but I also know that every line I write is informed by every other line I've written and read. I'm aware of syllables and stresses, of not loading all the "good words" at the ends of lines while having a list of prepositions (though I happen to like them: so useful and willing to get along!) at the beginnings, of the possibilities (and occasional unfortunate results) of enjambment, of what is musical and what is not and how even the latter can be pleasing. I am also happily unaware; I'm simply paying attention to the world and not Writing a Poem. If I say that I've "lost my line," I mean I'm not alert enough to take note of whatever is presenting itself. When I am paying attention, I tend to write lines that I know immediately are "accurate"—in terms of image, music, rhythm, visual presentation, rhetoric—or not. Revision—literally, re-seeing, more attention—is possible. The good lines cannot be translated or broken or otherwise parsed. Careful attention = accurate lines. This sureness is one of two things I like most about writing poetry. The other, interestingly, is uncertainty. Paying attention, writing a line at a time, means that I really don't know what will come next. In this sense, the line is exploratory, like boot prints in snow; I can look back and see where I've been but up ahead is uncharted. I write out of necessity, and thus my poems are useful (at least to me and, I hope, to others), sometimes even predictive. I might come to realize, for example, that I do know the source of my confusion or that I am already happy. I begin with a first line and, often, a title. That's it. Then, I write a line at a time, and, lately, end-stop most of my lines with a period or, my favorite form of punctuation, the shy semicolon. From there, I record slight shifts of "huh—" as closely as possible. If I have a "poetic" thought, I put it in.

If I'm hungry, I mention that. If the sky darkens, I record my noticing. All the while, the line coaxes me on: *What next? What else? How do you feel?* I read aloud, a lot. I walk away from my desk. I do the dishes. I pat the dog's head or take some advice from the cat. *Curling up is nice,* she seems to say, or *Look at my claw—*. I try to write the line that curls, the line that slumbers, the soft but fierce line. Mostly I try to sound like me, a person who thinks a cat might say *Look at my claw—*. I can and do write anywhere. No special pens. No special mood. The poems that hold my interest after their arrival still have some mystery and can be read as they appear on the page. Again, uncertainty + accuracy. I have favorite poems in each of my books, poems in which what is said cannot be separated from how it's said. Paraphrases fall short. It's nice to think poems always achieve this level of coherence, but we know that isn't true. Nonetheless, sometimes it does happen. I'll end with one such poem, which I wrote a line at a time and with all its current idiosyncrasies: the repeated line, the indented and italicized line, the lines that seem like questions but aren't, the much longer final line. This is a poem of, I hope, clarity *and* mystery: the sureness of the line *and* of discovery—line to line.

Make Them Howl or Breathe Fire

I was strung up.
I was my own angel.
Repeat: I was my own angel.
Something beeped to signal the end of mercy.
    Oh well—
Weather swirled just beyond my shoulder.
Had I not been on my knees already.
Had I not grasped the concept.
God likes firm resolve.
I detest all my sins. Above all, ingratitude, the color of which pales, like
    my skin. (36)

WORK CITED

Samyn, Mary Ann. "Make Them Howl or Breathe Fire." *Beauty Breaks In*. Kalamazoo, MI: New Issues, 2009.

Captivated by Syllabics

Robyn Schiff

My favorite line of poetry is the twentieth line of Marianne Moore's poem "The Jerboa." It goes like this: "Hippopotami." It may not seem like much when it's quarantined—but the line in poetry is funny, simultaneously demanding solitary confinement and full integration. All lines flicker between two lives; now an isolated unit, now a contiguous part of a sentence and stanza and poem. Lines move like time moves, both in contained moments, and boundlessly toward eternity. Maybe writing in lines fulfills our deepest and terribly contrary wish both to stop and to keep going at the same time. To hold captive, to be captivated, and also to let go and to be released. I digress to recall a stanza of Dickinson from poem #613:

> They shut me up in Prose—
> As when a little Girl
> They put me in the Closet—
> Because they liked me "still"— (302)

The word "still" so beautifully expresses the longing for stasis and the longing for endurance at the same time. Don't we put people in closets (tombs) because we still like them? But we lock the tomb door because of some deep-seated fear of unholy movement even after death; we prefer our dearly departed to remain still and refrain from wandering the cemetery, the countryside, the house. Every line-break is such a barricade for the body. Every line-break is also such a door for the soul.

Because she is a syllable counter, Moore's lines heighten the tension between the body and the soul of each word. I think of the body because words are chosen and placed according to their physical proportions, which lie somewhere between the pure textuality of their letters and the pronounced utterance of those letters literally sounded out and counted. I say soul because there's so much more to words than their physical attributes—the unaccountable part. As diverse as syllabic poems are in the history of English-language poetry, they do all seem to share an obsession with the crossroads of the material and the spiritual. Counting syllables brings to the fore the reckoning of sums, which puts us in the territory of summarizing and then reminds us quickly of all that can never be accounted for and what cannot be recounted.

"Hippopatami" is isolated on a line of its own in the menagerie of "The Jerboa" because it is a five-syllable word, and the second lines of all the stanzas happen to be five syllables long. So be it. The confinement of "hippopotami" is the result of the ancient procedure's arbitrary accounting that puts everything in its strange place, and "hippopotami" is literally penned in its position. In this poem about empire, the crucial confinement of "hippopotami" is a display of power and wealth, enacted through the arrangement of line. Furthermore, "hippopotami" rhymes in a closed asymmetrical couplet with "tie" that gives me the sensation of a gate locking shut. The rhyme tethers, the syllabics pen, and the syntactical closing couplet turns the key. But it's like fencing a monster, and those slats can look meager and pathetic, bound to break. Power like the one in this poem is tenuous at best; indeed, the poem is written in the past tense about a former superpower. Here's the whole sentence, followed by the rest of the stanza:

> They had their men tie
> hippopotami
>   and bring out dappled dog-
>   cats to course antelopes, dikdik, and ibex;
>   or used small eagles. They looked on as theirs,
>   impalas and onigers . . . (10)

Like so many displays of power, the confinement of the hippopotami, and likewise the very word "hippopotami," is a grandiose gesture of control. But in this poem which amounts to an inventory of a troubled royal court, the humble jerboa, after being identified in the title, doesn't appear until the ninety-sixth line, and when it does, it makes its home in the "boundless" sand, the very picture of freedom—not a piece of merchandise that can be sorted, but a living thing. "The Jerboa," like so many of Moore's poems, meditates on containment and freedom. I think her poem "What Are Years?" written, incidentally, in the summer that the Nazis finally invaded France, expresses this eternal struggle best:

in misfortune, even death,
    encourages others
    and in its defeat, stirs

    the soul to be strong? He
sees deep and is glad, who
    accedes to mortality
and in his imprisonment rises
upon himself as
the sea in a chasm, struggling to be
free and unable to be,
    in its surrendering
    finds its continuing. (95)

Syllabics heighten the contradiction between surrendering and continuing like no other form, demanding the most physical encounter with words both orally and textually—noticing how many times the mouth opens and closes in speech, and portioning the material of words into the tiniest components as we write them down—and the most metaphysical, as the very words transcend their physical sites to mean. Syllabics are a metaphor for the limitations of the body, but they are also a metaphor for imagination's range beyond the body's edges. And as the syllables clock through their abacus, I can't but consider the final countdown of my own mortality, and in that finite accounting toward zero, begin to encounter eternity.

WORKS CITED

Dickinson, Emily. *The Complete Poems of Emily Dickinson*. Ed. Thomas H. Johnson. New York: Little Brown and Company, 1961.
Moore, Marianne. *Complete Poems*. New York: Penguin, 1981.

Croon: A Brief on the Line

Tim Seibles

Whether we attend to the fact or not, poetry has deep roots in song. Beyond their meanings, words are sounds, *notes* if you will. A line—full of assonance or simply conversational—is, therefore, necessarily a kind of musical construct. For me, this means we poets have a good bit in common with singers. When vocalists *phrase* the sentences of song lyrics, it's clear that they are using *lines*— some enjambed, some end-stopped—to add emotional dimension to the tune. Of course, music allows a singer to bend and stretch words in ways that are not quite possible in conventional speech, but developing a sense of mood through pacing (to draw listeners into the lyrical spell) is essentially the same for poets and crooners. If we think of lineation as one of the engines that drives *tone*, it's easy to make yet another connection between poems and songs.

I realize that melody is an importantly distinct feature of musical expression. However, even melody resembles speech—with both sustained and short notes inflected in precise relation to silence—especially if we allow ourselves to see a note as a *word* that lives outside the realm of semantics. This is even more apparent if we consider the vocal gestures of, say, a saxophone solo. Isn't a poem a *spoken solo*, a musical composition built line by line for the express purpose of creating an emotional/intellectual experience for the audience?

Given this, I try to approach the line as both a singer *and* a reader. When I read a poem aloud or quietly to myself, I trust that the lines are made to offer me a particular set of intended effects: an exact rhythm of speech, a carefully considered pace for the intake of ideas, feelings, and other sensations. It strikes me that the sonic and semantic impacts of words can be nuanced in a hundred ways, depending upon their positions within a line and their connections to the lines and words that precede and follow. In reworking my own poems, these are the things that shape my sense of what should turn where.

Breadthless Length

Ravi Shankar

Rather than go from the inside out, from the breath to utterance, from enjambment to end stop, from Dickinson's hymn meter to Whitman's multitudinous
abode, let's go from the outside in: from the line as something to walk, to bet
the house on, to bunt down, to snort off a mirror, to make vanish with cream,
or to dangle from a prow. Because for the line—the basic syntactical unit of a
poem the way the sentence is for prose—to have continued relevance in a world
of text messages and hyperlinks, it's useful to begin peripherally and work
backward toward its multiple and moving centers.

    1. Pace: the stride of the line is a lap in a lake, else jagged, frenetic, broken-
toothed. Lilting and out-of-breath, forceful or stuttering, but when listened to
and crafted well, inflected with distinctive aesthetic personality. Denise Levertov, in her essay "On the Function of the Line," makes the point that the most
obvious function of the line-break is the hesitation between word and word, a
function of rhythm and a standard of prosodic interpretation, but that the effect
of the line-break on melody, which in turn is the place meaning is produced,
remains too little understood. Take William Carlos Williams's "XVII" from
Spring and All:

> Our orchestra
> is the cat's nuts—
>
> Banjo jazz
> with a nickelplated
>
> amplifier to
> soothe
>
> the savage beast—
> Get the rhythm

That sheet stuff
's a lot a cheese. (216)

Compared to Carl Sandburg's "Jazz Fantasia":

Sling your knuckles on the bottoms of the happy
tin pans, let your trombones ooze, and go husha-
husha-hush with the slippery sand-paper. (170)

While Williams breaks against the grain on the preposition "to" and shifts the possessive article "'s" to the couplet's underside in order to get the colloquialism of the phrase that follows, Sandburg extends his like a drowsy solo full of onomatopoeia and alliteration. It's bee-bop to big band because of their respective lines.

2. Gambling. Risk. Not just that of exposure, but that of choice. When the line scaffolds the stanza, the conscious or subconscious decision on how to use it informs the music of meaning. Take Robert Bagg writing on James Scully:

Scully's most brilliant insight into poetic technique is that the "line break,"—aka enjambment, a French term suggestive of a surefooted balletic "jump" from the end of one line to the start of the next—is most truly a keen weapon for unearthing and jacklighting buried truths, buried lies, buried bodies. Scully sees line breaks as muscular fulcra on which all poetic discourse hinges. Used bravely, line breaks can decode, implode, explode everything a manipulated language wants to hide.

The deadening body of language, its arteries clogged with bombast and rhetoric, can be operated on by the poet, a surgery which continues, in the end, to be un coup de dés, a hazard; there's no telling what will be disclosed when the words and their syntax are laid bare and segmented. Bust the house by just betting the line.

3. Sport and Intoxification: just as a tennis player hopes a smashed forehand catches the line, the poet demonstrates skill by ingenious confabulations, by weaving nets that take it all in, else by chipping away shards that somehow, in spite of brevity, cohere. Take the many, largely failed, nineteenth-century attempts by poets such as Longfellow and Arthur Hugh Clough to recreate a dactylic-hexameter line in English. Here's Longfellow in *Evangeline*:

This is the forest primeval. The murmuring pines and the hemlocks
Bearded with moss and in garments green, indistinct in the twilight. (13)

In a sense, this is Barry Bonds eyeing Babe Ruth; poets looking back at Homer
and Virgil, saying *I can do what you do!* and pushing the line in English further
and further toward the right margin until, save for the leg-irons of meter, the
line only precipitously resembles what we might consider the shape of poetry
to be.

Or take the opposite impulse. Here's an excerpt from May Swenson's "Riding
the A," which very rightly was chosen as a Poetry in Motion poem in the New
York City subway system:

Wheels
and rails
in their prime
collide,
make love in a glide
of slickness
and friction. (169)

Here the poem's form literalizes the train's journey underground, the staccato
motion of stopping and starting reminiscent of sex itself: urgent and hurtling.
Indeed the tradition of long skinny poems, from Neruda's "Elemental Odes" to
Kay Ryan's contemporary darkly witty truncations, also has at its root the dare
of sport. How much can be pared away and still continue to compel?

    4. Tradition and the Lure: trace the line back to Euclid, the father of geom-
etry. A one-dimensional entity without thickness, extending infinitely in both
directions. A "breadthless length," according to Euclid, that which "lies evenly
with the points on itself" (153). Thinking of memorable lines of poetry—"To
a green thought in a green shade" (Marvell, "The Garden"), "Nothing that is
not there and the nothing that is" (Stevens, "The Snow Man"), or "The nerves
sit ceremonious like tombs" (Dickinson, 341)—I imagine that they *do* extend
infinitely in both directions, toward the past and onward to the future, from
moment of conception to what will yet come. The power of such lines transcends
the parenthesis of time.

    The sense of line in my own work is something dynamic, to find what suffices
in any given situation, though I must admit that, speaking of geometry, the eye

is the measure by which I generally lineate. Within me is an inner carpenter who seeks to plane lines consistently throughout the course of a stanza or poem. While I love and advocate messy and serrated music, it takes conscious effort on my part to craft lines longer or shorter than the ones that come before it. I think this is related to my sense that as poets we are crafting something that when well-made can be held in the palm of the hand like an inlaid box. Ultimately, I have little use for a box that resembles a drunk rhombus or a ragged sleeve—I may look at such artifacts curiously, but I'm certainly not going to store anything in it.

WORKS CITED

Bagg, Robert. "Line Break." Curbstone Press. 5 Dec. 2000. Web. 5 Dec. 2009. <http://www.poevotes.com/line_break__poetry_as_social_practice_42007.htm>.

Dickinson, Emily. The Complete Poems of Emily Dickinson. Ed. Thomas H. Johnson. New York: Little, Brown and Company, 1961.

Euclid. The Thirteen Books of Euclid's Elements. Vol. 1. Ed. T. L. Heath. Cambridge: Cambridge University Press, 1908.

Levertov, Denise. "On the Function of the Line." New & Selected Essays. New York: New Directions, 1992. 78–87.

Longfellow, Henry Wadsworth. Evangeline. Ed. H. Y. Moffett. Gretna, LA: Pelican Publishing Company, 1999.

Marvell, Andrew. "The Garden." Selected Poetry and Prose. Ed. Robert Wilcher. New York: Methuen, 1987.

Sandburg, Carl. "Jazz Fantasia." The Complete Poems of Carl Sandburg. New York: Harcourt, 2003.

Scully, James. Line Break: Poetry as Social Practice. Willimantic, CT: Curbstone Press, 2005.

Stevens, Wallace. "The Snow Man." The Collected Poems. New York: Vintage Books, 1990.

Swenson, May. "Riding the A." The Great Machines: Poems and Songs from the Age of the American Railroad. Ed. Robert Hedin. Iowa City: University of Iowa Press, 1996.

Williams, William Carlos. The Collected Poems of William Carlos Williams. Vol. 1. New York: New Directions, 1967.

A Few Lines on the Line

Evie Shockley

(not all lines are straight.)

I thought it would be useful to begin thinking about the aesthetics of the line by revisiting some of my favorite prose poems. I pulled C. S. Giscombe's *Inland* and Harryette Mullen's S*PeRM**K*T off the shelf and considered. Despite differences in these poets' rhythms and the logics by which they proceed, both of their books suggest links between the prose poem and impatience. No matter how radical, how wide, the imaginative leaps it makes within and between sentences (or sentence fragments), the prose poem keeps right on going. The reader may keep up or catch up—or so it might initially seem. The lineated poem, on the other hand, foregrounds its relationship to time, flags us down at every turn.

Mullen's poem, propelled by the multiplicity of meaning and juxtaposition, offers words and phrases with layered significance and runs with them in (at least) two directions at once. Her book opens, as it happens, with a meditation not unrelated to the subject at hand: "Lines assemble gutter and margin. Outside and in, they straighten a place. Organize a stand. Shelve space. Square footage. Align your list or listlessness." She describes the structure of the supermarket fairly literally, even as she implicitly connects regularity and rigid linearity to issues of social control and containment through a quick series of puns. Alacrity and relentlessness characterize the progression of words and ideas in this work.

(a line is the manifestation of a unit of time passing; a line-break is, too.)

The lineated poem, by contrast, often uses line-breaks to create wordplay. It may invite the reader to linger on one understanding before turning to another: "Of course there was no mother / lode; of course it was unlikely," Brenda Hillman writes in "The Shirley Poem," a piece in her collection *Cascadia*, inspired by California geology (37). The pause accentuates the pleasure of the bait-and-switch. The line is crucial to this move, just as it would be an obstacle to the enjoyment of the rapid dance one is required to do in a prose poem like Mullen's. The lineated poem dances, too—but let's say it does the tango, offering us a series of dramatic poses.

(a line is the most direct route from point a to point b.)

In Giscombe's *Inland*, the prose paragraph suggests a single, long line, stretching out (but for the constraint of the page) across the flat expanse of the midwestern U.S. that his poem occupies. In what might also be read as a meta-commentary on this topic, he writes:

> Male, female. Black men say trim. An outline's sameness is, finally, a reference. Towns, at a distance, are content and reference both—how they appear at first, a dim cluster, and then from five or six miles off; how they look when you're only three miles away. In between sightings is the prairie itself to get across: trek, trace, the trick of landscape. (14)

Placing the outline in relation to the line of sight, Giscombe's poem, "Prairie Style (2)," emphasizes the way we visually anticipate what we cannot yet access, our eyes racing ahead of our brains. Yet, to do the poem justice, we must go back and slowly make the "trek" along the multi-sentence, wrap-around line of each prose paragraph, engaging the images and provocations we encounter, one by one, despite receiving no strong cues to pause.

Giscombe's structure is appropriate to his textual landscape—as the irregularly indented, roughly enjambed lines of Hillman's *Cascadia* are to the mountainous terrain they inhabit. The line-breaks, especially those that crack syntax mid-phrase, can be as grinding as movement along a faultline:

> The number of faults in middle California
>   is staggering—that is, we stagger
>   over them till it's
>   difficult to follow our own. Each tremor
>   is the nephew of a laugh—

sandstone, shale, chert from the Triassic
near I-Forgetville. He lined
them up, they made white sense,

stretchmarks on her body like
public transportation, very coastal . . . (12)

Lines interrupt logic, even when making sense. Lines like these, from Hillman's "A Geology," encourage careful reading, rereading, with that jagged back and forth which inhibits running, which forces you to watch your footing. If the prose poem can be deceptively unobstructed, then the poetic line can be utilized to trip the reader up until she learns to take her time.

(a line is the most direct route from point a to point b . . . and points c, q, and y.)

Along with the temporal aspect of the line, I am fascinated by its directional nature, how it begins and ends and moves in and through space. On this subject, I have more questions than observations to offer. For example, returning to Hillman's poem, we might consider the words that appear, one in each corner, on each page of "A Geology." What is the line in relation to those words? Is each "cornerstone" word itself a "line"? The two words in the top corners fall on the same horizontal plane, as do the two in the bottom corners. Does each pair make up a line, albeit a widely spaced out one? What would that imply about the relationship between the words in the top left and bottom left corners? Or the relationship between the top left cornerstone and the one on the bottom right? What more circuitous routes through a poem are closed off by our reliance on the line?

I've worked with vertical and diagonal lines in my own poetry. I write occasionally in a modified acrostic form I developed in which, instead of using the first letters of my lines to spell a word or name down the left margin, I use a line or two of lyrics from a relevant song to determine the first word of each line of my poem. For example, the first stanza of "you can say that again, billie" appears thusly in *a half-red sea*:

southern women serve strife   keep lines of pride open
trees are not taller than these broad vessels   femmes who
bear fully armored knights   clinking from the womb   but

a night in whining ardor   means black woman compelled   how
strange   brown vassal on a bed of green needles   ingests the
fruit of Georgia   let that gestate   but be-gets no child of the south

The vertical line is an integral part of the poem. Another of my poems, "not in
the causal chain," turns upon a diagonal line that emerges from the horizontal
ones. That poem, like John Cage's mesostic form, is of a sort in which the non-
horizontal lines are more critical to the work than the horizontal lines on which
we tend to focus. I don't know if I can identify precisely what appeals to me
about these other possibilities for the line, but I would guess it has to do with
how I think about poetry in relation to both music and visual art. These other
media don't operate on unidirectional or linear principles (even the written line
of music, as it moves from left to right, also exploits the vertical plane). I want
opportunities for visual (and aural) multiplicity available to my poetry.

(the dividing line)

On a related note, I find myself intrigued by the solid line, as opposed to—
and in relation to—the line of text. Ed Roberson, for instance, places a solid,
black line horizontally across the page in many of the poems in the "Lucid Interval as Integral Music" section of *Voices Cast Out to Talk Us In* and in *City Eclogue*.
What kind of relationship does that line create between the textual lines above it
and those below it? He has suggested that the voice below the line is "'singing
over' or 'singing under'" the speaker of the text above it (qtd. in Crown 210).
Might the solid line also represent a speaker's voice—and if so, whose? How
can we take seriously the fact that it also constitutes "a line of poetry"? Nathaniel
Mackey's serial poem "Song of the Andoumboulou" offers an interesting point
of comparison. Unlike Roberson's solid line, which effectively bisects the entire
page, the solid line Mackey uses is approximately the same length as his short
to mid-length textual lines. Further, wherever Mackey places the solid line—be
it a third, a half, or two-thirds of the way down the page—his text only appears
beneath the line, never above it. How differently should we read his solid lines
from Roberson's?

When I teach creative writing, I push my students to be conscious of and
thoughtful about how and why they break their lines of poetry, to understand
how significant the impact of lines can be on a reader, and to recognize that this
formal element of a poem need not (should not) be incidental to its language
and ideas. I urge them to choose carefully whether to place the strongest words

at the ends of their lines or frontload those words along the left margin, whether to enjamb their lines against the grain of their ideas or naturalize the right margin, whether to use short lines or long ones, and whether to use lineation at all. Then I tell them their work with the line has only just begun.

(the finish line)

WORKS CITED

Crown, Kathleen. "Reading the 'Lucid Interval': Race, Trauma, and Literacy in the Poetry of Ed Roberson." *Poetics Today* 21.1 (Spring 2000): 187–220.
Giscombe, C. S. *Inland*. Oakland: Leroy, 2001.
Hillman, Brenda. *Cascadia*. Middletown: Wesleyan University Press, 2001.
Mackey, Nathaniel. *Whatsaid Serif*. San Francisco: City Lights Books, 1998.
Mullen, Harryette. S*PeRM**K*T. Philadelphia: Singing Horse Press, 1992.
Roberson, Ed. *City Eclogue*. Berkeley: Atelos, 2006.
———. *Voices Cast Out to Talk Us In*. Iowa City: University of Iowa Press, 1995.
Shockley, Evie. *a half-red sea*. Durham, NC: Carolina Wren Press, 2006.

Life / Line: (Freaked)

Eleni Sikelianos

A car is driving down a dark road; suddenly, it must turn the corner, and the driver/writer/reader doesn't quite know what's after the curve. . . . That is the clinamen, the swerve that animates the poem. Lucretius held that this veering at both the atomic level and in the curves of human thinking is what makes possible new life forms and new ideas. The line-break provides the mystery-novel portion of the poem—that tension between sound, meaning, and interruption that is almost all of what a poem is to me.

A piece of Mylar wrap being pulled at opposite edges—one end is the poem itself (the whole), the other is its line-breaks. It crinkles and shimmers from the pressure between these two, it makes a kind of pleasing, disruptive noise. If it's Saran wrap, the whole thing gets slightly, permanently deformed, and that carries a certain pleasure, too.

As soon as we abandoned the mathematics that had for so long bound the line, a whole new slew of problems arrived. We still, instinctively, work with

line break (where the heart - meaning "possibility" — skips) : PULL HERE

poem (its "meaning", language, integrity) : PULL HERE

some kind of measure, but we have the freedom (?) imperative (?) to disrupt it at will. As Williams pointed out, "our lives have lost all that in the past we had to measure them by," and our verses "are left without any metrical construction of which you can speak" ("On Measure" 337). Our social and scientific understandings have changed. Williams and Whitman and Dickinson and Mallarmé created new lines according to some of those changes, and we are still, to a great extent, following their advances.

Williams scolded Whitman as a sloppy freedom-seeker in the line and called for some discipline, a measure that was not fixed or Euclidean, but flexible, and soon he invented the variable foot. I'm not sure how to proceed from Williams's idiosyncratic measure, but my own sense of the line is both mechanical and organic, linked in my mind to other forms of (human and nonhuman) animal industry.[1]

My first forays into the line were driven almost purely by music. My great teacher there, besides my own ear and my family's musical tendencies, was Lorine Niedecker:

Fish
  fowl
    flood
  Water lily mud
My life

in the leaves and on water (261)

As I began to expand my field of endeavor, I came to see the line as a kind of suspension system, something like the Brooklyn Bridge, with pylons at either end. The cable conducts energy, but the line-break, in its pressuring effect, electrifies it. In a project like The California Poem, I was interested in the potential for sag—how much weight could a line take? In a poem concerned with inventory (and the tedium/oppression of that), a sloppy fraying can become a gleeful

naughtiness (and wouldn't it be fun to be scolded by Williams?). That sag is akin to entropy, or population explosions and declines within an ecosystem.

> The bed is like a typewriter, sometimes I think the bed's a refrigera-
> tor with the holographic head of a man in dichroic color to be
> seen in ambient light on the door, I mean the cover of the
> book the bed is, you do look all the time at some of the same
> things until the names of the objects might as well fall off
> Then maybe you die, that's the scare of mornings, it's loose or lush
> like this or blood but darker than it ought to be, it all has a
> beauty and a structure I haven't seen all of yet like a story, I
> always forget the most important part (Mayer 24)

Is that two lines or nine? The line is arranged in a prose block after each initial promontory-like beginning, and the whole thing is stuffed to excess, like plankton-rich waters. Here are two more exhibits that exemplify the impulse to overload the line:

> For the next is GREEN of which there are ten thousand distinct sorts.
> For the next is YELLOW which is more excellent than red, tho Newton
> makes red the prime. God be gracious to John Delap. (Smart 37)

> ～

> California utterly more sky of the looking everything in the mouth of the
> tidelines
> the tip of the snail's horn caught in the eye & ice plant poppy bright by the
> highway deeps. (Sikelianos, *California* 189)

Such surfeit reaches toward the ecstatic (unbearable?) state of "everything," where the poet tries to put it all in.

Some lines might be seen as boxcar-like, an analogy that obviously fits parts of Ginsberg's *Howl* (where the sense of juxtaposition was learned from Cézanne and Apollinaire) and Cendrars's *La Prose du Transsibérien et de la petite Jehanne de France*. Whitman learned a form of line from the raggedy tides of the Atlantic, the sea's breath (which has its own mathematics), but this is a different kind of line, suggesting a system that laps but does not have the more mechanical, sharper-edged articulation and jointing of a boxcar or a bridge. (Whitman's line fit a particular era of expansion, with its particular problems of cohesion.) The later, more jagged joints in a line employed by poets like O'Hara suggest a momentary lapse or aporia that might resolve or dissolve via collision and/or connection, where two different kinds of things come together (leg bone connected to the hip bone, English connected to Arabic, technosphere connected to the biosphere) and either fit into a socket, or smash into each other. Although Whitman's lines certainly indicate points of contact, this later, more serrated line (updated from the surrealists, where the collision is borne out in content more than in form) allows for the rush and crash of information hurtling through the air as more and more points of the world intersect. It is a line that manages, even favors, excess, and it is one that still serves us (in various forms) today. The jointing is the gap between bits of information, or the split second when the web goes down and the world is blank, the dark matter peeking out from between the curtains. Everything can fall into or emerge from that hole.

Swerving away from the city, but holding onto the same techniques of conjunction, I have often seen the line as analogous to the jointed segments in arthropods (insects, arachnids, crustaceans), whose name means "jointed foot": the segmented, articulated parts in the line, which might be eco-kin to Williams's variable foot.

In each of the exhibits below, the hinges between the segments are palpable (as in, a spider's palps). Williams uses a break within the variable foot; Mayer uses a comma between parts; and I use dashes within a "prose" line. What is the effect? Each of these markers conveys the minute, rhythmic fluctuations in the pulse or breathing (of the animal body writing or reading the poem, and of the mind) within the line. They reflect the metonymic pile-up of the biospheric,

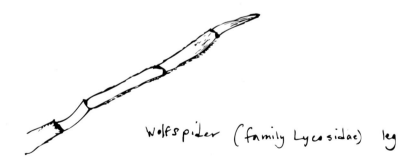

Wolfspider (family Lycosidae) leg

atmospheric, spatial, and imagined world and operate like little idling engines between revs.

> I cannot say
>> that I have gone to hell
>>> for your love
> but often
>> found myself there
>>> in your pursuit. (Williams, *Collected* 314)

～

Cosmetics, the crossbow, a drop in the sun's temperature,
The first gamma ray spectral line, the rings of Uranus. (Mayer 115)

～

THE PANIC ALPHABET—in water-voice packets—a longitudinal breaking—
the provisions of sang-froid that I collect—half of ordinary breathing—
(Sikelianos, *Monster* 120)

As Olson so long ago pointed out, the line is connected to the physicality (the heart, the breath, the head) of the maker. The line is the life of the poem, a spinal cord with its requisite vertebrae. Sometimes its expression is an organic vitality (as Olson professed), sometimes a telemetric one, burdened with (or excited by) the cyborg world humans have come to inhabit. Each poem or series of poems must find its own measure, be it a controlled symmetry or a wobbling between tightly phrased gestures and long, sloppy splashings. I tend to be interested in a more variegated measure (let's call it freaked), which probably reflects my various states of attention and inattention, and the kinds of information I operate within and that operate in the lines and curves as the world breaks and makes itself around me. I am curious about the measure of our times—what new line for the cybersphere, to reflect those points where the web of information greets the web of life?

1. The contemporary poet to have reimagined Williams's call for a modern measure most thoroughly might be Alice Notley, in particular with her experiments in a variable foot in "Beginning with a Stain," "Homer's Art," and *The Descent of Alette*.

Mayer, Bernadette. *Midwinter Day*. Bolinas, CA: Turtle Island Foundation, 1982.

Niedecker, Lorine. *Collected Works*. Berkeley: University of California Press, 2002.

Sikelianos, Eleni. *The California Poem*. Minneapolis: Coffee House Press, 2004.

———. *The Monster Lives of Boys & Girls*. Los Angeles: Green Integer, 2003.

Smart, Christopher. Extract from *Jubilate Agno*. In *Poems for the Millennium*. Ed. Jerome Rothenberg and Jeffrey C. Robinson. Berkeley: University of California Press, 2009. 34–40.

Williams, William Carlos. *The Collected Poems of William Carlos Williams*. Vol. 2. New York: New Directions, 1992.

———. "On Measure—Statement for Cid Corman." *Selected Essays*. New York: New Directions, 1931. 337–340.

A Few Attempts at Threading a Needle

Susan Stewart

A line is distinguished by a greater length than breadth: a cord or string: the span of a mortal existence, snipped to size: a breath exhaled in frozen air: a furrow in the face or hands (those instruments of making that cast lines into other forms).

As longer intervals unify passages made up of smaller intervals in oral poetry, the longer pauses point to the work's coming closure.

The patterned movements of dancers might indicate the unmarked, non-sacred space through which they gesture, and, beyond, the periphery of all their motion. (The patterned movements of bees, however, have no such negative space— pure significance.)

Arts of motion: singing, dancing, reciting. The dancers draw a geometry with their bodies; the shapes they make unfold and vanish.

In oral poetry there is no spatial appearance; the voice's time-bound shapes must emerge in a mind hearing, predicting, remembering a sequence.

In stichic verse all breadth comes from the theme; in stanzaic verse, the second-order pattern involves a spatial projection—the adonic lines of a sapphic, for example, are the pillars of the work's integrity. We can "see" through hearing alone.

A line of poetry is not weakened by being longer, or thickened, hence strengthened, by being shorter.

All the lines in a poem, including the opening and closing lines, are attached at each end to other lines. They also can snag other lines from anywhere within.

If a line cannot stand on its own, as a unit of—what? not sound alone, not sense alone, but some link between them—it cannot stand; yet however it stands on its own, the poetic line stands in relation.

Merleau-Ponty: "We have indeed always the power to interrupt, but it implies in any case a power to *begin*." Why emphasize line "end" and line "break" when, say, anaphora can just as easily be described as a practice of continually starting?

Someone will suggest: "The line of the plough, turning." All right, but the ploughman doesn't make shapes along the way, or create smaller turns within the turn.

Stroking in or banging out a tattoo on a drum, or beating your head against the wall—is the end of the line in these cases the drum, the wall?

Stories of the origin of visual art recount the outline of a hand or figure shadowed on a wall or, inscribed in a pot's clay, the afterimage of an animal's patterned leaping.

If the poetic line, too, begins in inscription, then its first determination is the skill of the hand up against the finite surface of the vessel or stone, the width and thickness of the papyrus scroll, or the shape of the codex page.

Line has an etymology with *linen*. Etymology is often a misleading line of reasoning.

In *Della pittura*, his 1435–1436 treatise on the new perspective theory, Leon Battista Alberti describes the technique for laying out the right-angled grid within a quadrangle that will make up the painting's field and then writes, "Within the quadrangle, wherever I like, I make a point that occupies that place where the central ray strikes." That point, a mark made freely, will found the relation between the beholder and all "painted things" in the work. A literal point of initiation, determined by desire, it enables the netted space within the painting to extend out into the "real" space of the work's beholder—and beyond into the imaginary continuation of the work's internal spaces.

Let's say I wanted to work as Alberti does, but in a poem. My quadrangle would be an octet and a sestet; I would use hendecasyllables for my measure; my end-rhymes would mark the rhythm and my internal rhymes confound it. My enjambments would undermine the line; my breaks on the clause would underline the line.

[Or is it that the line resists the syntax—unsuccessfully in enjambment or successfully in breaking on the clause?]

All my endings would be feminine unless they were masculine.

I would place a figure in the stanzas that would catch the attention of a person reading; the represented world would resemble the reader's world. Yet, following my symbols and puns, the reader would need another kind of line to save herself from drowning.

Every line has a hidden lining, and each hidden lining has a hidden lining; the motto of the Baroque.

The marks of orality in the written line are haunted typography. Ballad meter is 4–3-4–3 because it was seven, and seven is too wide for some pages. Hymns are split octometer. A refrain looks redundant on the page, but it once held the mind from chaos.

Arts of interiors, edges, and outlines: architecture, sculpture, painting, drawing, printed books. The line of beauty is an "S." Can a poem be shaded or stippled into form?

A poem has no skin to protect it; it feels the edge along a cut or perforation.

That is, the cut comes in to meet it and a sentence, startled, starts to sing.

A Broken Thing?

Stephanie Strickland

The line in digital poetry is not broken—

> it is extended, sometimes into a third dimension, sometimes into the semblance of a third dimension;

> it is apparent in space, as graphic arc, or sonic-graphic arc, or sonic-graphic-choreographic arc;

> it is always doubly located, in the code and at the interface.

In the code, the ensemble of lines, when read, makes things happen. Each line is exquisitely sensitive to change: any change magnifies as it ripples through the cascades of behavior it creates.

Lines of code are written to be readable by humans but to be read by a machine. The machine is a leaping, looping reader. We can see it in action in Brad Paley's *CodeProfiles*, his contribution to the CODeDOC show at the Whitney.[1] All the pieces in this show were made to connect and move three points in space. Paley's does so by highlighting its own inner working. It both reads—and displays itself reading—its own code. The amber point follows a straight, human, linear read down the columns; the green refers to the developmental order, how Paley broke it up as he composed it; and the silver-white, the most wildly active, shows the rhythm of machine reading, its execution order, how the routines call each other, passing control back and forth.

Paley chose not to visualize the parallel, multitasking aspect of the machine. However, another contributor to the CODeDOC show responded to *CodePro-files* with a remix that profiled Paley's program profiling itself, focusing on the parallel operations occurring at any given moment, rather than the sequential order Paley traced:

the line is not broken—layer upon layer of reflection on it is engaged;

the line is not broken: it has become parallel, multiple, orthogonal . . . .

The machine is also a reader of me, who is reading it. As much as I may scan the screen for new events, the computer—reading its lines of code—is scanning it for evidence of my hand movement. Each poem is a different instrument with a unique interface. To create a digital poem, a digital line, is to create, simultaneously, a way to evoke it, an entire interactional system, a means of—and potential for—producing *many* events without any intrinsic time of their own, events waiting to appear from virtuality.

To move from the code-line to the interface-line is to leave the tangible. The interface-line is the end result of a process, an evanescent, ephemeral *state*— one that cannot be known ahead of time with completeness, either by its coder or its viewer/reader, so dependent is it on the unknown condition of a vast web of interconnecting resources, those of the Internet and those on the reader's machine.

The onscreen line is *inflexional*, known only as it is transformed—an in-between, an on-the-way to we're not sure where. The line onscreen is morphing, or on the verge of morphing. It explores the felt togetherness of movement, feeling, color, thought, and connectivity. Choreographed, animated, folded across times, it can appear or disappear at will; sometimes it can appear, or disappear, at *your* will; it is perhaps generated once only, never to return.

The line in digital poetry does not break—

it reenters, it feeds back, it streams into sampled mixes, or recursive spirals, or . . . , or . . . , producing overlap, disintegration, newly created timespace . . .[2]

1. http://artport.whitney.org/commissions/codedoc/; to enter Paley's piece directly, go to http://artport.whitney.org/commissions/codedoc/Paley/code.html

2. More specific description at "Born Digital," http://www.poetryfoundation.org/journal/article.html?id=182942

The Thin Line

Terese Svoboda

My father takes oxygen before he gets out of bed in the morning. We joke that standing on his line is the only way to wake him up.

The poet stands on the line.

Lineation sounds like something official, step right up and join the others, file lockstep into the room, people lining up to be shot. A line is made to be broken—sometimes shattered. It's nearly a plane, for god's sake, practically glass. The eye follows it anywhere—it hugs the line no matter what happens to it.

The extremes: Mona Van Duyn's skinny sonnets destroy the line by punching up sound, C. K. Williams thickens the line with dramatic breadth and breath. Not to mention Paul Celan's lines, emptiness falling into emptiness. Line in prose poems doesn't disappear—it's a long string with a heavy kite that at last must lift. With some lines you can feel the toes tapping, or the cliff nearing, or the throat clearing, but line is best when all its effects—other than breath—disappear.

Lines curve in space—that's the most important thing about line. What you see is the infinite, delicate bending of meaning and sound coming together on the horizon where the line stops, where there's a gasp, and then the line falls in space.

Line lurks even in prose. Gordon Lish, prose ringmaster and editor extraordinaire, would insist that a sentence be changed because a line ended on a widow, that is to say, a word on a line all by itself. For him, prose was poetry. Is.

Dad likes his lines; he recites them: *Boomlay, boomlay, BOOM!* from Vachel Lindsay's "The Congo." Lindsay's largely forgotten except as the man who introduced Langston Hughes to the world, but he enlarged the definition of "the foot" by walking thousands of miles across country while composing; he walked his lines.

BOOM! repeats Dad. The end of the line. That's how I'd like to go out.

The poet tries.

The Broken Line: Excess and Incommensurability

Cole Swensen

Thinking of the crux of poetry as twofold—as excess and as incommensurability: the shape of sense and the shape of language simply aren't the same, and poetry is the form that, above all others, refuses to make light of that difference. And so it must, instead, address it. Poetry has historically addressed it through the line-break.

The line-break makes the line; there were no lines before line-breaks—there were sentences, there were phrases, there were all kinds of verbal structures, but there were no lines.

And so its broken-ness is at the heart of the line. Though a line may be a complete thought or a complete conventional metrical unit (iambic pentameter, say), it is nonetheless fractured. Which does not make it a fragment—that's another issue—instead, it's organized around a fracture, which marks a fissure, which is really a chasm, which is an abyss. And all the while remaining almost invisible. It goes by so quickly, and then there we are again on solid ground, but having glimpsed.

The line-break is born of severe necessity; it's born of pressure, the pressure of sense pushing against the limitations of language, causing language to enact the limitations of its own representation—that it is not presentation, that it cannot be present. And it's not just presence that goes missing, but much else.

That else overflows, is excess, and the poetic line, while it can't contain it, can by that very inability mark it and honor it. For centuries, from the symbolists and modernists on, poets have chosen to mark that overflow through enjambment, which, precisely by not giving way to prose, precisely because free verse has released the line from its metrical obligations, uses the line to show that the unit of sense can never precisely fit the linguistic unit, and that though sense may be entirely composed by language, there's a violence done to sense when it is forced into a linguistic structure.

But even before the flexibility afforded by free verse, the line was used to restrain sense, to bottle it under such an extreme pressure that its overflow was palpable—we feel it viscerally in the vertiginous suspension of pure end, with its thrill of weightlessness, that split second before the eye returns to the left margin, and thought flows again. The line-break enacts the rift between sense and language that language always tries to conceal, tries to heal.

Why? Perhaps because, of the pair, language is the human construct, while sense is not, and thus will not or cannot, despite all its claims to clarity, ever reveal its own source, which leaves language in the compensatory position.

The line-break has not been left alone to negotiate this difficult incommensurability; it has historically been aided by rhyme. Rhyme always posits an affinity, and yet in so doing, it often makes doubly apparent a disparity. Classical French prosody capitalizes on this, often rhyming opposites, or choosing pairs with a particularly striking, and uneasy, relationship to each other.

While the line-break is giving site to the incommensurability of sense and language, it's also using its capacity as a fissure to serve as an interstice through which the unsayable can enter. It cracks open the sealed façade of a finished expression and allows it to exceed itself, to emanate without the need to articulate. Ironically, this fissure is also what allows the reader to enter. It's the gesture that says, "This is not finished," with its implicit invitation to the reader to do, if not the finishing, at least some additional work. Thus the line-break is a gate; it both lets things out and allows things in. It's the point of permeability, the point of exchange between two worlds, not an inner one and an outer, not a constructed one and a real one, but simply two worlds that slip in and out of each other, and in the act of deep reading, become indistinguishable.

Line: So We Go Away

Sarah Vap

Of the seven directions, a line could move us all seven. Of all the directions, there is a single line down the memory that could return us.

Return us to the line of Tibetan prayer flags, strung from our kitchen window to the giant cedar that was struck with lightning. This half-burnt hollow black skeleton holds our son's sandbox inside of it.

Return us to the pale lines around my fingers when the rings are off; warm white worms.

The line moves us vertically, down the page. Line moves us horizontally, across the page.

The lifeline, from birth to death. Lines from before and after that. The lines of the face, of the palm, of the memory down a life.

The line moves us, as landscape and water move us. The line moves us, as any line will move us, or stop our movement. I was born on the Great Plain

—a horizontal stretch that is the basis of my imagination.

We moved into a small valley in the middle of the Rocky Mountains of Montana when I was very young. A verticality that has held my heart.

A verticality that has formed who I am.

Maybe one is open arms. One feels like open heart.

Line has the ability to open and close. To usher or prohibit. To slow or hurry a reader the cardinal directions of the page.

Then stand the cardinal directions on end: the crucifix. Extending its vertical line into the earth, and into the heavens. The arms of the crucifix, extended, wrap around the globe.

Then look at the heart of all directions, the intersection: that is center. The line could move us here, too.

A line could move the reader all the other directions, as well: backward, forward, earlier, later, spin you around, up in the air, back behind down into the ground at a spiral.

In poetry, as in life, each line will create a physical and an emotional resonance. Each line will have its physical and its ethereal truth.

I think of our grandparent poets. Whitman, the horizontal line I inherited, opened his arms wide to hold the whole body of world.

Dickinson, her vertical axis that is the basis of my own, opened to the heavens above and the heavens below.

I think of the line as direction. As movement within a landscape, tiny or huge. Physical or ethereal. As the speed of the movement. As the end of that moving.

There is a vertical line that is a mountain covered in snow outside our kitchen window. There is another line that is snow melting down the mountain in spring, drowning baby animals and trees on its way.

There is a line of corn, forever out from my grandfather's forehead.

There is a line that is heat and light and blue in the desert. Heat light blue.

There are lines that stop short as water stops at a dam. Lines that drop as the albatross drops to the ground, starved to death by her stomach full of sunglasses and cigarette lighters.

There are lines that linger, that cram. The line is an experience of movement, and the experience of not moving. Stuck. Stopped. Ended.

Moonscape-grid. I lived in Phoenix, in the Sonoran Desert, for seven years. There, the lines dropped underground, like the water, to cool. The lines shimmered like heat in front of light.

In the desert, line formed double rainbows during the monsoons, dry lightning in summer, and the grid of the pink canyon walls. Pink orange gold.

Now I live in the middle of a rainforest surrounded by seawater. Here, the line is a spiral. Line is a curl of moss, of stream, of algae.

There is no horizon here—all grows up or seeps down. The only horizontal movement is the river, turning through my valley.

Here in the rainforest, lines are the stretch, up and out, of the cedars covered with moss. Lines are the spirals down of the rain, months on end. Green. Gray. Brown.

In the thick of these spirals, in the thick of this mud, I write from memory in lines that are my enormous childhood mountains, covered in snow all year long.

Lines of herds pausing and moving, brown like the grasses in autumn. Lines of tiny animals burrowing deep into clay, to the cooler body of the desert.

Lines of heat settling down, heavy and bright to the grid of the city.

Where I live now, each autumn, during the start of the long rains, the river will choose one of the seven riverbed lines it has carved, through the millennia, down this valley.

Once, there was the line of the irrigation ditch in Wichita where my brother found, on his way to first grade, a little girl who had fallen into it.

There was the line of the eardrum that exploded. Ran yellow and slow out of my ear and down my cheek when I was three.

Lines of the igloo-shaped cast over my ear after they'd operated, and rebuilt the eardrum with a piece of skin cut out from behind the lobe of that ear.

My son has found this scar, a line as long as his fingernail, and rubs it as he falls asleep.

Right now, in this valley in the rainforest where I live, there are lines of salmon swimming down the river. Across the road, across the flooded fields to the winter creek behind our house.

They spawn there day and all night, just outside our bedroom window.

These salmon have followed a single unquestionable line their whole life. Back through memory. Back through switching channels and over dams.

Until here and now. They keep us awake us with their digging and dying. They thrash, then spill, then die—the end of the line of their memory. The full circle of their memories.

A single line etched to the memory of a whole species: *Go back.*

Go back through the line of dammed water. Through lines split, broken, clogged like waterways ruined. Lines like lines of dead salmon, foundered by the roadside.

Lines back before dying. Back through lovemaking and living. Back through one lifelong lovemaking, swimming back.

Lines through many lives, spilling and stilling and breaking. Lines back through mothers. Another line back through fathers.

Lines of the crucifix on my belly that the children gave to me: horizontal cesarean scar, vertical linea negra. And at the center, my belly button that held the line that held me to my mother.

There are the lines of Incan holy routes across a continent. Lines of constellations, the intravenous lines that mark a single life on earth.

There is a line, like a string through beads, that moves through each heart of my life. Back through the desert. Back through the mountains. Back to the prairie where I was born, shot-through with tornadoes—hard spirals across my life.

Back to the single line etched through my life, back to my poem. The single line that will move through those words.

That physical and ethereal line through a poem, like the long lines of children. Their lives: the intersect of every line. The line back through life. Back through the memory. Back, perhaps, to the four of us in matching scarves and mittens,

going outside for our paintings

that were drying on the laundry line.

Some Notes on the Poetic Line in
G. C. Waldrep and Lily Brown

Joshua Marie Wilkinson

Perhaps at least part of what the poetic line can do is debug normative syntax of its apparent seamlessness (like a paroxysm). Ten lines into the poem "Battery Alexander" by G. C. Waldrep, we encounter the following:

> Down a flight of stairs.
>   A cellar, a catacomb,
>   a landing.
>   A door. A grille
>   and beyond that grille
>   a perfumed garden.
>   A maze of pipes. Or,
>   nothing at all. (58)

Most obviously, the way these lines are arranged seems to mimic the content: the enjambed and variously indented lines can be read as a "flight of stairs" or going down into "A cellar, a catacomb" via the horizontally jutting lines like rungs or steps. Yet what's visually pleasing here is the way Waldrep's poem pulls us down, over, and then back (and repeat)—into this imagined terrain until we get to "A maze of pipes. Or, / nothing at all."

Waldrep produces this mastery with enjambed lines that invite us to fill in the gap of what might be next ("Or," . . .) and yet pushes us back out to "nothing at all." There is a sense of having arrived at some paradise of "a perfumed garden" because the form invites this as a possible end, the furthest indented line, and then cuts back to the interior—"A maze of pipes"—pulling us quickly back into the cellar or catacomb, or even further beyond the garden. But, crucially, the form doesn't merely mime the content. The lines' arrangement starts to mimic it, but then thwarts that expectation—cinematically leaping back to "A maze of pipes. Or, / nothing at all." And that hanging "Or" is the signal that the jig is up. This isn't the end of the poem (in fact, it goes on for another three pages), but the cinema of the line is the way that the form—that is, the lines' indentation, the lines' unpredictable enjambment—metaphorizes, bodies forth, and then thwarts, even playfully refuses, the content. In this way, the lines *carry over*, shift, and lure us in and out of the content. It's not that the form and content are inextricable, but that the form is always ahead of the content, oddly (the eye is drawn down, or over, before it can read the word). Waldrep's lines are a cinema of discord—here dissonant, there harmonic—but lyrically, playfully so.

In Lily Brown's work, we find something quite different in lineation than we encounter in Waldrep's work. Here is an excerpt from Brown's poem "The Return to Radical Innocence":

In the book, the last sentence circles
on siblings. Those who know
in a singular knowledge.
Like no one else. Like no one else
with whom we trade words. (24)

Brown's first *sentence* ("In the book, the last sentence circles / on siblings") is precise, and grammatically—in punctuation, syntax, etc.—a perfect line of prose, save the enjambment. So what does the line-break accomplish? Brown's poem is distinct from Waldrep's slippery rungs in that the break between "the last sentence circles" and "on siblings" brings out the peculiarity of the verb "circles" with regard to "the last sentence." (Does "circle" mean to focus *around*? To approximate? To highlight? To hone or zero in "on siblings"? To note, record, mark, or capture? And couldn't "circles" also gesture at something, but not overtly—like beating *around* the bush? Or, further, to circle around like vultures? That is, to hover in the space where something is *about* to happen?) Yet it's the quietly awkward break which is precisely less cinematic—despite the leap to an image—and more about the disruption of that odd verb "circles" from the relation of the subject ("the last sentence") to its object ("siblings").

The poems in Brown's *The Renaissance Sheet* are often an exploration of "correct" syntax, which is cut short or doubled by awkwardly unfitting locution to produce some new, discrepant—indeed, *othering*—sense. But it's always measured, seemingly plainly "spoken," and as often grammatically correct as it is truncated awkwardly like the following lines: "Those who know / in a singular knowledge. / Like no one else. Like no one else / with whom we trade words." Brown's lines are punctuated like a normal sentence, but they fragment from normal speech—inviting us to read in a sensible, sense-making way, only to be derailed. What's unique about her line-breaks is that they invite the normative thinking ("Those who know . . . ") which the line-breaks themselves derail. In other words, "Those who know" starts like a grammatically correct sentence, but where the line breaks ("Those who know / in a singular knowledge") is where the normative machinery of sense also falters, or shifts to something else.

Brown's punctuation operates similarly: the period following that line ("Those who know / in a singular knowledge.") is precisely what asks us to think along the lines of normative sense, but is simultaneously disrupted by where the period is placed—forbidding the "singular" ways of knowing we have come to expect when reading something grammatically seamless. But to me, what makes Brown's lines and enjambment stand out among so many others is that the moment our normative modes of thinking/knowing/reading are disrupted, we are lured back into the thought process of the poem as an experience of knowing (or finding out)—along a similar thread: "Those who know / in a singular knowledge. / Like no one else. Like no one else / with whom we trade words." And Brown does this through the disruptive line-breaks and breaks in thinking, which nonetheless operate in stride with the tenacity of "circling" around the same thread, or thing—the way that "In the book, the last sentence circles / on siblings." In which book? In Brown's book in which these lines appear? It's not as far-fetched as it sounds, since this poem keeps referencing The Renaissance Sheet (we come upon "The renaissance sheet is an entrance" about ten short stanzas after the one cited above). To entertain this leap, the "last sentence" of The Renaissance Sheet is composed of the final three lines of the following poem (entitled "From Left, to Right") and it reads:

When I say we I don't mean
we're the same, I mean

we fall on each other. (29)

There is a sense here that these final lines do indeed "circle" on the relationship of siblings. (How do we distinguish ourselves from one another? The physical differences are perhaps so obvious, perhaps clumsily so, it's still nonetheless a commonplace to speak for one another, to be recognized as united or bound or indistinct—even easy to be mistaken for one another, as my mother still accidentally calls me by my brother's name when she's fatigued or upset.)

But more striking than this is the way that Brown's poems—the perfect and then truncated syntax met with jarring line-breaks—invite us to imagine not the relationship of the siblings to one another ("I don't mean / we're the same"), but the ability of "the book," of any poetic text, to dislodge our most ingrained notions of what a relation to another might be. Indeed, in "the last sentence circles," it is the text which hovers, which beats around, which can never quite access but still manages to locate or spotlight this relation. Thus, in Waldrep and Brown, we discover new techniques of the poetic line to undo what we have unwittingly come to expect from poetry, from language, from one another: "Like no one else / with whom we trade words."

WORKS CITED

Brown, Lily. *The Renaissance Sheet*. Lincoln, NE: Octopus Books, 2007.
Waldrep, G. C. *Disclamor*. Rochester, NY: Boa Editions Ltd., 2007.

The Only Tool

Robert Wrigley

All the other attributes poetry is said to possess—rhapsodic language, say, or fierce compression, fragmentariness, juxtaposition, everything else—are bullshit. The only tool the poet possesses that is not also possessed by the writer of prose is the line. Give away the right margin and you give away the farm. You might be writing what you'd like to call a prose poem, but that moniker's all about the adjective, not the noun. I love prose (and even prose poems) because the same absolute attentiveness to syntax and rhythm and sound is required if one aims to approach the condition of literary art. But if you're not writing lines, you're not writing poetry.

A line, regardless of whether the poet's counting syllables or stresses or both, and regardless of whether she's ringing rhyme's implicating gong at the end of it, must have integrity. It asserts inside of syntax and sometimes even counter to syntax. It is the poem inside the poem and why the poem is a poem. Frost wasn't wrong about many things, but his idea that writing poems without meter or rhyme is like playing tennis with the net down is pure, cranky, stone-blind, wooden-eared, and most un-Frostian nitwittery.

It's not simply that the opening line (and sentence) of Richard Hugo's "Trout" is iambic tetrameter with the initial unstressed syllable (that implied "he's") lopped off: "Quick and yet he moves like silt" (3). It's that the subject of the sentence is dead center, preceded by an understood verb and coordinating conjunction that each, by virtue of its consonants, ticks by as quickly as the trout is capable of moving. And it's that the second verb, in the second tiny clause, along with the comparative "like" and the noun "silt," by virtue of their entirely other sorts of consonants, move as languorously as the trout is also capable of moving. When later in the same stanza, in the fourth sentence—two lines long—of a six-line unit, Hugo writes, "When evening pulls the ceiling tight / across his back he leaps for bugs," he plants an almost-rhyme with that earlier "silt," and by so doing mimics the there-and-not-there visibility of a trout in clear water (3).

And has evening pulled the ceiling tight *across his back*? Or is it that he leaps *across his back* for bugs? Exactly. It's both, and it is the fact that these are lines that makes that both-ways understanding immediate. Hugo's poem is an exemplary demonstration of how a poet extracts from his peculiar sculptural artifice more meaning and implication than the same words in the same order would ever be capable of doing in prose.

Mind you, syntax is holy. If you cannot write magnificent, musical, and fully-loaded sentences, find an art other than writing. But if you are a poet, your syntax must be arrayed across a grid of lines, thus enabling it to be much more than might otherwise seem possible. The line—all other abilities with the language being equal—is the poet's unique, most demanding, and most essential tool. Without it, you're a writer, but not a poet.

WORK CITED

Hugo, Richard. "Trout." *Making Certain It Goes On: The Collected Poems of Richard Hugo.* New York: W. W. Norton & Company, 1984.

The Economy of the Line

Rachel Zucker

My third book, *The Bad Wife Handbook*, is made up of five sections. Three of these sections are long poems. Part of what the book is about is how saying the same thing in a different way (for example, in a different form or with a different tone or from a different distance) is really saying something else. The five sections of the book restate each other, formal variation being the most obvious but not the only difference.

Longness is intrinsic to *The Bad Wife Handbook*, ineluctable. The book has long poems and long lines. The lines are long because the book is about monogamy and the reaching and reaching, the on-and-on-ness of marriage. The poems are long because the relationship (between husband and wife and between writer and reader) is long and imperfect, discursive and contemplative, not pithy or epiphanic. The lines are long because the speaker has children and has to say her say or think her thoughts in desperate, breathy, tumbling measures. In one of the long poems, "Annunciation," the lines zigzag down the page because this is the shape a mother's arm makes while cradling an infant and because the poem is all about insides and outsides (pregnant and not-pregnant bodies and gates around cities) and so the lines stretch out and out but also open (nearly break but don't!) with internal and end-of-line em dashes that create breaths and interiors within the long, vulnerable, straining line.

In 2007, I was faced with a difficult decision. During production, the budget for a wider-than-standard trim size fell through. My choice was to rebreak the long lines or pay the difference between the cost of a standard trim and the wider trim. I could afford to pay the difference; still, it was a lot of money, and I wondered what it meant that I was paying for (part of) the publication of my book.

All poets eventually come to understand that they will not make money from poetry. In fact, if one includes the cost of contest fees, paper, postage, not to mention the cost of an MFA (if one has an MFA) or the time one spends writing instead of doing something more lucrative, then we're all paying for our own books.

I was used to paying these poetry "expenses" and to paying my own way to conferences and readings, to spending money on my own publicity, to sending copies of my books to poets I adored. I no longer expected to make money, but writing a big check to the press to cover the cost of a wider trim felt different than spending more than I earned. Writing a check felt uncomfortably close to self-publishing, which at that time I held in low regard. (My feelings about self-publishing have changed dramatically since that time.)

In the end, though, I paid. I paid because I felt that the length and integrity of my lines were inextricable from the content and language of the poems. I paid because there wasn't a creative way to adhere to the standard trim size while maintaining the integrity of my poetry. To "reflow" or "rebreak" the lines (as the press suggested) was really to rewrite the poems, to write different poems.

Paying for a wider trim has made me think about the line in ways that are more practical and more philosophical. I know how much the integrity of a line matters to me. I know how much it's worth.

Contributor Notes

KAZIM ALI's books include two volumes of poetry, *The Far Mosque* and *The Fortieth Day*, the novels *Quinn's Passage* and *The Disappearance of Seth*, and a book of lyric prose, *Bright Felon: Autobiography and Cities*. Recently published is *Orange Alert: Essays on Poetry, Art, and the Architecture of Silence* (2010). He teaches at Oberlin College and in the University of Southern Maine's Stonecoast MFA Program and is founding editor of the small press Nightboat Books.

BRUCE ANDREWS, founding coeditor of the journal L=A=N=G=U=A=G=E, has maintained a consistent position and prolific record of activism at the radical edge of the literary avant-garde. Author of over thirty volumes of poetry, and one of critical essays (*Paradise & Method: Poetics & Praxis*), with books, interviews, essays, and recordings online at the Electronic Poetry Center, Ubu, PennSound, Eclipse, Jacket, and Wikipedia sites. In New York City, he teaches politics at Fordham University and collaborates with a widening circle of other artists (in particular, as music director for Sally Silvers & Dancers).

HADARA BAR-NADAV'S book of poetry *A Glass of Milk to Kiss Goodnight* (2007) won the Margie Book Prize. Her chapbook, *Show Me Yours* (2010), won the Midwest Poets Series Award. Recent publications appear in *American Poetry Review*, *Iowa Review*, *Kenyon Review*, *Ploughshares*, *Prairie Schooner*, and other journals. She is an assistant professor of English at the University of Missouri-Kansas City.

CATHERINE BARNETT is the recipient of a 2006 Guggenheim Fellowship, a Whiting Writers' Award, the Glasgow Prize for Emerging Writers, and a Pushcart. Her book, *Into Perfect Spheres Such Holes Are Pierced*, was published in 2004. She teaches at Barnard, the New School, and NYU. She also works as an independent editor and recently collaborated with the composer Richard

Einhorn on the libretto for "The Origin," his multimedia oratorio about the life of Charles Darwin.

CHARLES BERNSTEIN'S books include *Girly Man, Blind Witness: Three American Operas, Shadowtime,* and *Republics of Reality: 1975–1995.* Bernstein and Bruce Andrews edited a collection of essays on the line called L=A=N=G=U=A=G=E *Lines* in 1988; it is available at PEPC <http://writing.upenn.edu/pepc/contents.html>.

MEI-MEI BERSSENBRUGGE books include *Empath, Four Year Old Girl, Concordance,* and *I Love Artists: New and Selected Poems.* Her collaborations include artist books with Richard Tuttle and Kiki Smith, and theater works with Frank Chin, Tan Dun, Shi Zhen Chen, and Alvin Lucier. She lives in New Mexico and New York City.

BRUCE BOND'S collections of poetry include *Peal, Blind Rain, Cinder, The Throats of Narcissus, Radiography, The Anteroom of Paradise,* and *Independence Days.* His poetry has appeared in *Best American Poetry, Yale Review, Georgia Review, Paris Review, Poetry, New Republic,* and many other journals. Presently, he is Regents Professor of English at the University of North Texas and poetry editor for *American Literary Review.*

MARIANNE BORUCH'S most recent poetry collections include *Poems: New and Selected* (2004) and *Grace, Fallen from* (2008), which was brought out in paperback in spring 2010. Her books of essays on poetry are *Poetry's Old Air* (1993) and *In the Blue Pharmacy* (2005). She teaches at Purdue University and in the low-residency Warren Wilson College Program for Writers.

SCOTT CAIRNS is professor of English and director of creative writing at University of Missouri. His most recent poetry collection is *Compass of Affection: Poems New & Selected.* Other books include his spiritual memoir, *Short Trip to the Edge,* and his translations *Love's Immensity.* His book-length essay *The End of Suffering* was published in 2009. He received a Guggenheim Fellowship in 2006, and was recently named the Catherine Paine Middlebush Chair in English.

JOSHUA CLOVER is the author of one book on film (*The Matrix,* 2005), one on popular music and political history (*1989: Bob Dylan Didn't Have This to Sing About,* 2009), and two books of poetry: *The Totality for Kids* (2006), and *Madonna anno domini* (1997). He is a professor of poetry and poetics at the University of California-Davis.

AMONG NORMA COLE'S books of poetry are *Natural Light* and *Where Shadows Will: Selected Poems 1988–2008*. *To Be at Music: Essays & Talks* is forthcoming. Translation work includes Danielle Collobert's *It Then* and *Crosscut Universe: Writing on Writing from France*. Cole has received the Gertrude Stein Award as well as awards from the Foundation for Contemporary Arts, the Gerbode Foundation, and the Fund for Poetry. She teaches at the University of San Francisco.

BRENT CUNNINGHAM is a writer, publisher, and visual artist living in Oakland with his wife and daughter. His first book of poetry, *Bird & Forest*, was published in 2005. His second book, *Journey to the Sun*, is due out next year. He works for Small Press Distribution in Berkeley.

J. P. DANCING BEAR is the author of nine collections of poetry, most recently, *Inner Cities of Gulls* and *Conflicted Light* (2010 and 2008). His tenth collection is due out in 2012. His poems have appeared in *Shenandoah, New Orleans Review, National Poetry Review, Mississippi Review, Verse Daily*, and many others. He is editor of the *American Poetry Journal* and Dream Horse Press, and host of "Out of Our Minds," a weekly poetry program on KKUP.

CHRISTINA DAVIS is the author of *Forth A Raven* (2006). Her poems have appeared in *American Poetry Review, Boston Review, Jubilat, New Republic, Pleiades, Paris Review*, and other publications. She is the recipient of a Witter Bynner Fellowship (chosen by U.S. Poet Laureate Kay Ryan) and residencies from Yaddo and the MacDowell Colony. A graduate of the University of Pennsylvania and the University of Oxford, she is currently the curator of poetry at the Woodberry Poetry Room, Harvard University.

JOHANNA DRUCKER is the inaugural Bernard and Martin Breslauer Professor of Bibliography in the Department of Information Studies at UCLA. She has published extensively on the history of written forms, typography, design, and visual poetics within the twentieth-century avant-garde. In addition to her scholarly work, Drucker is internationally known as a book artist and experimental, visual poet. Her book *SpecLab: Digital Aesthetics and Speculative Computing* was published in 2009.

CAMILLE DUNGY is author of *What to Eat, What to Drink, What to Leave for Poison* (2006), *Suck on the Marrow* (2010), and *Smith Blue* (2011), editor of *Black Nature: Four Centuries of African American Nature Poetry* (2009), coeditor of *From the Fishouse: An Anthology of Poems That Sing, Rhyme, Resound, Syncopate, Alliterate, and Just Plain Sound Great* (2009), and associate professor of creative writing at San Francisco State University.

JOHN O. ESPINOZA is the author of *The Date Fruit Elegies* (2008), which was a finalist for a Northern California Book Award in Poetry in 2009. Espinoza holds degrees in creative writing from UC Riverside (BA) and Arizona State University (MFA). Born and raised in Indio, CA, by Mexican parents, Espinoza derives his poetic subjects from the population and landscape of southern California's Coachella Valley. He lives in San Jose, CA, with his wife.

KATHY FAGAN'S newest collection is *Lip* (2009). She is also the author of the National Poetry Series selection *The Raft*, the Vassar Miller Prize–winner *MOVING & ST RAGE*, and *The Charm*. Fagan is the recipient of awards and fellowships from the Ingram Merrill Foundation, the National Endowment for the Arts, Ohioana Library, and the Ohio Arts Council. She is currently professor of English at Ohio State and editor of *The Journal*.

ANNIE FINCH is author or editor of fifteen books of poetry, translation, and criticism, most recently *Among the Goddesses: An Epic Libretto* and *The Body of Poetry: Essays*. Her poetry has been released on CD, shortlisted for the Foreword Poetry Book of the Year Award, and reissued by Carnegie Mellon Classic Contemporaries. In 2009, she was awarded the Robert Fitzgerald Award. She lives in Maine, where she directs Stonecoast, the low-residency MFA program of the University of Southern Maine.

GRAHAM FOUST was born in Knoxville, Tennessee, and raised in Eau Claire, Wisconsin. The author of four books of poems, he works at Saint Mary's College of California and lives in Oakland with his wife, son, and daughter.

ALICE FULTON is the author of eight books, including an essay collection, among them, *Feeling as a Foreign Language: The Good Strangeness of Poetry; Cascade Experiment: Selected Poems*; and *The Nightingales of Troy: Stories of One Family's Century*. Her book *Felt* was awarded the Bobbitt Prize for Poetry from the Library of Congress. A recipient of fellowships from the MacArthur Foundation and the National

Endowment for the Arts, she is currently the Ann S. Bowers Professor of English at Cornell.

JOHN GALLAHER is the author of three books of poetry, most recently *The Little Book of Guesses*, winner of the Levis Poetry Prize, and *Map of the Folded World*, as well as the online chapbook *Guidebook*. He's currently coeditor of the *Laurel Review* and an editor at GreenTower Press.

NOAH ELI GORDON is the author of several books, including *Novel Pictorial Noise* (2007), which was selected by John Ashbery for the National Poetry Series and chosen for the San Francisco State Poetry Center Book Award. He's the co-publisher of Letter Machine Editions and an assistant professor in the MFA program in creative writing at the University of Colorado-Boulder. His latest book is *The Source* (2011).

ARIELLE GREENBERG is the author of the poetry collections *My Kafka Century* and *Given*; three anthologies, *Women Poets on Mentorship* and *Starting Today: 100 Poems for Obama's First 100 Days*, both co-edited with Rachel Zucker, and *Gurlesque* co-edited with Lara Glenum; and a college reader, *Youth Subcultures: Exploring Underground America*. She is an associate professor in the poetry program at Columbia College Chicago and founder/moderator of the poet-moms listserv.

SARAH GRIDLEY is the author of two books of poetry: *Weather Eye Open* and *Green is the Orator* (2005, 2010). Recipient of a 2009 Individual Excellence Award from the Ohio Arts Council, and a 2010 Creative Workforce Fellowship from the Community Partnership for Arts and Culture, she is an assistant professor of English at Case Western Reserve University in Cleveland, Ohio.

GABRIEL GUDDING is the author of *Rhode Island Notebook* (2007) and *A Defense of Poetry* (2002). He teaches ethics, critical poetics, literature, and creative writing at Illinois State University. His essays and poems appear in such venues as *Harper's*, the *Nation*, *Journal of the History of Ideas*, *New American Writing*, *Fence*, and *Mandorla*, and in such anthologies as *Great American Prose Poems*, *Best American Poetry*, and *Now: Best Innovative Writing*.

KIMIKO HAHN is the author of eight books of poems, including *Earshot* (awarded the Theodore Roethke Memorial Poetry Prize); *The Unbearable Heart* (an American Book Award); *The Narrow Road to the Interior*, inspired by Japanese forms; and *Toxic Flora* (2010). Hahn is the recipient of a number of awards—most recently, the PEN/Voelcker Award and the Shelley Memorial Prize—and she is a distinguished professor in the English Department and MFA program at Queens College/CUNY.

RAZA ALI HASAN is the author of two books, *Grieving Shias* (2006) and *67 Mogul Miniatures* (2009). He is originally from Pakistan and came to America in 1991. He received his MFA from Syracuse University. His poems have appeared in *AGNI*, *Shenandoah*, and *Blackbird*. He currently teaches in the English Department at the University of Colorado at Boulder.

H. L. HIX is a professor in the creative writing MFA program at the University of Wyoming. He has authored eight books of poetry, including *Chromatic*, a finalist for the National Book Award, and five volumes of prose, and he has edited three books. His poetry has been recognized with the Grolier Prize, the T. S. Eliot Prize, the Peregrine Smith Award, and an NEA fellowship. His most recent poetry book is *Incident Light*.

CYNTHIA HOGUE has published seven collections of poetry, most recently *Or Consequence* (2010) and the coauthored *When the Water Came: Evacuees of Hurricane Katrina* (2010), a collection of interview-poems and photographs. She is the coeditor of *Innovative Women Poets: An Anthology of Contemporary Poetry and Interviews* (2006). In 2010, she was a Witter Bynner Fellow in Translation at the Santa Fe Art Institute. She teaches at Arizona State University.

FANNY HOWE was born in Buffalo, New York, in 1940. She is the author of more than twenty books of poetry and prose. Her recent collections of poetry include *Lyric* (2007), *On the Ground* (2004), *Gone* (2003), *Selected Poems* (2000), *Forged* (1999), *Q* (1998), *One Crossed Out* (1997), *O'Clock* (1995), and *The End* (1992). Howe is also the author of several novels and prose collections. Howe was the recipient of the 2001 Lenore Marshall Poetry Prize for her *Selected Poems*. She has also won awards from the National Endowment for the Arts, the National Poetry Foundation, the California Council for the Arts, and the *Village Voice*, as well as fellowships from the Bunting Institute and the MacArthur Colony. Most recently, in 2009 Howe was awarded the Poetry Foundation's Ruth Lily Poetry Prize.

CHRISTINE HUME is the author of *Musca Domestica* (2000), *Alaskaphrenia* (2004), *Lullaby: Speculations on the First Active Sense* (2008), and *Shot* (2009). Her radio show/podcast *Poetry Radio* is available through iTunes U. She teaches in and directs the interdisciplinary creative writing program at Eastern Michigan University.

CATHERINE IMBRIGLIO is the author of the book-length poetry sequence *Parts of the Mass*, which received the 2008 Norma Farber First Book Award from the Poetry Society of America. Her work has appeared in *American Letters & Commentary*, *Conjunctions*, *Denver Quarterly*, *Iowa Anthology of New American Poetries*, and elsewhere. She teaches in the nonfiction writing program at Brown University.

KARLA KELSEY is author of two full-length books: *Knowledge, Forms, the Aviary* (2006), and *Iteration Nets* (2010). In addition, she edits and contributes to Fence Book's Constant Critic book review Web site. On permanent faculty at Susquehanna University, she has been awarded a Fulbright to teach at ELTE University in Budapest.

SARAH KENNEDY is the author of six books of poems, including *Home Remedies*, *A Witch's Dictionary*, *Consider the Lilies*, *Double Exposure*, and *Flow Blue*. An associate professor at Mary Baldwin College in Staunton, Virginia, Kennedy has received grants from both the National Endowment for the Arts and the Virginia Commission for the Arts and is currently a contributing editor for *West Branch* and *Shenandoah*.

BEN LERNER'S books are *The Lichtenberg Figures*, *Angle of Yaw*, and *Mean Free Path*. He teaches at Brooklyn College.

DANA LEVIN'S books are *In the Surgical Theatre* and *Wedding Day*; her newest, *Sky Burial*, came out in spring 2011. A 2007 Guggenheim Fellow, she teaches in the Warren Wilson MFA Program and is the Russo Endowed Chair in Creative Writing at University of New Mexico.

TIMOTHY LIU'S most recent books of poems are *Polytheogamy* and *Bending the Mind Around the Dream's Blown Fuse*. His work has been translated into nine languages, and his journals and papers are archived in the Berg Collection at the New York Public Library. Liu lives in Manhattan.

THOMAS LUX'S most recent book is *God Particles* (2008).

JOANIE MACKOWSKI is the author of two books of poems, *View from a Temporary Window* and *The Zoo*. She has received the Kate Tufts Discovery Award, the AWP Award Series in Poetry, a Rona Jaffe Foundation grant, and a Wallace Stegner Fellowship. She teaches at Cornell University.

SHARA MCCALLUM is the author of *This Strange Land* (April 2011), *Song of Thieves* (2003), and *The Water Between Us* (1999). Her *New & Selected Poems* will be published in 2011 in the UK. Originally from Jamaica, she lives with her family in central Pennsylvania, where she directs the Stadler Center for Poetry and teaches creative writing and literature at Bucknell University.

HEATHER MCHUGH is Milliman Distinguished Writer-in-Residence at the University of Washington in Seattle. She's a frequent visitor at the MFA Program for Writers at Warren Wilson College in Asheville, North Carolina. Her collection of poems *Upgraded to Serious*, published in the United States and in Canada, is her most recent offering among a total of thirteen volumes of poetry, translation, and literary essays.

WAYNE MILLER is the author of three collections of poetry—*The City, Our City* (2011), *The Book of Props* (2009), and *Only the Senses Sleep* (2006)—as well as coeditor of the anthology *New European Poets* (2008) and translator of Moikom Zeqo's *I Don't Believe in Ghosts* (2007). He lives in Kansas City and teaches at the University of Central Missouri, where he edits *Pleiades: A Journal of New Writing*.

JENNY MUELLER lives in St. Louis and teaches at McKendree University. Her book *Bonneville* was published in 2007.

LAURA MULLEN is a professor at Louisiana State University. She is the author of six books, including the cross-genre murder mystery *Murmur* (2007) and a collection of poems, *Dark Archive*. Her work has been widely anthologized, and she has been awarded the Ironwood Press Stanford Prize, a National Endowment for the Arts fellowship, and a Rona Jaffe Award, among other honors.

MOLLY PEACOCK is the author of six volumes of poetry, including *The Second Blush*, *Cornucopia*, and *How to Read a Poem & Start a Poetry Circle*. She is the coeditor of *Poetry in Motion: 100 Poems from the Subways and Buses*. Her newest work of nonfiction is *The Paper Garden: An Artist Begins Her Life's Work at 72*. She has been obsessed with the line since the age of ten.

V. PENELOPE PELIZZON'S *Nostos* (2000) won the Hollis Summers Prize and the Poetry Society of America's Norma Farber First Book Award. She is coauthor of *Tabloid, Inc: Crimes, Newspapers, Narratives* (2010), a study of the relations among sensation journalism, photography, and film between 1927 and 1958.

EMMY PÉREZ is the author of *Solstice*. Her work has also appeared in *Achiote Seeds, vandal: a journal of transformative activism*, the anthology *The Wind Shifts: New Latino Poetry*, and other publications. A recipient of the Alfredo Cisneros Del Moral Foundation Award (2009), she is currently a CantoMundo poetry fellow (2010) and a Macondo Writers' Workshop member. She is an assistant professor at the University of Texas-Pan American and also teaches creative writing in detention centers.

CARL PHILLIPS is the author of eleven books of poems, most recently *Speak Low* (2009), a finalist for the National Book Award, and *Double Shadow* (2011), as well as a book of prose, *Coin of the Realm: Essays on the Life and Art of Poetry* (2004). He teaches at Washington University in St. Louis.

PATRICK PHILLIPS'S first book, *Chattahoochee*, received the 2005 Kate Tufts Discovery Award, and his second, *Boy*, was published in 2008. His poems have appeared in many magazines, including *Poetry*, *Ploughshares*, and the *Nation*, and he has received fellowships from the John Simon Guggenheim Memorial Foundation, the National Endowment for the Arts, and the U.S. Fulbright Commission. He teaches at Drew University.

DONALD PLATT'S four books of poetry are *Fresh Peaches, Fireworks, & Guns* (1994); *Cloud Atlas* (2002); *My Father Says Grace* (2007); and *Dirt Angels* (2009). He is a recipient of a fellowship from the National Endowment for the Arts, the Paumanok Poetry Award, the "Discovery"/*The Nation* Prize, and two Pushcart Prizes. His poems have been anthologized in *The Best American Poetry 2000* and *2006*. He is a professor of English at Purdue University.

KEVIN PRUFER'S newest books are *In a Beautiful Country* (2011) and *National Anthem* (2008), named one of the five best poetry books of the year by Publishers Weekly. He's also editor-at-large of *Pleiades: A Journal of New Writing* and coeditor, with Wayne Miller, of *New European Poets* (2008), among others. The recipient of three Pushcart Prizes, he teaches in the creative writing program at the University of Houston.

PAISLEY REKDAL'S most recent book of poetry is *The Invention of the Kaleidoscope* (2007).

DONALD REVELL is the author of ten collections of poetry, most recently *A Thief of Strings* (2007) and *Pennyweight Windows: New & Selected Poems* (2005). Winner of the 2004 Lenore Marshall Award and two-time winner of the PEN Center USA Award in poetry, Revell has also received the Gertrude Stein Award, two Shestack Prizes, two Pushcart Prizes, and fellowships from the NEA as well as from the Ingram Merrill and Guggenheim Foundations. He is also the author of three volumes of translation: Rimbaud's *A Season in Hell* (2007), and Apollinaire's *Alcools* (1995) and *The Self-Dismembered Man: Selected Later Poems of Guillaume Apollinaire* (2004). Revell's critical writings include *Invisible Green: Selected Prose* (2005) and *The Art of Attention: A Poet's Eye* (2007). He is a professor of English and creative writing at University of Nevada-Las Vegas.

MARTHA RHODES is the author of three collections of poetry: *At the Gate* (1995), *Perfect Disappearance* (2000 Green Rose Prize), and *Mother Quiet* (2004). She teaches at Sarah Lawrence College and at the MFA Program for Writers at Warren Wilson College. She is a founding editor and the director of Four Way Books, an independent literary press in New York City.

ALBERTO RÍOS is the author of ten books of poetry, including *The Theater of Night*, winner of the 2007 PEN/Beyond Margins Award, and *The Smallest Muscle in the Human Body*, a finalist for the National Book Award. He holds numerous awards, including six Pushcart Prizes in both poetry and fiction, the Arizona Governor's Arts Award, and fellowships from the Guggenheim Foundation and the National Endowment for the Arts. He is Regents Professor of English at Arizona State University.

DANA ROESER is the author of two books of poetry, *Beautiful Motion* and *In the Truth Room*, both winners of the Morse Poetry Prize. She has received the NEA fellowship, the GLCA New Writers Award, and the Jenny McKean Moore Writer-in-Washington Fellowship.

MARY ANN SAMYN'S books of poetry include *Inside the Yellow Dress* (2001), *Purr* (2005), and *Beauty Breaks In* (2009). She also recently published a chapbook, *The Boom of a Small Cannon* (2010). Her poems have appeared in *Field*, the *Journal*,

Colorado Review, Meridian, Pleiades, and elsewhere. She teaches in the MFA program at West Virginia University where she is an associate professor of English and, currently, Bolton Professor for Teaching and Mentoring.

ROBYN SCHIFF is the author of the poetry collections *Revolver* (2008) and *Worth* (2002). Schiff was a 2008 fellow at the Brown Foundation Fellows Residency Program in Menerbes, France. She is an associate professor at the University of Iowa.

TIM SEIBLES, a native of Philadelphia, is the author of several collections of poetry including *Hammerlock* and *Buffalo Head Solos.* Currently, he is a member of the MFA in writing faculty at Old Dominion University in Norfolk, Virginia. He also teaches in the low-residency Stonecoast MFA program based at the University of Southern Maine.

RAVI SHANKAR'S poetry collections include *Seamless Matter, Voluptuous Bristle, Instrumentality,* and with Reb Livingston, *Wanton Textiles.* With Tina Chang and Nathalie Handal, he edited Norton's *Language for a New Century: Contemporary Poetry from the Middle East, Asia, and Beyond.* He co-directs the Department of Creative Writing at CCSU, founded online journal of the arts *Drunken Boat,* and teaches in the first international MFA program in creative writing at City University of Hong Kong. Norah Jones is not among his daughters.

EVIE SHOCKLEY is the author of *a half-red sea* (2006), *the new black* (March 2011), and two chapbooks: *The Gorgon Goddess* (2001) and *31 words * prose poems* (2007). She co-edits *jubilat* and teaches African American literature and creative writing at Rutgers University. Also a scholar, she recently completed a critical study titled "Renegade Poetics: Black Aesthetics and Formal Innovation in African American Poetry."

ELENI SIKELIANOS is the author of a hybrid memoir (*The Book of Jon*) and six books of poetry, most recently *Body Clock.* Her translation of Jacques Roubaud's *Exchanges on Light* appeared in 2009. She has received awards from the National Endowment for the Arts, the Fulbright Program, the National Poetry Series, and New York Foundation for the Arts, as well as the Gertrude Stein Award in Innovative American Poetry. Sikelianos teaches in and directs the creative writing program at the University of Denver.

SUSAN STEWART, a poet, critic, and former MacArthur Fellow, is the Annan Professor of English at Princeton. Her most recent books of poems are *Columbarium*, which won the National Book Critics Circle Award, and *Red Rover*. Her song cycle "Songs for Adam," with music by James Primosch, had its premiere with the Chicago Symphony in October.

STEPHANIE STRICKLAND'S most recent book, *Zone : Zero* (book + CD), includes two interactive digital poems, one of which, *slippingglimpse*, was introduced in Paris and shown at the e-Poetry festival in Barcelona. A director of the Electronic Literature Organization, her explorations of digital lit include the essay "Born Digital" and the *Electronic Literature Collection/1*, which she co-edited. Prize-winning print volumes include *V: WaveSon.nets / Losing L'una*, *True North*, and *The Red Virgin: A Poem of Simone Weil*. She is collaborating on a poetry generator with Nick Montfort and completing a book-length poem, "Huracan's Harp." Her Web site is http://stephaniestrickland.com.

TERESE SVOBODA has published fourteen books of prose and poetry including *Weapons Grade*, *Black Glass Like Clark Kent* (winner of the Graywolf Nonfiction Prize), *Pirate Talk or Mermalade* (2010), and *Bohemian Girl*, forthcoming. Winner of the Iowa Poetry Prize, Svoboda has taught at Columbia, Bennington, New School, Sarah Lawrence, Williams, and elsewhere.

COLE SWENSEN is the author of twelve books of poetry; the most recent, *Ours*, was a finalist for the *Los Angeles Times* Book Prize. Other volumes have won the Iowa Poetry Prize, the San Francisco State Poetry Center Book Award, and the National Poetry Series. A 2006 Guggenheim Fellow, she is the coeditor of the anthology *American Hybrid* (2009) and a translator of contemporary French poetry, prose, and art criticism.

SARAH VAP is the author of three collections of poetry: *American Spikenard* (2007), *Dummy Fire* (2007), and *Faulkner's Rosary* (2010). Her fourth collection, *Iris, Starless*, is forthcoming in 2012. She is poetry editor of the online journal *42 Opus*.

JOSHUA MARIE WILKINSON'S most recent books are *Selenography* (with Polaroids by Tim Rutili) and *Poets on Teaching*. He is an assistant professor at Loyola University Chicago.

ROBERT WRIGLEY'S seven books of poetry include, most recently, *Earthly Meditations: New & Selected Poems* (2006); as well as *Lives of the Animals* (2003), winner of the 2005 Poet's Prize; and *Reign of Snakes* (1999), winner of the 2000 Kingsley Tufts Award. A former Guggenheim and two-time NEA Fellow, he teaches in the graduate writing program at the University of Idaho.

RACHEL ZUCKER is the author of four books of poetry, including *Museum of Accidents* and *The Bad Wife Handbook*. Along with poet Arielle Greenberg she co-edited two anthologies: *Starting Today: 100 Poems for Obama's First 100 Days* and *Women Poets on Mentorship*. She teaches poetry and is a certified labor doula and childbirth educator. Her Web site is http://www.rachelzucker.net.

Index

Longenbach, James, 20–21, 85, 91, 167
Longfellow, Henry Wadsworth, 27, 114, 220
Longinus, 159
Lorde, Audre, 24, 89
"The Love Song of J. Alfred Prufrock," 8, 148, 175
Lowell, Robert, 156
Lucid Interval as Integral Music, 226
Lux, Thomas, 25, 155–156

Mac Low, Jackson, 24
Mackey, Nathaniel, 226
Mackowski, Joanie, 27, 157–160
"Make Them Howl or Breathe Fire," 214
The Making of a Poem, 44
Mallarmé, Stéphane, 228
Mann, Thomas, 165
Marvell, Andrew, 221
"Matins," 180
Mayakovsky, Vladimir, 173
Mayer, Bernadette, 229–233
McCallum, Shara, 27, 161–163
McGurl, Mark, 14
McHugh, Heather, 26, 156, 164–165
McPherson, Sandra, 14
McQueen, Steve, 79
Mean Free Path, 145
"A memory of the pond," 140
"Men," 153
"Mending Wall," 19
Merleau-Ponty, Maurice, 235
Merwin, W. S., 120, 168
mesostics, 226
metaphor, 58, 66
meter, 6, 9, 15–16, 22–23, 88–91, 116, 118–120, 178–181, 187–189, 196–198, 220, 241–242, 252
metonymy, 58–59, 105, 123–124
Mexico, 183
Millay, Edna St. Vincent, 176

Miller, Cristanne, 94
Miller, Wayne, 27, 166–169
Milton, John, 7
Misgivings, 194
Missing Measures, 88
Moby Dick, 108
modernism, 60, 122, 170
monostich, 115–116
Monster, 232
Moore, Marianne, 73, 215–217
Morgan, Robert, 15
"The Morning of the Poem," 194
"Morning Song," 173
Morrison, Toni, 79
Mozart, Wolfgang Amadeus, 54
Mueller, Jenny, 28, 31, 170–172
Mullen, Harryette, 223
Mullen, Laura, 31, 173–175
music, 86, 97, 112, 135–137, 147, 173, 218
"Mutable Boundaries," 44

Nabokov, Vladimir, 79
Naked Poetry, 19
narrative, 41, 46, 77, 83, 86, 94–95, 103–105, 194–195, 205, 207
Nemerov, Howard, 176
Neruda, Pablo, 221
New Formalism, 112
new media poetry, 10, 20, 37, 237–239
New Mexico, 52
New Poets of England and America, 23
The New Princeton Encyclopedia of Poetry and Poetics, 44
The New Sentence, 138–141
Newton, Sir Isaac, 65
Niedecker, Lorine, 229
9/11, 124–125
"Not Waving But Drowning," 197
"Notes for Echo Lake 4," 35
Notley, Alice, 232